Remembering THE Twentieth Century Limited

Remembering THE Twentieth Century Limited

BY

Matthew Stevenson

ODYSSEUS BOOKS

REMEMBERING THE TWENTIETH CENTURY LIMITED.
Copyright©2009 by Matthew Mills Stevenson.

ISBN 978-0-9709133-6-4

For information, address: Odysseus Books c/o Pathway Book Service, 4 White Brook Road, Gilsum, New Hampshire 03448.
Toll free: 1-800-345-6665. Fax: 1-603-357-2073.
E-mail: pbs@pathwaybook.com

Please use the same contact numbers for special or direct orders, group sales, or special promotions, for example, those available to book and reading clubs. To contact the author on any matter, such as to arrange a speaking engagement, please use: matthewstevenson@sunrise.ch.

Please visit the book's Web site: www.odysseusbooks.com

This book was printed on acid-free paper in the United States.

Edited by MICHAEL MARTIN and SANDRA COSTICH.
Jacket and book design by NANETTE STEVENSON.

Martin Daly, Michael Heslop, and Helen Boss Heslop
kindly read the galleys.

Library of Congress Cataloging-in-Publication Data
Stevenson, Matthew Mills, 1954-
Remembering the Twentieth Century Limited / by Matthew Stevenson.
p. cm.
ISBN-13: 978-0-9709133-6-4 (alk. paper)
ISBN-10: 0-9709133-6-2 (alk. paper)
1. Stevenson, Matthew Mills, 1954--Travel. 2. Voyages and travels. I. Title.
G465.S7447 2006   910.4--dc22
2009000052

10 9 8 7 6 5 4 3 2 1

Contents

Preface

THIS BOOK PULLS TOGETHER historical interests of mine from the last hundred years.

Older readers will recognize that the title comes from New York Central's *Twentieth Century Limited*, an overnight express train that ran between New York and Chicago. It was pulled from service in late 1967. A few months before, together with my father, I rode it for the last time. We went from Chicago to Kansas City, St. Louis, Omaha, and Wyoming—on a succession of trains that have vanished from timetables. It was on that trip, or others like it across the Great Plains, that I discovered the happy confluence of books, trains, and travel.

Even as a thirteen-year-old boy, I loved nothing more than to take a book to the observation car and to read about the landscape through which the train was crossing. In those days my imagination, pulled by the Burlington Northern or the Union Pacific, ran across the narrative of westward expansion, Indian wars, Manifest Destiny, the Civil War, and baseball. More recently, as I now live in Europe, my daydreams include Swiss railroads and eastern approaches. But the roadbeds and ballast of this history were laid on tracks of memory that crossed America in the 1960s.

Although it pleases me to think of life as a long train journey (with cloth tablecloths and upper berths), I have to admit that often the travels can be circular. This book begins at Gallipoli, on the Turkish coast, and ends almost a century later in the Lebanon cities of Beirut and Tyre. I would like to think that political thought has advanced from the butchery that sent men ashore to their slaughter in the Dardanelles, but from my writing in recent years about the wars in Turkey and Lebanon, I found little to distinguish the impulses that sent Allied landing boats into Anzac Cove in 1915 and the cluster bombs dropped in the Bekaa Valley, Lebanon, in 2006.

The wars of the Ottoman succession also run through the chapters about Serbia, Armenia, Mesopotamia, and Iran, preoccupations of both the modern political world and my bedside reading. Indeed, as this account wends its way to the press, I am mulling over other sleepers from Istanbul to Aleppo and wondering if it makes any sense to catch the night train to Tehran. The temptations are geographic and bibliographic, and I am never sure if I get more pleasure from my travels or my reading.

Not all of this book wallows in crusader fortresses or trenches overlooking the Mediterranean Sea. I have tried to describe individuals whose actions and lonely struggles have also helped to define—at least to me—the last century. For example, I have included an essay about a journey from Okinawa to Nagasaki, where my father was sent on occupation duty in October 1945, not long after the bomb fell on that southern Japanese city. During the preceding four years of combat in the Pacific, he had inspired the men under his command with acts of bravery on island battlegrounds. But his visit in a hospital ward, to the Nagasaki victims of the atomic bomb, may have taken more courage than the bayonet charge he led on Guadalcanal.

In the same vein, this book also recognizes other acts of individual bravery that have marked our age or those of earlier eras. In writing about medieval and recent bank failures, I found the lonely farmhouse in Tuscany to which Niccolò Machiavelli was exiled from the Florentine court and where he brooded (satirically, I think) on political and economic power. Machiavelli would have understood the political psychology that surrounds the strange case of the State Department officer Alger Hiss, who himself fell afoul of court politics. Both men went from diplomatic seniority to exile and ostracism, and lived out their days trying to illuminate the workings of imperial minds and the temperament of princes. Both, however, died without redemption.

A happier exile was that of Napoleon's critic and rival Germaine de Staël, who was forced out of Paris and settled beside the lake in Geneva, not far from where I live. From her chateau, Madame de Staël wrote books and letters, and held forth in salons, not to mention boudoirs. But to her principles of liberty, she is faithful and modern, an exemplar for the kind of personality that can emerge even from the political storms like those we have seen in the last hundred years. She outlasted Napoleon, as if to confirm his admission that "the sword is always beaten by the spirit." Many in the twentieth century, however, were not so fortunate, and some of their stories are told here.

—M.M.S.

Remembering THE Twentieth Century Limited

Summer Games:
The Bad Guys Are Winning
(2007)

ON ONE OF the nicest days of the summer in Switzerland, where I live, I drove my car through the back roads that skirt Geneva and parked in the lake town of Thonon, a setting from the old European world that, on its fringes, is laced with discount furniture outlets. On a road that I knew only from a Michelin map, I unloaded my bicycle and set off on a two-hour ride. To my right was a mountain stream and steep gorges. I might well have been peddling through the American West, not the French Alps. At first the traffic was heavy with lumber trucks and careening utility vans. Through a state forest the grade of the climb had me standing on the pedals. There was a plateau at around one thousand meters. Finally I could see a crest in the hills where I assumed I would find the alpine resort of Morzine and the cavalcade of the Tour de France.

Police barriers stopped cars from entering the mountain village. I passed through the barricades and labored up one last steep climb before I could see the *village du Tour* spread out in the gorge that separates one side of Morzine from the other. The *village* (always said, even in English, with its French pronunciation) is unfolded from trucks at the start of each day's stage and then, Potemkin-like, it is reassembled in the trailers and driven to the next point of departure, usually about 120 miles away. When in business, it buzzes like a Western saloon town. Before each day's race it is alive with journalists, racing celebrities—such as five-time champion Bernard Hinault—the current riders, and visiting corporate firemen who are *fêted* in hospitality tents. (Last year I met Senator John Kerry in the *village.*) Nearby the riders sign in for the daily stage, and then, at the sound of a gun, bell, horn, or cowbell—depending on where in France the Tour happens to be—the race disappears down the road, a beehive of spinning chains wedged between great convoys of publicity wagons.

Neither a daily journalist nor a corporate *hospitaler*, I nevertheless met up with my friends inside the cordons of the Tour *village.* One pleasure of the Bedouin racing tents is that many serve up local delicacies, and I had arrived early enough to enjoy a hot plate of scrambled eggs, local sausage, and espresso, my reward for having labored up the alpine pass. It was a day of brilliant, cool sunshine, more September than July, and the talk around the hospitality tables was of Floyd Landis's Great Escape. The day before, the American rider had gotten clear of the chasing pack, and ridden majestically over the peaks between Saint Jean de Maurienne and Morzine, to defeat his nearest rival by almost six minutes. Commenting on the win by phone, the three-time Tour winner, Greg LeMond, had called the victory "one of the great days in cycling." The breakaway victory had come the day after Landis had lost more than ten minutes and, effectively, the race. It was a rags-to-riches story, made even more appropriate for television as Landis had grown up in a Mennonite family near Lancaster, Pennsylvania. The press loved the plot line that allowed them cut-and-paste storyboards from the movie *Witness* into a remake of *Breaking Away*. Two days after I saw the Tour in Morzine, Landis rode into Paris as the winner at about the same time, presumably, that his adoring parents hitched up their buggy to go to church.

Only some weeks after the race was over did the Tour de France officialdom disclose that, on the day that he won his epic stage into Morzine, Landis had failed a drug test. Samples of his urine revealed levels of testosterone normally associated with a Bulgarian weight lifter. Landis protested his guilt. A testing of a second sample confirmed the suspicions of the first, causing his Swiss team, Cofidis—appropriately, a temporary employment agency—to fire him. Presumably at some date in the future, the Tour de France will strip Landis of his victory, and the International Cycling Union (commonly known as the UCI) will suspend him for several years from the sport, effectively ending his career and denying him the millions of dollars in endorsements that typically are due to Tour champions. The now unremembered second-place rider will be declared the winner of the yellow jersey (although no one will stop traffic on the Champs Elysées for him to try it on), and the sport of cycling can cope with a future that may relegate the most-watched sporting event in the world (after the World Cup) to something more analogous to the late-night encounters of professional wrestling.

DURING MY DAY in Morzine, no one I spoke with had a clue that Landis had been juiced. He was described as modest, hardworking, unassuming, and friendly. A few did note that the only reason Landis was still in contention at all was because, on the day before the Tour began, numerous top riders, including the great German hope, Jan Ullrich, had been denied starting the race because of their association with a doping investigation then unfolding in Spain. Other riders, like the American Tyler Hamilton, were still serving suspensions for having tested positive in the past. In Hamilton's case, he was suspected of having 'blood packed'—a transfusion meant to increase red blood cells and increase oxygen—prior to his gold medal win at the 2004 summer Olympics and then the subsequent Tour of Spain. When having my eggs in Morzine, I stood close to the English rider David Millar, a charismatic Tour hopeful who had just returned to the race after serving a two-year suspension for admitting to having taken human growth hormones. Lost in the good feelings at Morzine were the following questions: If such apparently good people as Hamilton and Millar were dopers, did that confirm that nearly everyone riding the Tour needed 'something' to finish the race? What about seven-time champion Lance Armstrong? If nearly all the top-ten riders had either confessed to or were suspected of doping, did that make him guilty by professional association, if not by his results, which were consistently better than those now suspected or confirmed to have been riding high?

Even during my brief encounter with the Tour de France, Armstrong hovered over the proceedings like Marley's ghost in cycling shorts. He was not in Morzine the day I was there, but he had visited the race a few days before, although, it seems, not to encourage his former lieutenant, Floyd Landis. By one account I heard, Armstrong had taken unusual delight when Landis had 'exploded' in the mountains. (It can only be assumed he thought the value of his legacy would stay higher if another American did not follow his seven consecutive victories with one of his own.) Armstrong remains a shareholder in his old team, now called Discovery Channel, so why should he root for a competitor, even one who had once been a teammate?

Even listening on the fringes of the Tour, I sensed that the world of cycling divides evenly between those who think Armstrong won his many victories on drugs, and those who believe that in France, in particular, there is a cottage industry devoted to smearing Armstrong's reputation with the drug label. In fact, he never tested positive to having taken banned substances and no one has ever come forward and said: "I saw Armstrong taking illegal drugs." As this game of shadows is now played out, Armstrong issues writs and libel suits against nearly everyone who hints that he was drugged for his wins. From his critics comes a near-endless parade of what might be called circumstantial witnesses, testimony from this former rider or that trainer who believes that Armstrong embraced the endemic cycling culture of doping. But no evidence exists to charge him with anything.

Most of the allegations against Armstrong are summarized in a book entitled *L.A. Confidential: Les secrets de Lance Armstrong*. Although one of the authors, David Walsh, is a correspondent for the London *Times*, the book came out only in French, as no English language publisher relished the idea of a multi-million-dollar libel suit from Armstrong. The 374-page book is what a friend of mine would call a "lid off" job, meaning that it was written to expose the deceits of Lance Armstrong. The authors interview just about everyone in the world of cycling who rode or knew Armstrong—trainers, teammates, race officials, doctors, etc.—and paint a portrait of the future seven-time Tour champion as a competitor obsessed both with winning and with the material trappings of success. As a young rider, Armstrong shows flashes of promise, but he lacks the endurance for the grand tours. After winning the World Championship in 1993, he is regarded as someone with promise in the one-day classics—a sprinter more than a potential tour rider. According to the book, when faced with the prospect of a middling career, and perhaps the loss of the team's corporate sponsorship, Armstrong tells his teammates that they need to embrace any fitness advantage (including doping) that they can. Before Armstrong shows promise as a Tour de France champion, the rider is diagnosed with testicular cancer, which, doctors in the book say, can be a specific side-affect of taking various synthetic stimulants.

Whatever the causes of Armstrong's cancer, he recovers courageously, inspires millions of others in the process, returns to racing, wins seven Tours, and earns fame and a considerable fortune. He mountain bikes with President George W. Bush and raises charity money with former President Bill Clinton. As someone said to me that morning in Morzine, "he's way beyond cycling now," meaning he is in the pantheon of superstardom, not just an athlete "who done good." But for the most part there are few flats on this golden climb. He proves a moth at the flame of celebrity and dumps his wife and the mother of his three kids for a romance with the singer Cheryl Crow. Yet the darker side of Armstrong isn't revealed in his love life so much as in his relationship with his former teammates.

Glimpses of Armstrong's encounters with former teammates show him to be something akin to the Godfather of cycling. Whenever a lieutenant, and he had many good ones, left Lance for another team, Armstrong responded as viciously as he has always chased down breakaways. From the beginning he would make it clear that he had no time for the ex-teammate. In more extreme cases, reports would circulate in the cycling press about veiled threats coming from Armstrong about certain former riders, especially ones that questioned whether Lance had won cleanly. Greg LeMond, among others, has reported that Armstrong threatened him and his wife for their suspicion that Lance had won with illegal stimulants. LeMond said: "If Armstrong's clean, it's the greatest comeback. If not, it's the greatest fraud." Armstrong, in turn, promised a parade of witnesses that would say LeMond had won his tours while doping, and he may have hinted at physical violence against LeMond and his family.

It is the group of former Armstrong teammates who could now make life particularly miserable for Armstrong. In recent years many of these same riders have either tested positive for drugs or, on their own, have confessed to using banned stimulants. Tyler Hamilton, Roberto Herras, and Floyd Landis are among the best known of Armstrong's lieutenants who have now tested positive for doping. Each of them was instrumental in some of Armstrong's seven wins in the Tour de France. Hamilton and Herras have been banned from the sport, each for two years. Presumably Landis will receive a similar suspension. But the confessions most threatening to Armstrong are those of another former rider, Frankie Andreu, once Lance's best friend in the sport and someone who now covers the Tour for American television.

In one of many Armstrong libel suits, Andreu and his wife, Betsy, testified that they had been present when the cancer-stricken Armstrong told doctors that he had taken performance-enhancing drugs. Who leaked such testimony from court records is unknown, but it is assumed that they are part of the "get Lance" constituency. Then, for reasons not clear, Andreu confessed to the *New York Times* that prior to the 2000 Tour de France (in which he rode on Armstrong's team and which Armstrong won) he had taken the banned drug erythropoietin, also known as EPO. He did not say that Armstrong had known he was taking EPO. Nor did he say that he had seen Armstrong take anything. But as I read the Andreu confession in the *Times*, I couldn't help but think that I was in a theater that was screening film noir. In the *Times* interview Andreu sounds scared and threatened. He says he is confessing to EPO as a way to "clean up the sport." But it raised this question: since doping revelations for the past ten years have only been repeated by even more doping confirmations, who or what was now forcing him, in 2006, to confess to dope taken in 2000? Was Andreu protecting his job, his family or his conscience?

Except to the millions of Frenchmen who turn out every year to watch the Tour de France, does it really matter if the sport is juiced? It may not be a scientific survey, but when I rode down the mountain from Morzine, in part through crowds waiting to see the race, I sensed little of the excitement as in years past. Maybe the French were voting with their feet? Clearly the UCI either cannot accurately test for doping or doesn't want to out of fear that the truth will set the race free from advertisers. For everyone except the fans, the stakes are high. Top professionals can earn millions in contracts and endorsements while those peeling bananas at the back of the peloton earn about $30,000 for a year's worth of hardship. A lot of the cynicism about the sport can be gleaned in the *Onion* headline: "Lance Armstrong Just Glad International Cycling Union Doesn't Test For Heroin," in which the last line of the satiric article says: "The UCI would not respond to Armstrong's comments, saying only that under current policies, any cyclist caught in possession of heroin within three days will have the drug confiscated by race officials." By all accounts the doctors for the dopers are a lot smarter than the testers for the UCI, and one way so many riders were able to blood pack was by using their own blood. The lesson that sends out about cycling, or professional sports in general, is that many are in the game to devour their own.

IN MANY WAYS, the scandals around professional cycling are similar to those in baseball, in which Barry Bonds, one of the all-time great champions, is rumored, but not proven in court, to have taken performance-enhancing drugs. By this time, to use the qualifier "rumored" in connection with Barry Bonds, must seem to most readers to be pedantic and legalistic. Who except diehard Giants fans doesn't think that Bonds doped to hit seventy-three home runs and then chase Henry Aaron's all-time home run record? Everyone has read the accounts of what Bonds looked like in his early seasons—a lean base stealer with some power—and who, by the time he is nearing age forty, starts to look like yet another East German shot putter. Isn't his personal trainer and syringe holder, Greg Anderson, serving time rather than incriminate his former boss, Barry Bonds? Did not a best-selling account of the Bay Area Laboratory Co-Operative (BALCO) conclude: "Of course Anderson's primary job was to provide Bonds with performance-enhancing drugs and to track his regime."

Down the hill from the Tour de France and on summer vacation in the United States, I heard a lot about whether Bonds would be indicted and whether, if he were, his records for single-season home runs or those for his career would be expunged from baseball records. As it was the North American sports conversation of summer, I decided to "look it up," by reading *Game of Shadows* by Mark Fainaru and Lance Williams, which has the subtitle: *Barry Bonds, BALCO, and the Steroids Scandal That Rocked Professional Sports*. Essentially, the book was published to blow the lid off Barry Bonds. It succeeded in that the book's conclusion that Bonds juiced is now widely accepted. Perhaps the authors got the ultimate "selling review" when the U.S. government empanelled a federal grand jury to weigh evidence against Bonds, who among other transgressions might have lied to an earlier grand jury about taking dope. But the facts about whether Bonds lied to a grand jury or used drugs in pursuit of baseball stardom have nothing to do with whether *Game of Shadows* is a good book. Having now read it, I can say that only a book as bad as this one can make anyone sympathize with the unsympathetic Barry Bonds.

Fainaru and Williams come to the ballpark through the murky world of investigative journalism, which, under the banner of crusading for the truth, often reprints innuendo, rumors, allegations, suppositions, and self-serving conclusions, usually from "informed" but always "unnamed" sources, whose vested interests are impossible to fathom. As a literary form, investigative reporting came to life with the Watergate dispatches of Carl Bernstein and Bob Woodward. Only thirty-three years later were readers informed that the person dropping the dime on the Nixon administration was the second ranking officer in the FBI, and thus someone motivated by institutional interests—outing the CIA's domestic operations, for starters—more than truth, justice, and the American way. In the case of Bonds, it is equally unclear who is ratting on the star and why, although those with grudges include a dumped girlfriend, an ambitious but not very thorough prosecutor, slighted ex-teammates, and authors with a large book contract to deliver the goods against Barry. From the book's footnotes (which are often laughable, as in: "A source close to Bonds"), it is apparent that Fainaru and Williams only believe what is leaked from grand juries or whispered in back alleys.

As described in *Game of Shadows*, Bonds is your basic prick. Whether or not he's terrific at baseball (I would say he is), he is also moody, controlling, vain, angry, secretive, and prone to rages. In building the case against Bonds, one source says: "I don't think he ever figured out what to do to get people to like him." (Bonds may be the first ballplayer indicted for bad manners.) At the ballpark he is surly to reporters (another capital offense) and installs a vibrating lounge chair near his locker. After Mark McGwire becomes an American idol for breaking Roger Maris's record of 61* home runs, Bonds avails himself of such mysterious products as "the clear" and "the cream" and wakes up a few months later with the body of an "NFL linebacker...with broad shoulders, a wide chest, and huge biceps." Even *MAD Magazine* satirized him with a ballad, "Barry At The Bat," in which a few stanzas read:

> *Big bashers got the headlines now—the rest were out of date;*
> *No sweat, the folks at BALCO Labs stepped smartly to the plate;*
> *For Bonds, their line of "nutrients" would surely help him out,*
> *To beef him up till he became the latest King of Clout.*

> *He'd earn a slew of MVPs, be hailed an all-time great,*
> *But trouble now was brewing—some would call it Steroidgate;*
> *Jose Conseco authored Juiced, which gave us our first clue;*
> *Big Mac was outed in the book, oh, yes, and Barry too.*

For the authors of *Game of Shadows*, proof of Bonds's doping lies, partly, in his unprecedented hitting tear, the likes of which baseball has never seen in someone his age. They write:

> Over the first 13 seasons of his career, from 1986-1998, Bonds hit .290 and averaged 32 home runs and 93 RBI. He hit one home run every 16 at-bats. But in the six seasons after he began using performance-enhancing drugs—that is, from 1999 to 2004, between the ages of 34 and 40—Bonds's batting line averaged .328, 49, and 105. That represented 17 additional home runs and 12 additional RBI per year. He would hit a home run every 8.4 at-bats.

One of the few comparable streaks came from Babe Ruth, who between the ages of thirty-two and thirty-seven averaged .354, 50 home runs, and 155 RBIs. But the only things Ruth was "on" in those years were hot dogs, beer, and female companions. (After games, the Babe would tell his teammates that he was going to see "a party.")

THE UNPLEASANT STORY of Barry Bonds is made more unpleasant when you realize the extent to which the federal government has spent millions of dollars to prove him a fraud. (Aren't the conclusions of fans with stadium banners enough?) Many passages in *Game of Shadows* put the Bonds investigation on a par with other notable government witch-hunts, such as that to bring down Lewis "Scooter" Libby. Fainaru and Williams write: "In hindsight, it was a startling thing to consider: Bonds, the greatest player of his era, secretly watched by federal lawmen who suspected him of using drugs to cheat his way into the record books." In congratulating themselves in the epilogue, the authors hint at the methods employed in this game of hardball: "If Agent Novitsky had not decided to dig through Victor Conte's trash, or if Don Catlin had not cracked the code for the THG, or if the Chronicle had not published the secret testimony of the baseball stars and inspired Jose Canseco to recast his autobiography into a memoir of drug abuse, nothing would have been done at all." Less tendentious, all *MAD Magazine* did was end its parody with: "But there's little joy in baseball— Barry Bonds has been found out."

I have no way of verifying whether Armstrong and Bonds played within the rules of their sports. For much of the time that Bonds was allegedly juicing, baseball had only vague policies against the use of artificial stimulants. (Mark McGwire openly displayed vials of androstenedione, so-called andro, in his locker.) In the witch-hunt of both Bonds and Armstrong, journalists and investigators have resorted to tactics as deceptive as those used by the Bush administration in the outing of Valerie Plame. In Armstrong's case, Tour de France testing laboratories mishandled his urine and blood samples and, at times, leaked results to the press that are at variance from what they told race officials. (It now turns out the same sloppy procedures were used in handling Landis's blood.) Against Bonds, the government and the press have collaborated to smear him with supposedly secret grand jury testimony. In the acknowledgements of *Game of Shadows*, the authors confide: "Finally, we reserve our greatest thanks to the sources who, at considerable risk, provided us with the confidential documents and information that revealed the true scope of the BALCO conspiracy." On closer inspection it seems neither the Feds nor the press played by the rules any more than did Bonds.

In the BALCO investigation, the target was Victor Conte, the owner of the nutrient outlet, who was dealing steroids on the side. Fainaru and Williams describe him as if he were the Broadway Danny Rose of the sports underworld: "Now in his early thirties, Conte was of average build and wore big, round glasses, had curly black hair, and sported a thin mustache that looked a bit cheesy....He was one of those guys who liked to play the angles, and he was good at it." According to the book and investigators, Conte gave steroids to Bonds's personal trainer, Greg Anderson, who then buffed up the Giants star. But something went terribly wrong in the government's case against Conte. Of the forty counts initially brought against him, he was only convicted of four and served four months in prison.

More bizarrely, although *Game of Shadows* is there to reveal "one of the dirty little secrets of American sports in the twenty-first century: that top-level athletes had become as enmeshed in the steroid culture as bodybuilders," an important source for Fainaru and Williams was none other than Conte himself. That came to light as the federal government was investigating leaks to the *San Francisco Chronicle* (and their reporters Fainaru and Williams), which published excerpts from the grand jury testimony. And it was the government itself, while investigating the newspaper, that accidentally revealed that Conte had been the source of the leaks. An electronic court filing neglected to cover up names.

In other words, Fainaru and Williams wrote an exposé about Conte and Bonds, using Conte as the main source against himself, but not telling their readers who was ratting on Bonds or why. Meanwhile the government is rummaging through Conte's trash and claiming victory while the BALCO owner beats about thirty-six of the raps against him. (Clearly he is good at "the angles," or the trash was just that, trash.) Then the *Chronicle* starts hiding behind the First Amendment, refusing to say how it got secret grand jury testimony while at the same time its reporters are publishing a best-selling book, beating their chests about how they used unnamed sources to out Bonds. In *Game of Shadows*, there is a line: "But that same morning, the Chronicle broke one more story: WHAT BONDS TOLD BALCO GRAND JURY." Casual readers might miss that "the Chronicle" in this case is also Fainaru and Williams, here writing about (and congratulating) themselves as if third parties. Barry Bonds could claim kinship with Scooter Libby when he heard the following:

> Whoever had given the newspaper the material had broken the law, Ryan contended. *The Chronicle* was breaking the law merely by possessing the documents and the tape. The newspaper was instructed to return everything to the government and name whoever leaked them.

But the *Chronicle* and its reporters thought nothing of both being fed such information and transmuting it into a page-one, best-selling story. (Now the judge in the case is threatening to imprison the reporters, as he claims, for not revealing who illegally released to the paper the grand jury transcripts. But, analyze this: it was the government's incompetence that outed Conte as one source.) Instead of explaining to its readers who was leaking to the *Chronicle* and why, the paper hid behind the First Amendment as its reporters were quoting themselves and were writing a book in which the alleged target, Victor Conte, was a main source against himself. ("Franz Kafka, call your office.") What prompts Fainaru and Williams to rail against the likes of Barry Bonds—"Competitive sports, it turned out, was part mirage, a game of shadows"—when they were also deep into the forest.

DURING THE SUMMER of 2006, tired of professional sports as lab cultures, I tried to take in a few baseball games. I had business meetings and family gatherings up and down the East Coast. By using the Internet, I could plan to attend games along the route. Strangely, the games that I saw diminished rather than revived my affection for the major leagues. Emotionally, I love the idea of professional baseball and summer afternoons at the park. A rite of passage when I was growing up was to go with school friends to Shea and Yankee stadiums. But now I resent the cost of tickets (over a hundred dollars in Yankee Stadium), the price of hot dogs ($7.95, assuming you don't want mustard), the organ music between pitches, and the ambiance of the stadiums (noisy strip malls with watered beer).

Nevertheless, on a business trip to Philadelphia, I did go to Citizens Bank Park, the new home of the Phillies. When I was a boy, the stadium in Philadelphia, Shibe Park, was a relic of pre–World War I baseball, a link to the Philadelphia A's and Connie Mack. I remember the feeling of violation when the wreckers' ball destroyed it in 1970 and the Phillies moved to the sterile confines of Veterans Stadium. From the 1960s into the 1980s, baseball stadiums were built with all the emotional warmth of urban renewal projects. Generally they were moved from downtown areas into nearby suburbs (so that fans could park cars), and the new ballparks were covered with Astroturf, which gave baseball the feeling that it was played with superballs. That was also the era of domed stadiums in which pop flies to second base would occasionally lodge in the roof. By contrast, Citizens Bank Park is cast in the line of retro-stadiums that follow the contours of Oriole Park at Camden Yards. In theory, these ballparks are built to evoke a nostalgic innocence about the city and the national pastime, as if the clock for each was being reset to the 1920s, before anyone had heard of "the clear" and "the cream" or taxpayer subsidized industrial revenue bonds, another pep pill for baseball's owners.

My meetings in Philadelphia ended early enough for me to get to the game by the third inning. The day was hot, sunny, and uncomfortably humid. I walked from the end of the subway to the ballpark. As all I wanted to see was the stadium, I assumed I would buy a cheap seat at the door. But the era of five dollar bleacher seats is as long gone as that of wool uniforms and home runs celebrated with slight tips of the cap. Because it was already the third inning, I ended up buying a $27.50 ticket from a scalper for ten dollars. Looking at the face value of the ticket, I thought I might be in a box seat. But all that $27.50 would have gotten me in 2006 was a seat in the upper deck, not far from the left-field foul pole.

I watched for three innings. During that time I wandered around the stadium, which is much larger than I expected. To be sure, it is a vast improvement upon the housing-project designs in Veterans Stadium. The outfield wall has a few nooks that no doubt will contribute to the number of triples hit. In the upper decks there is a selection of food courts (four dollars for bottled water), and the stadium is sited so that the Philadelphia skyline is framed over the centerfield wall. The problem at Citizens Bank Park isn't the design so much as how the game is watched and staged. Admittedly, I was jet lagged from my European flight, but nothing prepared me for the audio and visual assault from the scoreboard. Seemingly every pitch was serenaded with hard rock or those organ "charge" songs. No matter where I went in the stadium I found my eyes focusing not on the game but on televised scoreboard advertisements. To go to a game now is to be trapped inside a multiplex cinema. Clearly the owners of most teams have no confidence in the product of baseball, and its risk of pitchers' duels. They have turned baseball into another day at the mall, complete with Muzak, video games, juiced baseballs, and clownish figures. Barry Bonds got it right when he said: "We're entertainers," but he should have added that the players are part of a traveling freak show.

WHILE ON THE East Coast, I also caught the game celebrating the twentieth anniversary of the 1986 Mets. That team had won the World Series against the Boston Red Sox, most dramatically in game six, when the Mets rallied from a two-run deficit with two outs in the bottom of the 10th inning. (Tired joke: "What do Billy Buckner and Michael Jackson have in common?" Answer: "Each wears a glove for no apparent reason.") The 1986 Mets had many "one-name" players, including: Doc, Straw, Keith, Wally, Mookie, Bobby, Rusty, Davey, Ray, Kevin, El Sid, George, Lee, Gary (the Kid), Jesse, and Lenny (Nails). On the evening of their anniversary celebration, most of them answered a roll call and dramatically ran to the field from somewhere in the stands at Shea.

Like all of New York that season, I was a Mets fan when they won the World Series and well remember standing on a milk crate to glimpse their open cars in a Wall Street ticker tape parade. I could not help but juxtapose the feel-good evening for the 1986 Mets with the witch-hunt of Barry Bonds.

Even an adoring profile of that team, *The Bad Guys Won* by Jeff Pearlman, describes the drug culture that surrounded the team: "A decade before it became common for baseball players to consume steroids and human growth hormones, many of the Mets were popping amphetamines as if they were Advils. While it was common for the 1980s ballplayer to abuse the drug, New York likely led the league….The Mets were looking for a boost, and the pills—also known as "speed," "up," "fast," louee," "goey," "whiz," "pep pills," "uppers," and "greenies," and illegally distributed by an in-clubhouse employee of the club—did wonders."

Unlike *Game of Shadows*, in which the authors would like to think they are breaking the story of original sin, *The Bad Guys Won* is a frolic across the diamond. With no hint that he is investigating anything except boorish behavior, Pearlman writes: "To pop a greenie was to plug yourself into an electrical outlet"; or "Left fielder Tim Raines learned to dive headfirst so as not to puncture the bag of coke in his back uniform pocket." He goes on: "In 1986 the New York Mets spent every day under the giant-sized tent of the Big Apple Circus. Things moved at 10,000 mph—a hard-to-track swirl of baseball and booze and women and drugs and cars and fans and wins." They sneer at the other teams ("Rice cut the bag like a sixteen-wheeler turning into a McDonald's"), not to mention each other (Gary "Camera" Carter is thought to be "baseball's cleanest, most wholesome, most photogenic, most accessible, *most despised* player"). At one point Lenny Dykstra was discovered *in flagrante backseat* with a girl from a local high school. As pitcher Bobby Ojeda said: "We were throwbacks, man. We were like, 'gimme a steak, gimme a fuckin' beer, gimme a smoke, and get the fuck out of our way.'" Bonds may be no different, but even

in *Game of Shadows*, he is often out of the house at 6:00
A.M., together with his many fitness trainers, pumping iron
and shagging fly balls. Maybe his crime is that he is the
modernistic look of baseball's future (a rat pumped up in a
lab) while the 1986 Mets, more than any retro-stadium, are
a link to the bygone eras of Ty Cobb's cleats and the Black
Sox scandals.

I WAS THINKING about the battle over the future of baseball
when I got together in the Berkshires with former New York
Yankee Jim Bouton. He is the author of *Ball Four*, a diary
of a year in baseball with the 1969 Seattle Pilots, and, more
recently, *Foul Ball*, an account of trying to save a historic
minor-league stadium in Pittsfield, Massachusetts. Together
with our families and some mutual friends, we met over a
Sunday picnic, at which the children discussed school and
new movies, and the adults weighed in on the options for
peace in the Middle East. Before everyone scattered, I rum-
maged through our host's mudroom until I found a ball and
a glove. For the last fifteen minutes of that glorious Berkshire
summer afternoon, I had Bouton throw me knuckleballs. I
had never caught a real one, and his—which he threw professionally for the Seattle Pilots, Houston Astros, and Atlanta
Braves—break like screwballs and float like confetti. I felt
pretty good about handling so many wobbly pitches until we
stopped and Bouton said: "In a game, I would be throwing
them twice as hard."

After the picnic, my daughters and I drove north into
Vermont, and we stopped to look at Wahconah Park, which
Bouton and his partner, Chip Elitzer, had tried to save from
demolition by bringing an independent minor-league team
to Pittsfield. *Foul Ball* ends with the bad guys winning, in

that Bouton and Elitzer, despite three-hundred pages of good intentions, are turned away in their bid to lease Wahconah Park, fix it up, and bring in a team that would be owned locally. But in a twist of good fortune, after *Foul Ball* was published, Bouton and Elitzer were chosen to be the landlords of the historic, wooden stadium and to field a team. For a while it looked as if the ballpark where Casey Stengel and Lou Gehrig played would get a new lease on life and that Pittsfield would get an independent team of its own.

Foul Ball: Part II, issued in paperback by Lyons Press, updates the Wahconah Park story after the hardback edition was published. Although Bouton's first story ruffled many local feathers,[1] the voters in Pittsfield eventually turn out the rascals, and the administration of the new mayor awards Wahconah to a consortium that Bouton and Elitzer are putting together. To show good faith, the partners invest $250,000 of their own money to get the work started at Wahconah, and they are the impresarios for a game of vintage baseball, which is played according to the rules of the game in the nineteenth century. Bouton explains:

> There is only one umpire, positioned ten to fifteen feet behind and at an angle to the batter. The umpire is always addressed as "sir" by the players and may smoke a cigar. In the event the umpire does not have a clear view of a play he can request a "Gentlemen's Ruling," in which the players involved tell what transpired and a call can be reversed. And my favorite—the umpire has the option to ask for input from the fans in the stands.

---

1. "What's worse," Bouton writes, "than a lame-duck mayor with a chip on his shoulder? A lame-duck mayor with a chip on his shoulder who needs powerful friends."

The vintage players—for the most part local softballers and college players—parade through Pittsfield in antique cars. Many players grow handlebar moustaches for the occasion. ESPN broadcasts the game. Bouton pitches for one side. Former Boston Red Sox pitcher "Spaceman" Bill Lee pitches for the other. ("He was wearing a faded 1903 Red Sox uniform shirt, the one he keeps in the trunk of his car in case a game breaks out.") An era of good baseball feelings overtakes Pittsfield and the idea of a Wahconah revival until some local entrenched interests (whose feathers Bouton had ruffled in *Foul Ball*) decide to play bean ball with the idea of independent baseball.

Although Bouton and Elitzer are using private (starting with their own) money to repair a municipal stadium, and even though the team will be privately owned, they are told that, for the project to go ahead, they will need to play ball with local unions, as if this were a government contract. Bouton describes the visit they receive from the head of the New England Council of Carpenters, Local 108: "He looks like a cross between a child's bathtub frog and a linebacker from a small college. He has stab wound scars on his arms and chest, which he volunteered to show us."

Bouton and Elitzer are anything but scabs, but they quickly realize that making Wahconah a union-rules renovation will kill the dream. Elitzer asks at one town meeting: "Who is hijacking unionism's good name to kill baseball in Pittsfield?" Clearly, the answer is those slighted in Bouton's book and those not cut in on the action ("'You should have hired Potsy as a consultant,' said Nadeau"). The last and most eloquent word comes from Bouton's wife, Paula, who tells a town meeting: "And what do we get for our blood, sweat, and tears? Nothing but backstabbing and extortion and obstacles

and complaints. I've had it with Pittsfield and the Parks Commission and the newspaper and with all of you. No more. I
want out! Let's go home." Since that time, Pittsfield has been
without professional baseball. The game my daughters and I
walked in on was from a desultory summer league. We saw
a single stretched into a double, and a botched double play,
reminding me of what Dodgers manager Tommy Lasorda
said disparagingly about Darryl Strawberry: "Even a dog will
run after a ball."

HAD BOUTON AND Elitzer succeeded in establishing an independent baseball team at Wahconah Park, I imagine that it
would have resembled the genial madness of the St. Paul
Saints, a minor-league team run by the actor Bill Murray. He
owned the Northern League team in the mid-1990s when it
had a pig named Tobias act as the ball boy; a legless outfielder,
who was remarkably good; and Darryl Strawberry, who was
in the minors as part of one of his many last chances in the
game. The team might now be largely forgotten, as Murray
has moved on, except that it was memorialized in *Slouching
Toward Fargo*, in which Neal Karlen records a year of zany life
on the minor-league farm. Actually, the story has a happier
ending than was intended. Karlen worked for *Rolling Stone*
magazine, and its owner, Jann Wenner, commissioned him
to bury a hatchet in Murray's back. (At least Karlen's motives
in accepting the assignment, job preservation, are clearer
than those of Fainaru and Williams.) Karlen confesses: "If I
wanted to get this story and myself back into *Rolling Stone*,
I had to show him 'Bill Murray driving the Saints' team bus
while Darryl Strawberry is freebasing crack in the backseat.'"
On the road, however, Karlen falls in love not just with Tobias
and a few Baseball Annies, but with independent baseball

and especially the Saints that had as its motto: "Fun is good."
Murray only a makes a few cameo appearances with the
team. But when he does, he sometimes coaches third base,
works with the ground crew, or cheers up the ball boy ("You
look good, Tobias. You're a gamer."). Before a big game, he
flies in from a film location and motivates the team in the
voice of *Caddyshack's* Carl Spackler. ("So we finish the eighteenth and he's gonna stiff me. And I say, 'Hey, Lama, hey,
how about a little something, you know, for the effort.'") In
Hollywood, Murray has a reputation for moodiness. On the
diamond, he is closer to the screen version of himself—whim-
sical, slightly innocent, daring. "I like the rejects," he tells
Karlen, "and I like the carny part of minor-league baseball."
But with his millions he is making the point that Bouton and
Elitzer wished to replicate in Pittsfield: "The magic is that this
is how you remember baseball from when you were young.
And the fact that we're independent from organized baseball
meant we could make our own rules, with no interference."

While Murray comes and goes, the man running the Big
Top on a daily basis is Mike Veeck, the son of the legendary baseball owner and stuntman, Bill Veeck. To clarify the
pronunciation of his last name, the father titled his autobiography: *Veeck as in Wreck.* The father described what he did
in baseball as "running his circuses." Mike Veeck describes
his father to Karlen: "The fans loved my father, but organized
baseball, the other owners, all hated Bill Veeck. He wrote
two books—*Veeck as in Wreck* and *The Hustler's Handbook*—
where he made fun by name of the people who controlled
baseball, and they never forgave him his apostasy." Mike
himself shares some sense of being a refugee from the major
leagues. When his father owned his last team, the Chicago White Sox, Mike organized Disco Demolition Night,

probably the most notorious promotion in baseball history, although whether you loved or hated it probably depends on what you think of the Bee Gees.

The 1980s White Sox were terrible, and Comisky Park resembled a shooting gallery. To boost attendance, Mike conceived the idea to have a bonfire of disco records between games of a double header. Instead of the usual 3,500 die-hard Sox fans, some 60,000 showed up at Comisky and another 40,000 were turned away. All came clutching albums by the likes of Donna Summer. Karlen describes what happened at the pyre set up in center field: "Between games, a buxom fire goddess dubbed Loreli ignited the records in a great explosion. Suddenly seven thousand fans were scaling the walls and on the field, running wild, stoned, and amuck...whipping their albums like Frisbees." It was the first and probably only Disco Riot. The police had to be called in to quell "the fever," and the White Sox forfeited the second game. Even the audacious Veecks were repentant. Afterward his father sold the team, and Mike had to wait until Bill Murray gave him the chance to advance the baseball cause that "fun is good." In Saint Paul he greets fan at the turnstiles. Among his many promotions he puts on a Jerry Garcia Night during which, when an opposing player hits a home run, the announcer mumbles: "Whatever."

Mike Veeck is just one of the saints discovered on the road to Fargo. The rest, a combination of pheenoms and fading journeymen, inhabit a world that Karlen calls "The Life." It involves: "Sleeping until noon. Playing ball at night. Guzzling beer until closing time and chasing what ballplayers call 'puss' after the game. The Life, be it baseball, rock & roll, or the carnival: where time is turned upside down, and the straight nine-to-five world is looked upon with contempt." Girls who hang around the team are called "flies," and the scoreboard girls are local celebrities. The team song is the theme from the movie *Shaft*, and Karlen refers to the Saints' best reliever as "the Closer," although it refers to his after-hours abilities more than his performance in save situations.[2]

The Saints' manager is the bemused Marty Scott, who deals empathetically with the likes of the legless outfielder ("Dave reminded me of what baseball is supposed to be about. It's about *trying* when everybody says stop."); the rehabbing Strawberry, who hits towering home runs and then signs with the Yankees; and the ever-present ball boy pig. "This," he says, "is the league of the last hurrah," echoing sentiments of St. Paul resident Garrison Keillor, who found himself defending Tobias in a column: "Once a player from an opposing team was offended by the pig and turned to the umpire and said, 'That is so bush league,' and the ump said, 'This *is* the bush league.'" But the Saints never fail to live in contrast, especially, to their crosstown rivals, the Minnesota Twins, who play inside the Metrodome. Karlen remarks: "During the summer on Minnesota's rare golden days, going inside to watch baseball seemed depressing, sad, pathetic, and very expensive."

LATE IN THE summer, when my sons were back from camp, I wanted to take them to a ballgame before we headed home to Switzerland. We were in Maine and toyed with the idea of a night at Fenway Park. But on a similar outing a friend of mine spent $900 with a ticket broker and then fifty dollars on hot dogs. While trolling the Internet, I learned that

---

2. Karlen writes: "Wade Boggs once went to the trouble of figuring out that he hit .333 with his mistress in Fenway Park and only .229 when his wife was in attendance."

Bill Murray had sold the St. Paul Saints ("Whatever...") and had purchased the Brockton Rox, a minor-league team that plays south of Boston. It had even inherited the Saints motto, "Fun is good," and the best seats in the house cost seven dollars. I bought eight seats behind home plate and invited my boyhood friend Nick Seamon and his family. They brought a picnic, which we ate while the teams warmed up. But it was my friend Nick who noticed that the awning near the hot dog stand read "Concessions...Confessions...Contentions."

Before I had read *Slouching Toward Fargo* or knew of the connection with Bill Murray, I had heard of the Brockton Rox when they had offered Theo Epstein the position of general manager, after he had quit the Boston Red Sox, apparently in anger. In part, the Rox press release making the offer read:

> November 3, 2005 - BROCKTON – The Brock-
> ton Rox will officially offer the position of General
> Manager to former Red Sox GM Theo Epstein today.
> After three years at the helm of the Red Sox, it's
> assumed that Epstein is looking for a greater challenge.
> "We haven't won a championship in two years," said
> Rox President Jim Lucas. "But we're bringing in a new
> manager, scouring the waiver wires and we can't think of
> a better candidate to manage our $87,500 team payroll
> than Theo Epstein."

Some months later, when the future Hall of Fame pitcher Roger Clemens was wavering between retirement and playing, the Rox tried to outbid the Yankees, Red Sox, and Astros:

> Money is no object. The Rox will offer Clemens the maxi-
> mum monthly salary of $3,000 on Opening Day (May will
> be pro-rated). As for living quarters, the Rox will offer him

accommodations with a host family in Brockton where he can stay free of charge and will arrange for a special rate for his family, when they come to visit, at the local Residence Inn.

Clemens can have his choice of uniform numbers, although numbers 21 and 22 have been claimed by other players on the roster. In addition, Rox hats have a "B" on them, a letter he is familiar with from his Red Sox days. In the locker room, Roger will have a corner locker and his own rocking chair that will have "Roger" printed on it (on removable duct tape). Lucas adds, "As a special promotion, we will produce a special bobble called 'The Brocket' showing 'The Rocket' in a Brockton uniform.

We loved our evening at Campanelli Stadium. After parking the car, the attendant saw that I was with young boys, one of whom had a glove, and he disappeared into a shed and returned with two baseballs—presumably from home runs that had rattled around the lot. During the game we loved watching the curves break and the speed of even routine ground balls. The fathers, anyway, enjoyed the blonde belly dancer employed to gyrate with hula-hoops on top of each dugout. The rest of the between-inning entertainment failed to live up to my St. Paul Saints expectations, but after Tobias they may have been exaggerated. A bit wistfully the boys and I recalled the lobster toss that is staged at the games of the Portland Sea Dogs and the recording of breaking car glass that is played every time, in Trenton, a foul ball goes out of the stadium. But it was as close as we would get that summer, to what it was Bouton had dreamed about. He writes about saving Wahconah Park: "Here was an opportunity not only to save an old ballpark but to turn The System upside down—a system that extorts taxpayer dollars to build new stadiums for migratory teams. We'd replace the same old threat with a brand new offer: We'll spend *private* dollars to renovate an *existing* ballpark for a *locally* owned team."

At the picnic in the Berkshires, I had asked Bouton what he was doing now that reviving Wahconah Park was no longer an option. He said he had founded an association for vintage baseball teams. He was selling them uniforms and equipment plus explaining the concept and rules. Already he had about fifty teams in the association, and it clearly pleased him that vintage baseball had a following. He writes in *Foul Ball: Part II*:

> Most important were the vintage uniform and behavior codes, which I personally would like to see enforced today: no batting gloves, helmets, wrist bands, elbow pads, skin guards, sunglasses, logo shoes, pajama pants, gold chains, or earrings. No arguing with the umpire, stepping out of the batter's box, calling time out, charging the pitcher, posing at home plate, curtain calling, chest bumping, high-fiving, pointing to the sky, or kissing jewelry.
> Just baseball, dammit!

Not having played vintage baseball, I cannot say whether it is fun or not. I suspect it is. The gloves are little more than leather mittens, the pitching is underhand, and routine fly balls are never sure outs. The language of vintage baseball, unlike faux traditional stadiums, recalls an era when America was clear, literate, direct, and witty in its speech. In vintage baseball, when the bases are loaded, they are "drunk." Pitchers are called "ballists" or "hurlers." The word "ginger" describes determination. Errors are "muffs." A hard grounder is a "daisy cutter." A "sky ball" is a pop. A run is an "ace." Fans are "cranks." Home plate is the "dish." I also like the idea of vintage baseball as a political statement, as it speaks, literally and figuratively, of grassroots. It sounds like the game can be played in sandlots and cornfields, and the only needed concessions (confessions?) are picnics. Teams are clubs, in the best sense of the world, and it is impossible to imagine the sport ever needing juiced superstars to fill multimillion-dollar stadiums. Perhaps the nicest aspect of vintage baseball is that, no matter what you take for your tired muscles, there is no system to beat. Playing the game is all that matters.

Hell Heaped Up at Gallipoli

(2004)

Here lies the servant of God
Sub-Lieutenant in the English Navy,
Who died for the deliverance of Constantinople
from the Turks.

—Headstone of Rupert Brooke, who died
on the Greek island of Skyros, on the way
to Gallipoli with the invasion forces.

MY FIRST TRIP to the Sublime Porte came at the end of a
Grand Tour. In June 1976, I had paid my library fines and
graduated from college in time to join a family vacation
that began in Naples, meandered across southern Italy and
Greece, and ended on the M.V. *Adjaria*, a Soviet Black Sea
steamer that linked Beirut with Odessa, not to mention the
then-hostile capitals of Greece and Turkey.

At sunset on that overnight passage, we rounded Cape
Sounion, its white-marble columns shimmering above the
brown cliffs and Homer's wine-dark sea. The next morning
we entered the Dardanelles, with Troy to our right and the
forgotten trenches of Gallipoli to the left, "corners of a foreign
field," like those that Rupert Brooke described as "for ever
England," but which he never saw.

Most of the other passengers on the *Adjaria* were vaca-
tioning Georgians or Russian diplomats fleeing the civil war

in Lebanon. We arrived in Istanbul in the late afternoon, when a summer haze and the setting sun framed in velvet a skyline of minarets, the Blue Mosque, and Agia Sophia, where East meets West under once-Christian domes that now call the faithful.

Thirty years elapsed between my visits to the Golden Horn. On this occasion I arrived on a flight from Geneva and rode into the modern city in a cramped yellow taxi, a distant echo from the old Chevys that roamed Istanbul in the 1970s. In between appointments, I toured the Blue Mosque and drank coffee overlooking the Bosphorus, which I find as visually hypnotizing as the New York or Hong Kong harbors. I never tire of its parade of ships, even though coping with modern Istanbul can be exhausting. If crusaders ever succeed in retaking Constantinople, they will find that they have inherited a city of twelve million people, not simply the mixed metaphors of Arabic script on the walls of Christian monuments. But it was the Fourth Crusade in 1204 that caused more damage to the Byzantine capital than did the conquering Turks in 1453.

Gallipoli: *"Who in this generation has heard of Lancashire landing?"*

TOWARD THE END of my week in Turkey, I decided to visit the battlefield at Gallipoli. After seeing the Dardanelles from the rail of the *Adjaria*, I had read the histories of Alan Moorhead and Geoffrey Moorhouse, seen the Peter Weir film *Gallipoli*, and traveled extensively through Australia and New Zealand, where in each country I collected books and memoirs about the campaign—notably Maurice Shadbolt's excellent *Voices of Gallipoli*. But until I visit a place, I find it an abstraction.

It took four hours at warp Turkish speeds to traverse the farmland that rolls along the coast. We crossed the Dardanelles at Gelibolu—a village of rusting howitzers and pistachio salesmen—from which the peninsula takes its name.

To the Turks the Gallipoli campaign is known as The Battle of Çanakkale, a town on the southern side of the straits, where I spent the night at ANZAC House, an Australian youth hostel near the ferry landing. "Who in this generation has heard of Lancashire Landing or Gully Ravine or the Third Battle of Krithia," is a question posed by the Australian war correspondent and historian, Alan Moorhead. He was evoking images of failure that once were as resonant as the Battle of the Bulge or Tawara. Nevertheless, each year about 10,000 young Australians and New Zealanders (hence the word ANZAC) visit the battlefields, to pay respects to an equal number of their countrymen who died on the imperial road to Constantinople.

Little can match morning coffee in Çanakkale, overlooking the Dardanelles. Along this narrow channel of destiny was an armada of oil tankers, grain ships, naval destroyers, container vessels, and tramp steamers, ships of the line that connects Istanbul and the Black Sea ports to western markets. Control this café, the thought passed my mind, and you control much of the world's trade.

On March 18, 1915, with the Western Front stalemated in mud from the English Channel to the Swiss border, the British decided to force the Dardanelles with a naval squadron of eighteen battleships and thus, in one bold stroke, seize Istanbul, bolster the faltering Russians, knock Turkey from the war, isolate Germany's flank and, maybe, restore Christianity in what had been Constantinople.

The First Sea Lord, Winston Churchill, supported the end run, which failed for the absence of competent mine sweepers off Çanakkale. Turkish mines provided by Germany, plus mobile batteries hidden among the hills, sank three battleships and crippled three more, killing 700 sailors, which convinced the British high command, including Churchill, that ground troops would be needed to silence the artillery and open the straits for the crusade.

Not often since 1066 had an English army landed from the sea. When General Sir Ian Hamilton departed for the invasion beaches, he sailed into what one historian has described as "a disagreeable atmosphere of confusion and irresolution." Thirty-seven days had lapsed between the failed naval attack on the Straits and the army invasion, giving the Turks ample time to defend against the landings. Army commanders had no control over the navy, which put the ANZAC battalions ashore one mile from their designated landings and in the lee of thorny cliffs. At Cape Helles, where British troops came ashore, one platoon of Turkish gunners killed or wounded 60 percent of a Lancashire battalion. As the historian John Keegan concluded: "Nothing was more improvised than the plan."

Nine months later, defeat at Gallipoli cost Churchill, perhaps unfairly, his job and almost his career, which was resurrected in the 1930s only after the Germans invaded the rest of Europe. But even if the strategy had merit, which in my view it did, the Gallipoli offensive bogged down on the beaches. In retrospect, the 1944 battle of Normandy was the only victory at Gallipoli, as lessons from the peninsula, applied twenty-nine years later, made that similar operation a success.

Anzac Cove: *"Hell heaped up"*

AFTER MORNING COFFEE, I joined a tour that started its day
at ANZAC Cove, a bend in the coastline that is the Little
Bighorn of Australian history. Keegan describes it: "To the
north and south, high ground comes down to the sea, so
that ANZAC takes the form of a tiny amphitheatre—the
smallness of the Gallipoli battle-ground is the most striking
impression left on the visitor—dominated on three sides by
high ground." Over nine months it became a city of the dead:
"for all the world like a great foundry...where shells were
bursting great fiery showers." "Hell heaped up," was how a
New Zealander described it.

Between April 1915 and January 1916, when the Allies
finally withdrew, ANZAC forces never advanced more than
two or three miles inland. After the amphibious landings, the
Turks rushed regiments into defiles that came to be known
as Lone Pine, The Sphinx, Shrapnel Valley, The Nek and
Gun Ridge. (The Atatürk hagiography includes his desperate
command: "I'm not ordering you to attack. I am ordering you
to die.") The Turks never relinquished the high ground. "On
the hills," Aubrey Herbert, later an MP, wrote, "we are the
eyebrows, and the Turks are the forehead."

Much of the tour was spent retracing the trenches that
snaked among the jagged ridges, in terrain as forbidding as
some of the canyons of California. In the close quarters of
the peninsula, Allied dead were 156,000 and the casualties
were 256,000. The reported number of Turkish dead was
86,000. But a graves commission in the 1920s was still turning up Turkish bodies, and the numbers on that side killed or
wounded may have exceeded 300,000. ("You'll want flowers

on your grave next," was the stock answer at ANZAC to another soldier's complaints.)

One in five of the Australians and New Zealanders who went to the peninsula never left, and this loss of 10,000 men, from the small towns Down Under, strained the umbilical cords of empire between Mother England and her colonial offspring—seeds of doubt first planted by an enterprising Australian journalist, Keith Murdoch (father of Rupert), who toured the trenches in September 1915. In the Peter Weir film, Mel Gibson goes over the top at The Nek, where, in the actual fighting in August 1915, 300 Australians were found dead in an area the size of a tennis court. We were "just anybody's mutton," is one veteran's recollection. "Gladiators with the eyes of children," was how General Hamilton described the Aussies.

My tour ended on Chunuk Bair, which has views down both sides of the peninsula—east to the Dardanelles and west to the Aegean. Moorhead describes this promontory as having "the grandest spectacle of the whole Mediterranean." Here the campaign was decided.

Led by an intrepid and brave colonel, W.G. Malone, a battalion of New Zealanders took the high ground by surprise on August 8 and were poised to drive a wedge across the peninsula. But while reinforcements never arrived, the Turks did. In the distance, while they clung to their martyrdom, the New Zealanders could see British troops coming ashore at Sulva Bay, pausing on the beach for a spot of afternoon tea.

With a courage that is difficult to comprehend, the New Zealanders attacked the Turks repeatedly with bayonets. But an errant British shell killed Colonel Malone, if not the heart of the offensive. Of the 700 Kiwis who climbed to Chunuk Bair, only seventy were unwounded two days later. Today a

Great War monument remembers their last stand. But the lasting tribute to their valor lives in their now silent trenches, which, like so much of New Zealand, were carved from rugged landscape, perched above azure seas.

Cape Helles: *"You have ten minutes to live"*

LEAVING THE TOUR bus at Maidos, near the ruins of an Ottoman fortress, I found a taxi to take me to Cape Helles, the western cape of the peninsula from which the Hellespont of mythology takes its name. At Krithia, the forlorn objective of so many British "pushes," we paused at a small museum, with sad cabinets of shell casings and rusted entrenching tools. Then making our way to the cape, we crossed open fields edged with flowering dogwoods that in 1915, "for all its openness," wrote Robert Rhodes James, "was a prison, which became a tomb."

Coming ashore ten miles to the southwest of the ANZACs, the British, supported by French colonials, were to march inland that first day and take Achi Baba—more high ground on Gallipoli's spine. "Casualties? What do I care about casualties?" is a remark attributed to the British ground commander in this sector.

Presumably he found little to bother him in the 6,000 killed or wounded in the Second Battle of Krithia—taken for what someone called "five hundred yards of bad grazing ground." As James concluded: "Even in the long catalogue of futile valor in the Great War, the advance…up Krithia Spur can still inspire an incomprehending wonder." ("You have ten minutes to live," was how one British officer rallied his troops.) Instead of rolling up the Turkish flank, as Churchill had dreamed, the Allies bogged down in the same entrenchments that, by attacking the Hellespont, they had sought to envelop.

Before returning to Çanakkale, I stood on the steps of the soaring, classically-inspired British war memorial that gives Cape Helles its feeling of immortal tranquility. To my right was the Lancashire Landing ("hell's foundation," to use Moorhouse's description), where volunteers from Bury were cut to ribbons. Down to the left was the narrow beachhead where the British landed combined elements of two regiments in the *River Clyde*, a hollow steamer towed ashore as if a Trojan horse. But without the wily Odysseus as their leader, men from several companies were killed almost to a man.

The afternoon had turned chilly, and the sea was fleeced with white caps, making it easy to imagine dreadnoughts on station or Jason and his argonauts. Across the Hellespont, vivid in the setting sun, were the beaches where Menelaus fought, Achilles sulked, and Patroclus was killed. In tragic voices like Brooke's, or that of his friend Patrick Shaw-Stewart, the campaign for Gallipoli brought the Renaissance men of classical England to the choices of death and dishonor that only the likes of Hector could understand:

> *...I will go back this morning*
> *From Imbros over the sea;*
> *Stand in the trench, Achilles,*
> *Flame-capped, and fight for me.*

As Keegan reflects: "It is difficult to say which epic Homer might have thought the more heroic."

Welcome to the Hotel Armenia
(2004)

IN THE OLD city of Jerusalem I first got the idea of a trip to Armenia.

During the 1990s, I made a number of business trips to Israel. On three or four occasions, one set of meetings ended before the Jewish Sabbath and others did not begin until the Christian work week started on Monday. To pass the time, I read books on the beach in Tel Aviv, ate lunch on the ramparts at Jaffa, and, when feeling adventurous, rented a car from a small office in the hotel and toured the Holy Land.

Writing in 2004, I find it hard to imagine that earlier moment of peace when it was possible to drive a rented car across the West Bank or down to Gaza. One weekend, I drove from Haifa, in the north, to Capernaum—Jesus's home town on the shores of the Sea of Galilee—and then down to Jericho after a detour through the Golan Heights. On another weekend, I made a grand tour of Gaza and the Dead Sea, passing along the road that, if the Palestinians ever get a national homeland, will be as controversial as the Polish corridor.

Often I tried to end my travels in Jerusalem, the part of Israel where I feel most at home. My wife and I first went there in 1985, staying in East Jerusalem at the American Colony Hotel, made famous by T.E. Lawrence. Since that trip, in the early days of the first intifada, I have often retraced our steps around the old city, with its quarters of Christians, Jews, Arabs, and Armenians.

I remember my initial surprise at discovering an Armenian quarter in Jerusalem. I had assumed its sacred ways only had the grubstake claims of Christians, Jews, and Arabs. I must have come across the Armenian quarter by chance, on an old-city ramble. Since that time, I have returned often to its forlorn courtyards and the museum on the second floor of a rundown palace. Elsewhere Jerusalem has the feel of a warrior-ant farm, a labyrinth of tunnels through which armies of the faithful try to sink foundations in what is otherwise a city built on sand.

At the Armenian Museum—one of those sad collections where the curator walks ahead of you flicking on lights—I made my first effort to connect the dots of the Armenian nation. Many Armenians had settled in Cilicia, on what is now Turkey's southern, Mediterranean coast. Others lived on the shores of Lake Van, and still more were in the Caucasus of the Russian empire. Other than a common language, what bound such a far-flung nation was Christianity, first embraced in 301 AD, and a faith sustained in an archipelago of remote monasteries, which appeared on the museum walls as lonely stone chapels, tucked away in the crevices of a mountainous land.

On other trips to Jerusalem, I began collecting histories of the Armenian holocaust, some purchased from a small shop that otherwise sold votive candles, icons, and Armenian newspapers. The shopkeeper sold me a pamphlet called "Documents of the Armenian Genocide" and tried to interest me in other literature, without ever ascertaining why I was drawn to such a corner of the world. It was a question I myself had a difficult time answering. To my knowledge, no one in my family is Armenian. Nor was anyone I knew caught in the vortex of that genocide. Early in our courtship, my wife gave me a copy of Michael Arlen's *Passage to Ararat*, a description of his trip to Soviet Armenia. But even when I read it, I doubt I could have accurately found Armenia on a map, and I read Arlen's account more as a travel narrative of the Soviet Union than as a history of a forgotten people. Nevertheless, thanks to my lazy afternoons in Jerusalem, I now had Armenia and its capital Yerevan amongst my travel daydreams.

MY CHANCE FOR a passage to Ararat came after a week's business in Moscow. I had not been in Russia for more than five years and found the darkness at noon now illuminated with neon branding and late-model cars. It was a cold evening in Moscow. The night flight for Armenia departed from a desolate corner of Sheremetyevo Airport. When I arrived at the airport, I stood in line at security while a group of men squeezed a refrigerator through the metal screening devices.

The plane for Yerevan departed after midnight, as did another late flight for Kazakhstan. The lounge, furnished as I could imagine the Krushchev living room, had a gloomy, smoke-filled atmosphere. I felt I was the only passenger not wearing a leather jacket or drinking brandy shots. After my flight was called, a group of us stood for a long time on the freezing tarmac. We were finally taken to the plane aboard a dimly lit bus, one that looked like it had seen shuttle service in a five-year plan. The aircraft was a Tupolev 134, the workhorse of the Soviet fleet, and the flight seemed over-booked. I recalled travelers' tales from the early 1990s when Aeroflot captains used to make money on the side by letting standby passengers fly in the lavatories—proving that even Aeroflot can be competitive with Western, no-frills airlines.

By good fortune I was flying revisionist class. As a result, I can offer here a few kind words about the Russian national airline. The beer was cold. My reclining leather seat was suit-able for a commissar. Even though the stewardess asked me if I wanted water "with gasses" during dinner, the fish served was excellent. After take-off, I was surprised how quickly the lights of Moscow gave way to the vast darkness of the steppe. We flew south toward Volgograd, once Stalingrad, and then passed over Chechnya and the Caucasus, where Armenia is one of the rugged lands that straddle the Black and Caspian Seas.

Immigration formalities in Yerevan, the capital, are a casual affair. I paid thirty dollars for a passport sticker, which no one bothered to stamp. At 4:20 A.M. I passed with my suitcase into the Stalinist nightmare that is the city airport. I am sure in daylight it would have seemed less threaten-ing. At night the soaring concrete buttresses seemed drawn from the House of Escher. Then I had the surreal experience of explaining to a customs officer why I was carrying into Armenia a watercolor of Venice (purchased in Moscow)—not something easily declared at dawn's early light.

On the Internet I had booked into the Hotel Armenia and had even arranged for an airport pickup. We drove to the hotel that is centrally located on Republic Square. My room was a suite, which meant that for a hundred dollars a night, instead of having one room with a narrow bed and plastic furniture, I had two. From a balcony I looked across what had once been Lenin Square to the Foreign Ministry and the National Museum. Like many state buildings in Yerevan, their façades were lined with soft, pinkish stones—those more synonymous with the Byzantine or Roman empires than the harsh concrete of Soviet rule.

Lenin was dragged from his square after Armenia became independent from the Soviet Union in 1991. As I heard often during my stay, Lenin's mark on Armenian history was almost as catastrophic as that of the Turks. Toward the end of World War I, after the events of the Armenian genocide, when some refugees fled into Soviet Russia, Lenin spoke favorably of restoring Armenian lands in eastern Turkey. The 1920 Treaty of Sèvres even stipulated guarantees for Armenian repatriation. Briefly an Armenian nation-state struggled for recognition. Then in 1921 Lenin concluded a peace with Turkey, which agreed that even Mount Ararat would be Turkish, forsaking Armenian claims for the kind of power politics that the Bolsheviks had abhorred in the tsars. By 1922, Mustafa Kemal, also known as Atatürk, had pushed the Turkish-Armenian frontier to the outskirts of Yerevan, which by then was under Soviet control. To paraphrase Lenin, peace for the Armenians was "one step forward two steps back."

THROUGH THE ARMENIAN ambassador in London I had arranged to meet a driver in front of the hotel. At the appointed hour, Gor, a generous man in his early thirties, arrived in a red Korean hatchback—a note of sportiness in a market that is otherwise dominated by sedans the color of Brezhnev's suits. We had time before my first meetings to drive around the city, which I mistakenly assumed had been devastated by the 1988 earthquake. That tremor, however, struck Spitak, several hours to the north. All that was felt in the capital were faint shocks, whose fissures are hard to distinguish in a city already coming apart at the seams.

Like Mexico City and Seoul, Yerevan spreads out in a dish that has mountains on several sides. On clear days, it faces the snow-capped peak of Mount Ararat, although that symbol of the Armenian nation is on the other side of a sealed border. Imagine Mount Fuji as a part of North Korea. A memorable feature of the city are the shops selling tires, oil, soda, plastic chairs, household goods, step ladders, wire baskets, bicycles, and sofas along the street, as if everyone in Yerevan had decided that today was the day for a garage sale. I had seen similar sidewalk shops on other trips to the former Soviet Union, and there the marketing hinted at desperation. Here curbside Coca Cola meant business. As at Home Depot, I saw numerous happy customers leaving the malls with purchases tied to car roofs.

Downtown Yerevan has a number of state ministries. Gor pointed out the principal sites, many in the past tense: the old KGB complex, the party headquarters, and the central-planning departments. In their place, we passed newly formed banks and renovated office buildings, although such is Yerevan's thin line between the old world and the new that it was easy to imagine the tenants of these corporate headquarters embracing privatization as though it were part of a great leap forward.

Beyond the capital district, Yerevan is a city of broken dreams. One of the housing projects is called Bangladesh, an allusion both to its summer heat and shanty-like apartments. Elsewhere, we drove through an abandoned chemical plant, acres of rusted steel and decaying pipelines, what Pittsburgh would look like if its last investments had been made in 1962.

Stalin's idea for the Soviet Union was that each socialist state would get one of the engine rooms to turn the means of production. Armenia drew straws for chemical plants and nuclear power. The cooling towers of the atomic reactor are visible on the Yerevan horizon. Otherwise Armenia is down-sizing its heavy industry, having found that western businessmen rarely put up seed capital for the residual rights to a central plan.

I had a short meeting with my business hosts, men in the hydro-electrical business. After we had arranged to spend the following day together, I was free for the afternoon. At my suggestion Gor drove me to the Museum of the Armenian Genocide, located on a hillside outside the city, near the football stadium. We parked in an empty lot—it being a Friday in late autumn—and walked toward the monument, great slabs of tilted granite that encircle an eternal flame.

Alongside one of the paths, I came across many newly planted trees and bushes, each with the name of a celebrity or a world leader who had broken this earth in remembrance of the 1915 holocaust. Small plaques recalled the visits of presidents, prime ministers, the California state assembly, even the Pope, lest the world forget the 1.5 million Armenians who died in 1915 as the Turkish authorities claimed their houses and towns, and then marched hundreds of thousands into the summer heat of the desert.

A planting that caught my eye was dedicated to Dr. Hampar Kelikian by Senator Robert Dole, whom I have never met but whose biography I sometimes think I am writing. On my trip to Albania, I was told that the senator's mother had Albanian origins. On another trip to Italy I rode my bicycle through Tuscany not far from where Dole's 10ᵗʰ Mountain Division fought in World War II and where the senator was grievously wounded in the back and shoulder. By chance, it was an Armenian doctor who had reconstructed his arm and who had given him hope. They met in 1947, when Dole was looking for a surgeon to repair his damaged arm:

> His friends called him Dr. K. He was a short man, but a giant in the operating room. As a boy Kelikian had escaped the blood-splattered landscape of his native Armenia. Three of his sisters were less fortunate; a fourth sibling, a brother, was killed in Italy during World War II....He was a pioneer in the surgical restoration of otherwise useless limbs. For his contributions to military medicine, Harry Truman gave him a medal. Those whom he rescued gave him their love.

The senator wrote in his autobiography that the doctor had largely failed in the operating room—Dole never regained the mobility of his right arm—but succeeded in the heart. "Learn to make the most of what you have," Dr. Kelikian often said to Dole. "Don't worry about what you have lost." He, himself, had lost more than most.

Clearly the purpose of the museum is to make the case that the genocide happened, that it followed the orders of top Turkish government officials, and that it was not an unhappy byproduct of World War I fighting in Turkey—all of which are points contested in the Turkish version of history. Near the entrance is an accounting of Armenian deaths by region, estimating that some 1.5 million people died in the holocaust, which began in April 1915 and lasted eight years. Specific display cabinets tell the story of the regions that were drained of their Armenian populations. In all, two million Armenians living in central and eastern Turkey, but still subjects of the

Ottoman empire, were forced from their homes and marched toward Syria, which few ever saw.

Then, as now, few took note of these population displacements. Nor did the Turks believe that the Armenian losses constituted genocide. On October 6, 1915, Viscount James Bryce told the House of Lords: "Things which we find scarcely credible excite little surprise in Turkey." But an American consul in Aleppo was one of the few to witness the arrival of these human caravans:

> Few are permitted the opportunity of riding except occasionally on an ox or a donkey, the sick drop by the wayside, women in critical condition giving birth to children, that according to reports, many mothers strangle or drown because of the lack of means to care for. Fathers exiled in one direction, mothers in another, the young girls and small children in yet another.

EARLY THE NEXT morning I had an appointment with an official from the European Bank for Reconstruction and Development, one of the lifelines for the otherwise moribund Armenian economy. Some seven hundred million dollars in aid has come to Armenia in the past ten years. He was supposed to join me for a hotel breakfast, but he never showed. My table quickly filled up with American pilgrims, who even at 8:00 A.M. confessed to anticipating tired feet.

With Gor and a group of local businessmen in another car—it reminded me of a politburo limo—we left after breakfast for a day in the country. I had slept poorly; the headlights from Republic Square had danced on my ceiling like bedtime dragons. But the crisp fall weather, perfect for college football and apple cider, washed away whatever jet lag I was feeling.

Our destination was a hydroelectric plant not far from the Georgian border. In the three-hour drive we had ample opportunity to visit monasteries and look around Spitak, the city that was devastated in the December 7, 1988, earthquake. Rural Armenia, parched brown for much of the year, has the forlorn qualities of the Scottish highlands. Its snow-capped peaks are desolate and craggy, and the hillsides are covered with what looks like heath, recalling the words Robert Louis Stevenson wrote in *Kidnapped*: "By day, we lay and slept in drenching heather; by night, incessantly clambered upon break-neck hills and among rude crags." As they have for centuries, Armenians prefer to live in towns, which spelled doom for those caught in Soviet housing when the tremors began. The quake, measuring 6.9 on the Richter scale, struck near Spitak at 11:41 A.M., killing eight thousand citizens in that mountainous town. It then rolled down the long valley toward Vanadzor, the provincial center of a region on which Stalin bequeathed another huge petrochemical plant. Altogether twenty-five thousand died in northwest Armenia, many from exposure as rescue workers from Yerevan were unable to breach the seismic trenches that crossed the only road north from the capital.

The international aid community has moved on from Armenia, although it left behind various relief headquarters, which have been turned into health centers and recreation halls. Otherwise Spitak is another forgotten town in the Caucasus. Surprisingly, despite having sprawling apartment complexes, Vanadzor was spared significant damage. Of more serious consequence to Vanadzor than the earthquake is the future of the petrochemical complex, which finds the market economy a less generous benefactor than the five-year plan. With the collapse of the Soviet Union went the last speculators in such heavy industry—in their place are Western investors unwilling to "take Armenian risk"—and the last hope of easy money.

After a stop in Vanadzor for water and to pick up my host's brother, we continued north through a narrow valley that leads eventually to the border with Georgia. I found it difficult to comprehend that this twisting two-lane road, near a single line of track, was one of Armenia's few passages to the world economy. The borders with Turkey and Azerbaijan are closed, as if on a war footing, and the Iranian mullahs view the Christian enclave with tolerant suspicion.

Although I did not know my hosts for more than a day, I trusted them implicitly, even when we changed cars to an old Soviet jeep and headed deep into what I judged was the Armenian Grand Canyon. The road we climbed for more than one thousand vertical meters would have tried the footing of a donkey. Many of the rock-strewn potholes were filled with deep puddles. It took thirty minutes to traverse the mountainous hump, and then we descended toward a reservoir in the spectacular Droza Valley, one that provided the headwaters for a hydroelectrical plant down in the valley where we had started our climb.

The plant, dating to the 1960s, produces 2 percent of Armenia's energy requirements. Of the three turbines in the station only one was operating. But, as a business, there was a felicitous quality to the Arax River Station. Most ex-Soviet companies come with enough employees to fill several sanatoriums on the Black Sea. But this operation had less than ten workers, who mostly repaired the turbines and controlled the cascade of water two kilometers down the mountain. The owners were searching for funds to repair the broken turbines, so that more power could be fed into the local electricity grid, a web of power that explains a lot about Armenia's economic isolation.

Nearly half of the power in Armenia comes from the Soviet-era nuclear power station, whose cooling towers are as visible from Yerevan as are the twin peaks of Mount and Little Ararat. The central planners of the Soviet Union allocated nuclear power to Armenia much the way they kept the arms merchants near Moscow and foisted cotton production onto Uzbekistan. The rest of Armenia's power comes from imported gas, much of it from Turkmenistan. The problem for Armenia is that it cannot afford to pay market rates for the gas any more than it can cover the maintenance on the nuclear station, which places Chernobyl technology on seismic fault lines. Nor is there a market for the surplus power that Armenia generates. Were the border open with Turkey, my hosts explained, almost two billion kilowatts could be available for export. The Turks would pay $0.07 per kilowatt hour while the Armenian cost of production was only $0.03. No one I met in Armenia had ideological reasons for not selling to Turkey, but, for whatever reasons, the Turks weren't buying.

WE ATE LUNCH in a restaurant perched on a cliff hanging over the Debet River Valley, not far from the hydro-electric station. I obliged one of my hosts by playing chess before the meal, and he obliged me by kindly pointing out whenever my Queen was in harm's way—much as parents prolong a game with eager children. Back in the car, we drove toward Lake Sevan, one of the wonders of the Armenian landscape, crossing near Mount Majmech on a series of switchbacks that climbed 2,000 meters above sea level. At the summit we went through a village that has been Russian for several hundred years—it had the feel of a white clapboard New England town—and, descending, we saw the tunnel that will link Dilijan to Sevan through the base of the mountain.

A small sign said that the work was thanks to the generosity of the Lincy Foundation, which I remembered was credited for the restoration of the National Museum and several monasteries that we had passed. My hosts had only vague details about the Lincy Foundation, saying it belonged to Kirk Kerkorian, the movie and casino mogul. On my return from Armenia, I spoke with Harut Sassounian, the foundation's vice chairman, and got more of the details.

A newspaper columnist in the Armenian Diaspora and the president of the United Armenian Fund, which contributed more than 100 airlifts after the earthquake, Sassounian said that the Lincy Foundation, thanks to the generosity of Kerkorian, had thus far committed $170 million in aid to Armenia. They had earmarked only projects that would make an immediate contribution to the Armenian economy. For example, the Dilijan tunnel would cost $8 million and be ready in late 2004. The foundation had also pledged $45 million for apartments in the earthquake zone, $73 million to fix roads, $14 million for the streets of Yerevan, and $18 million for cultural sites, including $2 million for the opera house. It had already made $20 million in loans to small businesses. In exchange, Kerkorian had not even wanted favorable publicity. All the signs I had seen had been put up locally. Nor did Kerkorian have any direct investments in the country. In this instance, he had tilted the roulette wheels so that only Armenians would benefit.

I was grateful that the foundation had given so much to restore the country's monasteries. During my visit, I was continually asking Gor to show me yet another remote chapel. All over Armenia, and no doubt in western Turkey, are small stone churches, made from granite, that speak of Christianity's lonely vigil across desolate valleys of Asia Minor. At Echmiadzin, where sits the patriarch of an Armenian church (there are two), I came across monks in flowing robes and smelled incense that reminded me of Jerusalem. All that is left at Zvartnots is the footprint of a seventh-century Armenian church. The toppled Roman columns lying nearby, however, connect this field in the shadows of Mount Ararat to the passages of Edward Gibbon.

My favorite monastery was Khor Virap, which dates to 1669 and has achieved immortality on the walls of Armenian restaurants around the world. It sits on a small escarpment that rises from the plain near what is now the Turkish border. From the walls of this most holy shrine, it is possible to look down on the no man's land, sealed with razor wire that separates Armenia and Turkey. No troops were in evidence—indeed Armenia has few displays of militarism despite its painful history. But just over the border is Mount Ararat. From a village at the foot of Noah's mountain, I heard a muezzin calling the faithful to prayer. I mused about the fault line between Christianity and Islam, running from Sarajevo to Kashmir, until my hosts convinced me to climb down twenty feet into the dungeon that had held St. Gregory the Illuminator for thirteen years for advocating Christianity. I felt as though I had been swallowed by Jonah's whale.

On this Saturday afternoon, we stopped at two chapels overlooking the dark blue waters of Lake Sevan, which is lined on nearly all sides with sharp barren hills and mountains. It was necessary to hike a kilometer along a stony hillside path to get to the chapels. Inside, weekending Armenians were lighting candles for friends and family. Although called monasteries, the Armenian churches are better understood as shrines to the nation, almost civic in their testimony to past struggles. The atmosphere is casually reverent. Only at the larger churches are priests in evidence. At only a few monasteries that I visited were services being offered. Nevertheless, I sensed that Armenians spend a large part of their free time lighting candles in these mountainous chapels which, if seen as a whole, might illuminate the constellation of the Armenian nation.

WHAT THEN HAS been the fate of Armenia? For most of its 2000 years, it has not been a contiguous country, but national pockets within larger empires. Donald E. Miller and Lorna Touryan Miller write in *Survivors: An Oral History of the Armenian Genocide*: "From the sixteenth century, Armenians were ruled by the Ottoman Turks and existed as a semiautonomous *millet* in a multinational empire...relatively free to practice their religion, and they had considerable autonomy in civil matters, as did other *millets* within the empire, such as the Greeks and Jews." Cilicia was an important Armenian center since before the Crusades, as were Van and Yerevan. But the country today known as Armenia is approximately one-tenth the size of what was Great Armenia, which if it existed today would lay claims to parts of Turkey, Georgia, Azerbaijan, Iran, and Iraq. More Armenians, some 3.5 million, live in the Diaspora than those now within the borders of newly independent Armenia.

The 1878 Treaty of Berlin attempted to impose an orderly liquidation on the collapsing Ottoman Empire. It contemplated a constitution for Turkey and basic human rights for such indigenous groups as Armenians. But by the turn of the twentieth century, the Great Powers were too preoccupied elsewhere to think much about the Armenians or impress upon the sultan the small points of a largely forgotten treaty.

When the Young Turks seized power in 1908, they embraced, in response to the decline and fall of the Ottomans, Turkish nationalism. G.S. Graber writes in *Caravans to Oblivion: The Armenian Genocide 1915*: "To the Young Turks, the disgust with which the more cultured Turks of Constantinople viewed the Turkic peoples of central Asia was a cynical abandonment of all that was valuable in Turkey. 'Fatherland for the Turks is neither Turkey nor Turkestan,' so the Young Turks' spokesman Ziya Goeckalp wrote in a famous poem, 'Their fatherland is a great and eternal land, Turan.' Thus Turanism was adopted." While such nationalist sentiments were gaining currency, the Ottoman Empire lost a series of wars in the Balkans, which reduced the empire, according to Graber, by "424,000 square miles of territory and some 5 million persons out of its population of 24 million."

As the Ottoman Empire contracted, the importance of Armenians, as a minority within the realm, grew, especially because their communities were present in so many Turkish cities and towns. But the Armenian nation, in a further accident of history, found itself straddling tsarist Russia, at a time when the German Kaiser saw his expansion dreams running down the track of a Berlin-to-Baghdad railway. Before World War I, two million Armenians lived within the Ottoman Empire, but the same number were subjects of the tsar. Graber writes that, on average, Armenians felt more protected within the polyglot Ottoman Empire, fearing that under the tsar "they would lose the individuality of their historic religion." In the days leading to World War I, the Armenians were perceived as a people with divided loyalties. As the Millers write:

> From the Armenian perspective, the boundary between Turkey and Russia was artificial—their historic home land for twenty-five hundred years had spanned this border at the foot of Mount Ararat. But the Young Turks viewed the Armenian response as treasonous, proclaiming that the Armenians would side with the Russian army if it advanced onto Turkish soil.

Here is not the place to detour into a discussion of the Great Power politics that surrounded Turkey in the First World War. But even a summary indicates how it was that the Armenians found themselves hostage to the fortunes of war. Prior to the war, Russia had liberated Romania and Bulgaria from the Ottoman sphere. At the same time England, the traditional ally of the Sublime Porte, sided with Russia to blunt German expansion. Germany moved to fill the imperial void in Constantinople. At the outbreak of war in 1914, Turkey sheltered two German battleships and thus found itself at war both with Russia and with the western allies, England and France, who—when they bogged down in the trenches of Flanders—thought they could outflank the Germans by seizing the Dardanelles and Constantinople.

Whether by historical coincidence or consequence, the destruction of the Armenian nation began the same day that Allied armies landed near Gallipoli, April 25, 1915. Graber writes: "The invasion, which ended ingloriously with Allied withdrawal some nine months later, is often called the Gallipoli campaign. It has been labeled the worst-prepared invasion in history. It has even been called 'the coming of age of Australia.' But it also...ushered in the death of the Armenian nation."

WHILE OPPOSING THE Allied landing at Gallipoli, Turkey was fighting the Russians on its eastern borders. Sandwiched between the two fronts was Turkey's Armenian population. "The relationship between Armenians and Turks before the deportations of 1915 was complex," writes the Millers. "In some locations, Armenian and Turkish houses were intermingled; other areas had a separate Armenian quarter; and in still other places, the entire village or city was Armenian." But as Graber writes, the Dardanelles landing "produced the changeover from a form of national consciousness to a type of brutal chauvinism." What followed was the "the decision of the leaders of the Young Turks to arrange the physical annihilation of the Armenian people."

The Millers conclude: "First, the Armenian Genocide was not inspired by religion. The ideology that drove the Young Turks was nationalism, not Islam." After the genocide, the Turkish minister Talaat said that the Armenians were killed because: "In the first place, they have enriched themselves at the expense of the Turks. In the second place, they are determined to domineer over us and to establish a separate state. In the third place, they have openly encouraged our enemies."

The best eyewitness accounts of this holocaust come from diplomats, many of them American, then posted to the Ottoman Empire. The U.S. ambassador in Constantinople was Henry Morgenthau, whose memoirs record the horror of the Armenian deportations. He writes: "The caravans of death could be seen winding in and out of every valley and climbing up the sides of nearly every mountain—moving on and on, [those deported] scarcely knew wither, except that every road led to death." But his account relies on dispatches from the interior, especially as these caravans of death marched from central and eastern Turkey into the Syrian desert. In most cases the Armenians were rounded up and sent on forced marches to oblivion. It was a holocaust carried out by exhaustion.

Writing for the British government in 1916, Arnold J. Toynbee summarized a typical caravan, of which there were hundreds:

> From the moment they left the outskirts of the town they were never safe from outrage. The Moslem peasants mobbed and plundered them as they passed through the cultivated lands, and the gendarmes connived at the peasants' brutality.... When they arrived at a village they were exhibited like slaves in a public place, often before the windows of the Government Building itself, and every Moslem inhabitant was allowed to view them and make his choice of them for his harem....There were still more horrible outrages when they came to the mountains, for here they were met by bands of 'chettis' and Kurds....The first to be butchered were the old men and boys...but the women were also massacred....But while the convoy dwindled, the remnant had always to march on....Women who lagged behind were bayoneted on the road or pushed over precipices, or over bridges....The lust and covetousness of their tormentors had no limit. The last survivors often staggered into Aleppo naked....The only chance to survive was to be plain enough to escape their torturers' lust, and vigorous enough to bear the fatigues of the road.

In theory the caravans were destined for Aleppo or Deir el-Zor in the Syrian desert, but as the U.S. consul J.B. Jackson wrote: "One of the most terrible sights ever seen in Aleppo was the arrival early in August, 1915, of some 5,000 terribly emaciated, dirty, ragged and sick women and children, 3,000 on one day and 2,000 the following day. These people were the only survivors of the thrifty and well-to-do Armenian population of the province of Sivas, carefully estimated to have originally been over 300,000 souls!" Half of the Armenian population in Turkey perished, which amounted to almost one-third of all Armenians worldwide.

Peace proved no easier for Armenians than did war. In 1918, an independent Republic of Armenia was proclaimed in Yerevan, the center of what had been Russian Armenia. Toward the end of the war, the front lines between Turkey and Russia had been west of Mount Ararat, giving Armenians hope that they could resettle lands around Van and elsewhere in eastern Turkey. Nevertheless, at Brest-Litovsk, the peace conference that governed Bolshevik Russia's exit from the war, the victorious Germans allowed the Young Turks to make their claims in the Caucasus, based on Turanism. With the war ending on the Western Front, Russian forces withdrew from eastern Turkey. Graber writes: "The abandonment of Armenia by Bolshevik Russia left the Armenians again at the mercy of the Turkish forces." After the Allied victory, the August 1920 Treaty of Sèvres recognized Armenian independence. For a brief period the United States considered exercising a mandate to run the country. But the U.S. Senate backed away from an Armenian protectorate. In September 1920, Atatürk invaded Armenia, pushing the frontier east of Mount Ararat, on the edge of Yerevan.

In effect, the Great War in Asia Minor did not end until 1922, when the Greek invasion of western Turkey failed. That war ended with the sacking of Greek Smyrna, now known as Izmir. A British historian, Michael Llewellyn Smith, has described that cauldron:

> The Armenian, Greek and 'Frankish' or European quarters were almost entirely destroyed. Only the Jewish and Turkish quarters remained.... With a horrific appropriateness, the fire expressed in symbolic terms the rooting out and destruction of Greek and Armenian Smyrna. Hellenic Smyrna was dead. Christian Smyrna, too, one of the great ancient Christian foundations of Asia Minor, was dead. The phoenix to rise from these ashes was a Turkish Izmir purged of two thousand and more years of history.

In 1922, Atatürk finished what the Young Turks had begun. It could then be proclaimed that the Armenian question had been settled.

After the 1923 Treaty of Lausanne, the Republic of Armenia disappeared officially. Instead Armenia became another socialist republic of the Soviet Union, in which Josef Stalin played one nationalist group off against another, so that Russia remained first among equals. For example, he created Azerbaijan as a Caucasian counterweight to the Christian republics of Georgia and Armenia. In 1923 he awarded to Azerbaijan the mountainous Armenian enclave of Nagorno-Karabakh, which has remained a flash point in the skirmishing wars between Armenia and Azerbaijan.

Armenia was left with a memory of a nation, captured in novels, plays, short stories, and paintings. An aunt of Peter

Balakian, who wrote *Black Dog of Fate*, tells him: "We have a dream instead of a country.... The more our geography shrinks, the more our imaginations expand, the more we're like owls flying in the dark." In this American 1960s coming-of-age memoir that returns to the Armenian holocaust, Balakian quotes his grandfather, who wrote in 1922: "Our generation has more friends in the next world than in this one. There are places where I walk with anguish as if I were crossing a graveyard of memories."

DESPITE THE LOSS of more than a million Armenians in 1915, the Turkish government continues to deny that what happened to them constitutes genocide. As early as 1919, Talaat Pasha said, from his sanctuary in Berlin: "The responsibility for these acts falls first of all upon the deported people themselves." In 1982, a Turkish ambassador wrote: "What took place was a complex tragedy which claimed Turkish as well as Armenian lives. Indeed, it was a civil war within a global war stemming from an armed uprising of the Armenian minority at a time when the Ottoman state was fighting for survival during World War I. Many more Turks than Armenians perished." Those denying an Armenian holocaust hold to the belief that there was "no intent to annihilate either group, only to relocate its members" and that all sides "were equally at fault."

On my own trips to Turkey in recent years, I have tried to assess the extent to which denial remains in circulation. When I have been with someone I feel might be open to discussing the Armenian holocaust, I ask for the Turkish version of the story. One articulate friend, who studied diplomatic history in Ankara, spoke of the tragedy of World War I and the disintegration of the Ottoman Empire. Armenians, in her version, were caught between the front lines of the Russian and Turkish armies fighting on the eastern front. In this telling, the death of so many Armenians was a misfortune of war, not a planned genocide. Many populations, from the Balkans into Egypt, suffered a similar fate. Turks, themselves, were killed by the tens of thousands as the Ottoman Empire was slowly defeated on lines north from Salonika and east of Suez. She ended: "But no one speaks of these Turkish losses as a genocide."[1]

More recently the Canadian filmmaker, Atom Egoyan, produced a movie about the legacies of the Armenian holocaust, including that of denial. Titled *Ararat*, the film cuts between numerous plot lines in which the characters confront their legacies of the Armenian holocaust. One subplot involves the making of a movie about Clarence Ussher, an American diplomat at Van whose dispatches to Ambassador Morgenthau describe the agony of the deportations. The name of the filmmaker is Saroyan, a link to the great Armenian-American writer by the same name, William Saroyan. In an interview with *The Guardian*, Egoyan says: "He is making a film about the event, the genocide. I have made a film about the negation of that event."

Everyone in the film is confronting "the ghost of my father." In other scenes the artist Arshile Gorky paints, from a photograph, a portrait of his parents, who vanished in 1915. Another story involves the complex relationship between an art historian, there to analyze Gorky's painting, and her troubled son, whose father died in the act of trying to assassinate a Turkish diplomat. (Between 1973 and 1985, Turkish officials

---

1. The First World War historian John Keegan writes that no accounts were ever tabulated of Turkish losses, but estimates them in the "many hundreds of thousands." He estimates that 300,000 Turkish soldiers died fighting at Gallipoli.

claim eighty-six Armenian terrorist incidents killed thirty-one diplomats.) At one point in the convoluted plot, the son meets an actor of Turkish descent, who then summarizes the view that it was not a systematic idea of holocaust, but that the Armenians were war victims, like so many at that time. Plus he makes the point that the Armenians had sided with Russia, which was at war with Turkey.

What I admire about *Ararat* is that, in the age of Hollywood stunt thrillers, Egoyan made a serious film about a difficult subject: holocaust denial. A man in his forties, he grew up in Canada as the descendant of Armenian immigrants, but had never expected to make a movie about the deportations. At university, he wrote a thesis on "Woodrow Wilson, Lenin and Armenia." But only later in his career did he return to the world of his forebears. "To me," he said in the interview, "the real Armenian cause lies at this level. It hinges on one's relationship with authenticity. It involves not only the truth about what actually happened, but also the possibility of making truth apparent, and then getting it accepted as such." In a pamphlet on the deportations, Richard G. Hovannisian writes: "It has been said that denial is the final phase of genocide."

PERHAPS THE BEST response to those who deny an Armenian holocaust comes from the pen of Ambassador Henry Morgenthau, whose memoirs of diplomatic service in Constantinople first appeared in 1918, before the war ended. Morgenthau served as U.S. ambassador there from 1913 to 1916, and he was on intimate terms with the government of the Young Turks, many of whom were responsible for the atrocities. Not only did he keep diaries and records of his conversations with the Ottoman government, but he received many of the dispatches sent from places like Van and Aleppo, in which his consular officers bore witness to the atrocities. A rare individual who could both listen and write, Morgenthau had a gift for historical narrative that undoubtedly inspired his granddaughter, Barbara Tuchman, who, when she wrote *The Guns of August*, incorporated her grandfather's eyewitness account of the flight to Constantinople of the German warships *Breslau* and *Goeben*.

Morgenthau's premise is that the Kaiser subverted the weak Ottoman government so as to protect Germany's flank against Russian encroachment. He concludes: "Germany precipitated the war to destroy Serbia, seize control of Balkan nations, transform Turkey into a vassal state, and thus obtain a huge oriental empire that would form the basis of world domination." For Germany to control Turkey was a way of controlling the eastern front, and to control Turkey the Kaiser dispatched, as ambassador, Baron von Wangenheim, whom Morgenthau sketches as a case study in power policies: "Like the government which he served so loyally, he was fundamentally ruthless, shameless, and cruel." In *The Road from Home*, David Kherdian writes: "Germany wants us out of the way, as we alone are capable of guaranteeing economic and political independence for Turkey in Asia Minor."

Nor was Morgenthau blinded by the intentions of the Young Turks, who, he believes, "were not a government; they were a really an irresponsible party, a kind of secret society, which, by intrigue, intimidation, and assassination, had obtained most of the offices of state." He describes Enver Pasha, one of its leaders, as a "cog in the Prussian system."

Morgenthau not only concludes that Turkey became a German client, he believes that the Kaiser's government had a strong hand in articulating policies that led to the destruction of the Armenians. He writes: "The violent shifting of whole people from one part of Europe to another, as though they were so many herds of cattle, has for years been part of the Kaiser's plans for German expansion." As part of its wartime intrigues, Germany tried to foster an Arab revolt against their colonial overlords in London and Moscow, thus weakening the Allied supply lines that ran from India to the Western and Eastern fronts. ("Deutschland Über Allah" was one phrase that described this subversion.) Morgenthau continues: "[Germany] aroused in the Mohammeddan soul all that intense animosity toward the Christian which is the fundamental fact in his strange emotional nature, and thus started passions aflame that afterward spent themselves in the massacres of the Armenians and other subject people." Turanism, or the idea of pan-Turkism, was what he calls "government by massacre."[2]

In the Near East, Morgenthau observed that "nations talked to each other with acts, not words." After Gallipoli, he bore witness to a national degeneration: "New Turkey, freed from European tutelage, celebrated its national rebirth by murdering not far from a million of its own subjects....When the British and French withdrew from Gallipoli that action turned adrift this huge hulk of a country to flounder in anarchy, dissolution, and ruin." Morgenthau believed Germany "acquiesced" to the deportations and quotes Wangenheim, after the Turkish victory at Gallipoli: "Turkey has settled with

---

2. From 1913 to 1916, when Morgenthau was keeping a diary of Turkish atrocities, the United States remained neutral, one reason he had the confidence of Armenians, Turks, and Germans. The comedy of American imperialistic innocence can be seen in 1914, when the Ottomans pleaded with the Americans for a sovereign loan of $5 million. The American banker C.K.G. Billings agreed to review the proposal by calling at Constantinople in his yacht—after diplomatic exchanges on the thickness of the flannel to be worn ashore.

her foreign enemies....She is now trying to settle her internal affairs." Nor does Morgenthau believe that the Armenian losses were casualties of war. He wrote: "Deportation proved to be merely a euphemism for extermination.... The physical destruction of 2,000,000 men, women, and children by massacres, organized and directed by the state, seemed to be the one sure way of forestalling the further disruption of the Turkish Empire."

Morgenthau pays particular attention to the so-called "Revolution" at Van, to answer those critics who believe that the deportations were in response to a rebellion aimed at toppling the Ottoman state. He writes: "I have told this story of the 'Revolution' at Van not only because it marked the first stage in this organized attempt to wipe out a whole nation, but because these events are always brought forward by the Turks as a justification of their subsequent crimes....The famous 'Revolution,' as this recital shows, was merely the determination of the Armenians to save their women's honor and their own lives, after the Turks, by massacring thousands of their neighbors, had shown them the fate that awaited them." The resistance at Van consisted of about 300 Armenian rifles against a corps of Turkish soldiers: "The police fell upon them just as the eruption of Vesuvius fell upon Pompei."

Most convincing are Morgenthau's conversations with some of the Young Turks in the aftermath of the deportations. Enver Pasha explained: "The Cabinet itself has ordered the deportations. I am convinced that we are completely justified in doing this owing to the hostile attitude of the Armenians toward the Ottoman Government, but we are the real rulers of Turkey, and no underling would dare proceed in a matter of this kind without our orders." Talaat Pasha was more cryptic: "Why can't you let us do with these Christians as we please?"

He boasted: "I have accomplished more toward solving the Armenian problem in three months than Abdul Hamid [known for pogroms against the Armenians] accomplished in thirty years." He concluded: "Yes, we make mistakes, but we never regret."

In From the Cold War:
Alger Hiss and
the Accidents of Truth

(2005)

*"Hiss remains in the strange position of a man
who is held in contempt by most of his country
and yet esteemed by almost all who know him
well."*

—Dr. Meyer Zeligs

MY FIRST ACQUAINTANCE with Alger Hiss and his celebrated
case came in 1973. I was a sophomore at Bucknell University
in Lewisburg, Pennsylvania, where, by coincidence, Hiss had
spent his forty-four months in prison, after conviction for
perjury—in effect for denying under oath that he had been
a Soviet spy while working in the State Department. That
summer, rather than dwelling on the Cold War, I worked at
a marina on Long Island Sound. My job was that of "night
habormaster," a glorified title for someone who acted as the
desk clerk at a boat motel. I reported to the docks in the
middle afternoon. Until 2:00 A.M. I was on duty to run the
launch, assign yachts to overnight slips, and coil up the hoses
on the gas dock. Watching the sun set over a boatyard didn't
teach me too many life lessons, idyllic as it was, although I
did figure out that not all couples reporting to the bridge of
cabin cruisers were husband and wife. That was the charged

summer of Watergate revelations and Richard Nixon's discontent, although that didn't stop me, sometimes after work, from sailing my small boat under the Throgs Neck Bridge, which even at that hour of the dogwatch was alive with barges and tugs, flickering city lights. Now those memories appear fixed in time; then it was a summer job.

Toward the end of the summer, my parents' friend Bill Rodgers and his wife, Katie, came to stay at our house on Long Island. They had all met in 1951, on a dance floor in Bermuda. Bill, sixty, had been a familiar face throughout my childhood, but until that visit I had never really spoken to him or known much about his life. I knew he had written a best-selling history of IBM and loved Rignes beer made in Norway. Before any of Bill's visits, my father would lay in a case of Rignes. That summer Bill and I talked about my college courses, the books I was reading, the papers I had written. A man of infectious enthusiasm, especially after a few Norwegian beers, he loved it that I spent the short winter semester helping farm workers in California. I, in turn, admired his work in the campaign of George McGovern, for whom he had written position papers arguing that the candidate should make a stand on the issue of President Nixon's corruption—not as apparent in summer 1972 as it was a year later.

As he was leaving, Bill and I promised to keep in touch. The summer ended, and I drove my 1966 Volkswagen back to Lewisburg, a town of colonial elegance on the west branch of the Susquehanna River. Sometimes during my college years its banks would flood, and students would evacuate residents from low-lying houses. But generally it was celebrated as the longest un-navigable river in the country. Lewisburg combined redbrick and gaslight elegance with touches of a midwestern small town: for example, along main street cars were parked at an angle. Both the university and federal peniten-tiary were built alongside Route 15, a kind of thirties highway that in those days attracted tired motels, gas stations, and diners that served hamburgers at odd hours. If Bucknell's campus copied the Georgian quadrangles of Mr. Jefferson's university in Virginia, the prison chose Gothic morality for the design of its central tower, factory-brick windows, and Dickensian high walls. Lewisburg is a town that celebrates both the liberal and dark arts.

DURING MY COLLEGE years I would sometimes ride my bike past the penitentiary—Saturday afternoon excursions I recalled later when I read Tony Hiss's memoir of his father's prison days, *The View from Alger's Window*. In one letter to his family Alger captures the landscape of Lewisburg: "The day was gloriously bright + the sunset again very exciting. By standing on my bed I can see the rolling fields to the south + the lane of young sycamores that leads to the entrance (all yellow, they are now) + with a sunset glow the view is very fair indeed." According to Tony, prison had a humanizing affect on Alger, as if he had attended the university in town, not the penitentiary. Tony writes: "That was also when Alger began to put less faith in government as a force for moving humanity forward and more trust in private acts of friendship and in the study of the human heart."

That September in 1973 Bill Rodgers wrote me a letter and thus we began a correspondence that would last more than twenty years, until, in his early eighties, time laid waste to his lively mind. All his letters were typed on a heavy 1960s-era IBM typewriter, which he nursed through the years with new carriages and ribbons. I still have hundreds of his let-ters—the files holding them are two-feet deep. Mostly we wrote to each other about daily life and politics. But that first message invited me to spend the weekend with him and Katie at their house on Maryland's Eastern Shore. He remembered that I had a Volkswagen and suggested that I drive down in early October, something I did in the company of migrating birds, which were also following the Susquehanna to the Chesapeake Bay.

Lewisburg to Centreville, Maryland, is a memorable drive. I followed Route 15 to Harrisburg, picked my way through the capitol district, headed east toward Lancaster, and then discovered the heart of Amish country in hamlets like Bird in Hand, Paradise, and New Providence. From Intercourse—the latter being worth a detour, at least to a college sophomore—I followed rolling farmland along Route 896 to Elkton, once General Washington's encampment at the head of the bay, and then headed south on Maryland Highway 213, which since that day has been among my favorite American roads.

In a few places, such as crossing the Chesapeake and Delaware Canal, 213 glimpses the bay and its estuaries. Mostly it rolls inland through fields of wheat, corn, and soy that often stretch to the horizon. Parts of the Eastern Shore remind me of Kansas, but at sunset, especially in winter, it becomes the Low Countries, seemingly linked with rivers, dikes, and canals. Ten miles north of Centreville, 213 cuts through Chestertown, with its colonial townhouses overlooking the Chester River. Having grown up in Baltimore, Alger Hiss spent some of his summers in Chestertown, and it is also where Christopher Tilghman has set some of his stories and novels, including *Mason's Retreat*, in which he writes of the mansions you can sometimes glimpse from the road: "I think these big family places run out of luck, sooner or later. I think bad things begin to happen in them."

Instead of a "big family place," Bill and Katie, who had no children, owned what they called the Captain's Houses, four small row houses overlooking the backwaters of the Corsica River. Each house was small, not more than single rooms stacked on two floors. But Bill and Katie had connected the houses with a greenhouse and spiral staircases. Katie was an artist, and thus part of the front hall was a pebble garden. Perhaps for dramatic effect, the bathtub was just inside the front door. Wood stoves maintained the heating; fireplaces warmed the bedrooms. In one house Bill had his writing studio, and in another Katie worked her sculpture. In between was a small dining room table where the three of us, over the next several years, ate many of Katie's memorable meals. At that first dinner I heard of Bill's friendship with Alger Hiss, who not long before had visited the Captain's Houses.

During World War II Bill served in the merchant marine, mostly on Liberty ships to Liverpool and Murmansk. He also served on convoys that went to Basra in Iraq and Alexandria. After the war, he worked on *PM*, an evening New York newspaper, and then the *Herald-Tribune*, where he was an accomplished writer of political features. During the 1950s, he left newspapers and worked for a stationery company to promote the cause of letter writing—a job ideally suited to his epistolary temperament. At the same time, he was friendly with the couple that published the *Nation* magazine, Elinor Ferry and George Kirsten. One weekend they invited Bill and Katie to spend the day with Alger and his family, who came from Greenwich Village to the country for the luncheon. Alger was then just out of prison and working on the book that became *In the Court of Public Opinion*, more a legal brief about the case than a memoir of his experience. It was hoped that Bill might help Alger give the book some life. In 1986,

Bill wrote to Alger remembering their first meeting—"that day you came out to our place near Tarrytown, on the border of Rockefeller's estate, accompanied by Elinor Ferry and a couple of friends, with young Tony in tow." He continues:

> We talked about your manuscript, which you gave me to study. I felt the text too bland, devoid of the terrible injustice that had wronged you, a wrong that altered my outlook and, I often think, changed my life. For better or worse? Maybe it just fueled a concern for fairness and justice awaiting the flint to set it off.... When I think about it, I'd rather have lived your life, incapable as I would no doubt have been to endure with grace what befell you, than a single day of Nixon's.

From that day, Bill began keeping a file on the Hiss case, and when Bill died many of the clippings and books came into my possession. Some I shipped off to the Howard Gotlieb Archival Research Center at Boston University. Much of it I copied, and those boxes have accompanied many of our moves in subsequent years, with my wife asking, "Do we still need the Hiss case?"

IN MANY WAYS, no one needs the Hiss case, which raged between 1948 and 1950, and officially ended when Hiss was released from prison in 1954. Maintaining his innocence until he died in 1996, Hiss wrote two books, delivered lectures, and eked out a living as a stationery salesman. He failed in an attempt to have the Supreme Court strike his conviction from the record, but enjoyed measures of recompense when his chief accusers, Richard Nixon and J. Edgar Hoover, fell from grace and power. His nemesis, Whittaker Chambers, lived for eleven years after the trials and either died of a heart attack or a suicide. Chambers's best-selling memoirs, *Witness*, were serialized in the *Saturday Evening Post*, and his champions included William F. Buckley, Jr., and Ronald Reagan, plus a phalanx of historians and social critics for whom Chambers mixed the redemptive qualities of born-again sinner with the verisimilitude of a spy coming in from the cold. During the Reagan years even Chambers's pumpkin-patch Maryland farm was awarded National Landmark status.

Nevertheless, for the balance of his life, Hiss was a political symbol. To his defenders, he was railroaded to conviction by the FBI, Nixon, the House Un-American Activities Committee, and the likes of Senator Joseph McCarthy and the subscribers of magazines like *Reader's Digest*. To Hiss loyalists, his only transgression was that of naïveté, in not readily recognizing Whittaker Chambers as George Crosley, a freelance writer whom he had befriended and helped during the Depression. Hiss was convicted as a metaphor, someone to pillory, in the absence of Franklin Roosevelt, for the lost illusions of Yalta and the collectivism of the New Deal. To Hiss's friends, Bill among them, Alger's persecution, conviction, and harassment embodied everything that had gone wrong in American politics ever since 1919, when Attorney General A. Mitchell Palmer first raised the red scare.

Bill defended his obsession, saying he felt compelled to press the issue of public comprehension in the Hiss case "as a paradigm of the long assault on the decent, ethical, vibrant promise of America."

Think back now on the ugliness of the people who provided the leadership and the script for what so many people believed. Think of J. Edgar Hoover and his secret files destroyed at his death, of the odious Roy Cohn, of the racist Senators, of Richard Nixon, the legions of phone-tappers, the invidious HUAC, loyalty boards, a president [Reagan] even today running an illegal war against a small impoverished country [Nicaragua], a president engaged in Watergate morality of deceit and lies.

To those convinced that Alger was guilty of espionage—even though technically he was only convicted of perjury—Hiss represents the so-called enemy within, the betrayal of America by those who would have it embrace Marx and Engels. Hiss is the American Kim Philby, one of the country's elite who passed state secrets to the Russians in the dead of night. Or he's a descendant of Benedict Arnold, there to collaborate with the Soviets at Yalta and in the back alleys of the New Deal. His detractors further resent his refusal ever to come clean with a confession. (As Marlow writes in *Edward II*: "Ah, traitors, will they still display their pride?") This suspected hubris is the subject of a recent book, *Alger Hiss's Looking Glass Wars: The Covert Life of a Soviet Spy*, in which Professor G. Edward White of the University of Virginia Law School concludes:

> For Hiss, convincing the public that he had been an innocent victim of a malevolent political culture, not a Soviet agent, was intimately connected to the overriding goal of helping the ideals of Soviet Communism spread throughout the world. He was prepared to betray the trust of loyal friends, and family members, to pursue that goal.

The *New York Times* assigned the review of White's book to its former executive editor, Max Frankel, who minced few words: "If you are too young to care much about Alger Hiss, move on. Turn away also if you recall the case and still believe Hiss never fed secrets to Soviet agents. But if you accept Hiss's guilt, as most historians now do, you will profit from G. Edward White's supplementary speculations about why, after prison, that serene and charming man sacrificed his marriage, exploited a son's love and abused the trust of fervent supporters to wage a forty-two-year struggle for a vindication that could never be honesty gained." In the minds of these faithful, Frankel and White among them, Hiss is a sinking witch.

WITHOUT TURNING AWAY, I knew Hiss for the last seventeen years of his life. I don't want to imply that we were confidants or best friends. But I did know him, admire him, share meals with him, speak with him on many occasions, and get to know his family. It was Bill Rodgers who introduced us in 1979, when Bill was adding to his voluminous Hiss file and wanted to interview Alger on some aspect of the case. As Bill needed a quiet place to record their interview, I offered my apartment. I must have sat through the interview, but I do not recall the specifics of the conversation. I do, however, have a clear memory of serving Alger tuna fish, and then watching with horror as one of our cats liberated the sandwich from Alger's plate. Leaving aside for the moment whether Alger was a Soviet spy, he *was* a gracious guest and amiably fed the cat the rest of the tuna.

After that initial meeting, even though I was in my mid-twenties, I summoned the courage to invite Alger to lunch. He was then seventy-five. By then I had read a few books about the case, and I was interested to hear more about it from him. That first lunch evolved into periodic meetings. We would meet at a restaurant off Gramercy Park. The conversation would move from the case and the New Deal to current political gossip. He spoke about Oliver Wendell Holmes's experiences in the Civil War, about which he had heard directly from the justice. We shared that interest of stretching personal links well back into American history.

Sometimes his son Tony would join us, as he and I were working for magazines. I had heard from Bill that Tony, as a young boy, had suffered understandable anxiety when Alger went to prison, and that once his mother had to jerk him back from the train tracks in Lewisburg where he had lingered far too long just to see if, in fact, the engine was coming around the curve. At those lunches I admired the apparent easy intimacy between father and son, their natural give and take during the conversation. I heard Alger more than once express his pride in Tony's successes as a writer for *The New Yorker*. (His classic account, *All Aboard with E.M. Frimbo*, remains my favorite book about American railroads.) In his book, White makes Tony to be a dupe of Alger's Marxist cunning, there to deflect Alger's guilt. But then White was never at our meals nor had he ever met either of the Hisses.

After one of our lunches, I asked Alger if he would speak to a group of my friends on the subject of the New Deal. I knew he was weary of discussing the case—who wouldn't be? But I sensed in him a reservoir of passion on the subject of the Roosevelt presidency. During the 1930s and 40s, Hiss had served in the Agricultural Adjustment Administration (AAA), on the so-called Nye Committee investigating arms sales, in the office of the Solicitor General, and lastly in the State Department. Ronald Reagan was president, and much of the New Deal was under attack, although in the 1930s Reagan's views closely matched Hiss's. Alger was eager to defend the New Deal, and thus we fixed a winter weekend afternoon for him to meet my friends over lunch at my apartment.

That apartment on West 85ᵗʰ Street had neither direct sunlight nor a dining room table, so we sat around the small living room on my sad collection of furniture. I remember Hiss as tall and thin for his age, with an erect bearing, even when seated. He wasn't the kind of person, I suspect, who ever slouched on a sofa. On most occasions when I saw him, he wore an English tweed sports jacket and sometimes carried a raincoat on his arm—as if he were a Harvard law professor, as well he could have been. His smile was engaging. While he didn't have a lot of small talk—on things like the weather or baseball—he had many passions: wine, railroad stations, public places, speeches he had heard, etc. When he grew up in Baltimore, it was still a southern city, and he inherited its graciousness, making him endlessly grateful for small favors. He was meticulous in answering letters and phone calls. He did not seem excited about travel; that part of the modern world did not engage him. But he was at home with political narrative, which in my mind marked him as a Washingtonian. New Yorkers tell stories about broken elevators, stalled subways, and failed relationships, while Washingtonians describe their proximity to men of power and politics. In that art, Hiss had a Faulknerian sense of narrative and irony.

JUST BECAUSE HISS was a gracious luncheon guest or fed table scraps to a cat does not mean he was or was not a celebrated spy. But several hours in his company, on the subject of the

New Deal and the Roosevelt presidency, did suggest outlines of his personality. Clearly he felt the New Deal the most profound influence on his life. Hiss had come of age politically and emotionally in the company of men like Jerome Frank at the AAA, Abe Fortas, a confidant of Lyndon Johnson, and Telford Taylor, who later tried war crimes at Nuremburg. The men he most admired were Oliver Wendell Holmes, the Supreme Court justice for whom he was a clerk, and President Roosevelt, who allowed these many headstrong young bureaucrats to reshape the American polity. A passage which later appeared in his memoirs, *Recollections of a Life*, could well have been spoken at the luncheon: "Young men of my generation tended to be self-conscious about matters of belief and principle. If asked, I would have said my code consisted of honor, loyalty, pride, an aversion to exploitation of others, and independence." He described Eleanor Roosevelt as "my favorite woman in political life."

Later, reading *Witness* by Whittaker Chambers, purportedly an account of his spying times with Alger, I was struck by the inaccuracy of his Hiss profiles. One passage reads: "Hiss's contempt for Franklin Roosevelt as a dabbler in revolution who understood neither revolution nor history was profound....He startled me, and deeply shocked my wife, by the obvious pleasure he took in the most simple and brutal references to the President's physical condition as a symbol of the middle-class breakdown." Perhaps to someone who had never met Alger, such a description could be plausible. But to anyone who spent time in his company, it's inconceivable that he would ever have mocked Roosevelt, his infirmity, or pounded the table like Nikita Khrushchev. Hiss was an idealist, not an ideologue. In his memoirs he writes: "I recall few if any references in Johns Hopkins classes to the Soviet revolution, which in no way excited my interest." His favorite book was Somerset Maugham's *Of Human Bondage*.

Nevertheless, another passage in *Witness* describes Hiss as a hardened revolutionary, the kind of man uncomfortable with any newspaper other than *Pravda*. Chambers writes:

> For our friendship was almost entirely one of character and not of the mind. Despite his acknowledged ability in the legal field, which I was not competent to explore with him, Alger Hiss is not a highly mental man.... Ideas for their own sake did not interest him at all. His mind had come to rest in the doctrines of Marx and Lenin, and even then applied itself wholly to current politics and seldom, that I can remember, to history or to theory.

In college at Lewisburg, I had professors who adorned their offices with revolutionary posters. In my travels across Eastern Europe and Russia, I have met any number of union organizers, for whom the workers of the world are always in need of uniting. But to think of Alger Hiss in such company is to confuse the Ivy League with the Shining Path. As I judged them, his habits of mind were those of an Anglophile, and his literary tastes focused, not surprisingly, on *The New Yorker* magazine. "Apart from Mencken," he wrote of his college reading, "we had only the sages of New York to look to—figures like Dorothy Parker, Alexander Woollcott, music critic Chotzinoff, and Franklin P. Adams of 'The Conning Tower.'" Alas, no one ever accused Hegel of writing casuals.

In our Saturday lunch, Hiss spent a lot of time talking about Pearl Harbor, the outbreak of war, and his presence at Yalta, where he had accompanied the Secretary of State, Edward R. Stettinius, Jr. Hiss was then involved in the organization of the United Nations, but when the war broke out he was in the Far Eastern division, thus charged with interpreting Japan's war aims, if any. We asked if Roosevelt could have invited a Japanese attack, as a way of leveraging the United States into the war. Hiss dismissed such cynicism, as he later wrote: "With no thought of our impending catastrophe, those of us who were responsible for our Far Eastern policy had not stayed late in our offices on Saturday, December 6. I got home by midafternoon with no sense of crisis....The Navy reported that a Japanese fleet had been observed off the coast of Indochina headed south."

Toward the end of the war, Hiss had responsibility for planning American participation in the United Nations. Although he was not a senior State Department official, he was invited to accompany President Roosevelt to Yalta, as high on FDR's agenda for that conference was to win Russian acceptance for the world organization. At Yalta in winter 1945, Hiss recounted how, up early one morning, he had watched Churchill march to the water's edge, shed his bathrobe and, wearing only a cigar, float on his back in the warm waters of the Black Sea. When a wave washed over the British prime minister and his cigar, Churchill made a rude gesture to the sea and sullenly trudged back to his room.

At our luncheon Hiss defended the terms of Yalta, arguing that Roosevelt's overriding goal had been to bring the Russians into the Pacific war and to secure their participation in the United Nations. Hiss, personally, opposed three votes for the Soviet bloc in the UN. But Roosevelt, eager for Russian involvement, overruled him. Hiss believed that relations with the Soviets would have been less confrontational had Roosevelt lived, but acknowledged that even in February 1945 Russian troops were well entrenched in Eastern Europe.

On the way home from Yalta, Hiss spent a day in Moscow with the Secretary of State. In some versions of the case, while in Moscow he (with the codename ALES) supposedly received a decoration for meritorious service from Soviet military intelligence. Recently, a retired Soviet spymaster for the Americas scoffed at such an award ceremony. But it lingers in case mythology. In the same vein, I asked Curtis Roosevelt, grandson of FDR whose mother, Anna, was at Yalta, if Hiss could have driven a Communist line with Secretary of State Stettinius. Curtis laughed that Roosevelt laugh and said: "And FDR never asked Stettinius his views, either."

WHO THEN WAS Whittaker Chambers and why did he accuse Alger Hiss of spying for the Soviets? Small libraries of books address this question. For anyone interested in learning more about the case, I can save them time, as follows: if you are prepared to like and admire Chambers, and want to believe his confessional, read *Witness*, *Perjury* by Allen Weinstein, or a relatively new biography of Chambers by Sam Tanenhaus, who subsequently became editor of the *New York Times Book Review* and who presumably commissioned the Frankel review. Nixon has a chapter in *Six Crises* that lionizes Chambers, and William F. Buckley, Jr., collected Chambers' correspondence with Hiss's accuser and published it as a book. On the other hand, if you want to think well of Hiss, the books to read are those by John Chabot Smith, Fred Cook, The Earl Jowett, Dr. Meyer Zeligs, Tony Hiss, William Howard Moore, and a someday-to-be-published history by William A. Reuben, the author of *The Honorable Richard Nixon* and someone who has defended Hiss since the 1950s.

Alas, no one, in my experience, is neutral on the subject of Whittaker Chambers. William Buckley, Jr., who found in

Chambers an emotional father figure, describes their first meeting as if an encounter from the lives of the saints:

> I was taken to his bedroom. The doctor had forbidden him even to raise his head. And yet he seemed the liveliest man I had ever met. I could not imagine such good humor from a very sick man, let alone anyone possessed by the conviction that night was closing in all over the world, privately tortured by his continuing fear that the forces aligned against him would contrive to reorder history, impose upon the world the ghastly lie that he had testified falsely against Alger Hiss, and so erase his witness, his expiation for more than ten years' complicity with Communism.

In contrast, Bill Rodgers wrote that the belief in Hiss's guilt required a leap of faith:

> It also required the attribution of religious and patriotic righteousness to Whittaker Chambers, who had held such attributes in contempt all his life until he was laundered clean by the visitation of the Lord, the 1939 German-Russian alliance, his renunciation of homosexuality, and the prospects of promotion at *Time*. After his redemption, he emerged recanting but still suicidal, loyal to God and country, faithful to all he had previously loathed, speaking the truth as presumably only a professed atheist and practiced liar could speak it.

Unlike Hiss, I never met Whittaker Chambers, who died when I was seven years old. I do, however, share a few things in common with him. We both grew up on Long Island

and both attended Columbia University. We both edited and wrote for monthly magazines. He also spent a long period at *Time* magazine, where I have known many editors and writers, some of whom knew Chambers. I have read his writings and seen him on film. We both knew Alger Hiss.

Other than his court testimony against Hiss, what we have of Chambers is *Witness*, his memoirs that were serialized while Hiss was in prison and later published as a book. Contemporaneous in many ways with film noir, *Witness* is 799 pages of melodrama in which Chambers is the suspect, judge, and jury of his effusive imagination. He begins: "All the props of an espionage case are there—foreign agents, household traitors, stolen documents, microfilm, furtive meetings, secret hideaways, phony names, an informer, investigations, trials, official justice." He intones: "At heart, the Great Case was this critical conflict of faiths; that is why it was a great case. On a scale personal enough to be felt by all, but big enough to be symbolic, the two irreconcilable faiths of our time—Communism and Freedom—came to grips in the persons of two conscious and resolute men." He concludes: "A Communist breaks because he must choose at last between irreconcilable opposites—God or Man, Soul or Mind, Freedom or Communism." Such thinking informed the foreign polices of presidents Nixon and Reagan, if not George W. Bush, who over the years has made his own communion with the disciples of Whittaker Chambers.[1]

IN RECENT YEARS, it has been in vogue to reissue *Witness*— my copy is the fiftieth anniversary edition—and add it to the

---

1. On July 9, 2001, the 40th anniversary of Chambers's death, the Bush White House played host to a memorial conference.

canon of Western literature. It was voted one of the influential books of the century. But in the vein of modern novels, the subject never strays very far from the importance of being Whittaker. He writes of an earlier attempt at authorship: "I called the book: *Defeat in the Village.* It was to be an autobiography of mood, but not of factual reality." That description also works for *Witness,* but the only moods the reader ever gets are those of Chambers. Read fifty years later, his portraits of communism in America, of Richard Nixon, of Hiss himself read like outtakes from an airport rack spy novel. (*"I was the contact man between a powerful Soviet espionage apparatus in Washington, and my superior in New York City. Each of us was a link of unequal size in the invisible chain of Communist command that laces the world."*) Other than what he learned in books, he knows Russia not at all. Much of *Witness* is what in the trade is known as a "clip job," something rewritten from clippings. Nor does Chambers ever let facts get in the way of his notes from the underground. God has organized his escape from the pages of Dostoyevsky, so he can bear witness, and those left behind are consigned fiery retribution—Hiss coming across as the Washington cousin of the brothers Karamazov.[2]

When you read about Chambers's childhood on Long Island, it's not hard to see how he emerged akin to one of Gogol's dead souls. From his mother came his gift for languages and from his father a taste for surreal literature.

---

2. In Patrick O'Brien's novel *The Wine-Dark Sea*, Stephen Maturin recalls similar confessions: "But all the time I was reminded of a cousin, a priest, who told me that the most tedious, squalid and disheartening part of his duty was listening to penitents who having made the act of contrition recounted imaginary, fictitious sins, unclean phantasms. And the most painful was the giving of an absolution that might be blasphemous."

"In justice to my father," he writes, "it must be said that he regarded himself first and foremost as an artist....Curiously enough, he did own three volumes of Dostoyevsky—*The House of the Dead*, *The Idiot*, *Crime and Punishment*." But his father, a commercial illustrator, abandoned his family during Whittaker's childhood, only to return later as a figure as reclusive as Boo Radley. "For years," his son writes, "all my father's meals were served to him on a tray in his room....We were four people, living in emotional and physical anarchy." Also present in the house were his brother, who eventually succeeded in committing a gruesome suicide, and his grandmother, who is cast as a raving lunatic. (*"I suppose nobody ever sleeps quite peacefully in a house where a woman sometimes wanders around with a knife."*) Just to add to the fallout from this nuclear family, Chambers's mother sleeps with an axe under her bed. When in 1948 Whittaker testified on his flight from communism—*"For a year I lived in hiding, sleeping by day and watching the night with gun or revolver within easy reach"*—little did the congressional committee know that he was upholding a family tradition.[3]

Witness was written after Hiss's conviction and after Chambers had worked at *Time*. He boasts of his magazine career during the 1940s: "I also became *Time's* most controversial foreign news editor; in the middle of World War II, I reversed the magazine's news policy toward Russia, making

---

3. As a Long Islander, I find absurd Chambers's account of a typical pub-crawling day with his grandfather. He claimed that they started in Freeport, crossed by motor launch to Long Beach, took a "cross Long Island trolley" to the North Shore, drank in bars near Manhasset and Hempstead bays, and ended their excursions "in the taprooms of Brooklyn or Jamaica"—the kind of trip, I can say from experience, that is probably beyond the reach of a high school senior driving a Corvette. Plus in those days few trolleys ran from the South Shore to Manhasset, where I later lived.

it clear on the basis of the weekly news that Russia was not a friend, but an enemy, who was actively using World War II to prepare World War III." In fact, Chambers was a gifted rewrite man, there at Henry Luce's magazine to give political spin to dispatches from the field. In that sense, *Witness* can be read as the longest *Time* cover story in history (something along the lines of *Espionage Comes Home*). In fact, much of the research for the book was provided by the two Hiss trials, endless FBI wiretaps and investigations of Hiss (several hundred agents worked, at one time, on the case), and the yards of congressional testimony, from which Chambers would have had the pleasure of quoting himself. All he had to do was rewrite the cables.

Chambers was a restless, frustrated intellectual, someone whose Columbia friends, such as Lionel Trilling, had made names in literary circles. In *Witness*, as with his espionage charges against Hiss, my belief is that he chose to experiment with literary forms that we now view as commonplace, but which then touched off criminal investigations. As an account of the Communist threat to America, Chambers's stories are recycled clichés, delivered with newsreel breathlessness. (*"There was Marxist-Leninst political instruction and discussion in the Group."*) As fiction, however, *Witness* is an attempt to have Dostoyevsky describe Washington in the 1930s, with characters, like Hiss, drawn from people Chambers had met but didn't know well. He uses real names, but then makes up the characters. I still think it's a bad novel, but at least it places the author in the tradition of fabulist characters and writers—Walter Mitty, E.L. Doctorow, and Gabriel Garcia Marquez come to mind—rather than as a creditable prosecution witness. As one biographer concludes: "In his ordeal of living, he was, in effect, a person come to life from the pages of Hugo and Dostoyevsky." A friend described Chambers "as a writer who preferred to live his novels rather than write them." In *Witness*, he could do both.

ANOTHER WAY TO read *Witness* is as an early work of gay literature. If in reading *Witness* you substitute the word *homosexual* for *communist*, and exchange one underground for another, the book makes sense as an attempt of a gay writer to describe the many valleys of his temptations. Chambers's father had left his family when Whittaker was a boy to have an outing with the gay lifestyle. His son did the same in the 1930s. During the Hiss trials the FBI covered up the matter of Chambers's homosexuality, fearing he would have been discredited as a witness. Indeed, Hiss's lawyers, among themselves, wondered if Chambers's motivations against Hiss were those of a rejected lover. Hiss, who was not homosexual, said Chambers had never made advances when they knew each other in the 1930s. A juror at the second trial, Vincent Shaw, said that Chambers's being homosexual does not address the question of whether Hiss was guilty. But, he said, if it had been known at the trial, Hiss would have been acquitted.

In an FBI document, which was only released in the 1970s, Chambers confesses to cruising movie theaters in the 1930s at exactly the same time in which he claims to have been a Soviet spy. (*"Since that time, and continuing to the year 1938, I engaged in numerous homosexual activities, both in New York and Washington."*) Who knows which underground Chambers is describing when he writes: "Sometimes the initial contact was made at a movie, followed by a long ramble around the city, winding up at a restaurant." Cut then to several passages in *Witness* between Chambers and his intelligence master, Colonel Bykov. It's Bykov who, through Chambers, is running secret agent Hiss. It's Bykov whom Hiss meets in Brooklyn. It's Bykov who often awaits Chambers in remote places. *("Most of our meetings took place in New York City. We always prearranged them a week or ten days ahead. As a rule, we first met in a movie house. I would go in and stand at the back. Bykov, who nearly always had arrived first, would get up from the audience at the agreed time and join me.")* Lastly it is Bykov who invents the way for Hiss to commit treason. *("[Bykov] proposed that the Advokat [Hiss] should bring home a brief case of documents every night.")* But Bykov is interesting on several levels. No one in America, including the FBI, or in Russia has ever been able to prove that such a spymaster existed, and, second, Bykov is the name of a character in Dostoyevsky's first novel, *Poor Folk*.

Chambers told the FBI "that three things of some great importance happened during the year 1938. First, my cessation of my homosexual activities, my final break with the Communist Party, and my embracing for the first time, religion."[4] Chambers's staunch defender, Professor Allen Weinstein, writes: "No evidence has emerged to contradict Chambers's assertion that he ever mixed the Communist Party's secret work with his private homosexual encounters"— making it sound like a declined office perk. Hiss, however, stated in 1979: "Years later, I learned that in the mid-1930s, when I knew him as Crosley, Chambers was a closet homosexual. I now believe that my rebuff to him wounded him in

---

4. To leave the underground, Chambers needed security, as he wrote: "Shortly before my break, I began to organize my life preserver. I secreted copies of Government documents copied in the Hiss household, memos in the handwriting of Alger Hiss and Harry Dexter White, microfilm of documents transmitted by Alger Hiss and the source in the Bureau of Standards."

a way that I did not realize at the time. I think the rebuff, coupled with his political paranoia, inspired his later machinations against me."

DURING THE SUMMER of 1948, public sentiment against Alger Hiss turned on his belated recognition of Whittaker Chambers as someone he had known in the 1930s as George Crosley, a freelance writer. Before a congressional committee, Chambers testified that Hiss, among many others, had been a Communist whom he had known in the underground. Chambers described Hiss's devotion to the cause and his passion for paying party dues. Hiss denied having been a Communist or that he had ever known a man named Whittaker Chambers, but later, seeing him in person before the House Un-American Affairs Committee, he changed his story to say he now recognized his accuser as Crosley.

Crosley, the writer, had come to the Nye Committee, researching a story on armaments, and Hiss had befriended him and his young family for a time—even letting them sublet an apartment and use an old car. Hiss recalled: "We talked backwards and forwards about the Munitions Committee work. He told various stories that I recall of his escapades. He purported to be a cross between Jim Tully, the author, and Jack London. He had been everywhere." As a witness, Chambers could recall intimate details about the Hisses—aspects of their houses, Alger's interest in bird watching—and such familiarity lent credence to the larger charge that Hiss had been a fellow-traveler in the underground. That some of these details later were proved to be fabricated or sketchy hardly mattered at the time he first testified. They were explosive. Nixon, then a congressman, personally appeared before the grand jury to press evidence against Hiss, who was subsequently indicted for perjury—a way to circumvent the expired statue of limitations on treason.

What had the Ivy League lawyer, then working for an important congressional committee, seen in the itinerant freelance journalist? According to one biography, Chambers had qualities that Hiss recalled in his older brother, Bosley, who had died tragically in his twenties. Dr. Meyer Zeligs, who wrote *Friendship and Fratricide*, a psychological profile of Hiss and Chambers, describes the connection:

> "Bosley Hiss" and "George Crosley" were both high intellect; colorful and magnetic personalities. Both were knockabout, nonconformist character types. Both had lived unwisely. To Alger, the proper and obedient boy grown into the conventional gentleman, the "rough and tough" style was something he had always admired in others, a style of life he had pleasantly brushed but not really engaged in.

Why did not Hiss take a better measure of someone like Chambers? Zeligs observes: "Despite Hiss's exceptional skills as an administrator and his wide experience with many character types, his appraisals of people are more idealized than worldly. Indeed, from a close study of him as a person one senses a lack of those very attributes of character—shrewdness and cunning—which characterize his public image. In his need to seek out the good in people, he unconsciously prevents himself from recognizing guile and deceit." Nevertheless, it would be wrong to read too much into the friendship of Hiss and Chambers, which, by Hiss's account, lasted from late 1934 or early 1935 into 1936.

In 1936, after some months as acquaintances, Hiss felt Crosley was taking advantage of his generosity and dropped him as a friend. According to Hiss, they had an abrupt phone conversation. He recalled: "I can't remember when it was I finally decided it wasn't any use expecting to collect from him, that I had been a sucker and he was a sort of deadbeat; not a bad character, but I think he just was using me for a soft touch." Could such a brush-off explain the subsequent motivations of Chambers to describe Hiss as first a Communist and then a spy to the FBI, a White House official, various congressional committees, a grand jury, at two federal trials, and in an 800-page memoir? Hiss said this on reflection: "I can't imagine a normal man holding a grudge because somebody had stopped being a sucker."

BUT WAS CHAMBERS normal? In my view he had a Jekyll and Hyde personality. To men like Henry Luce, Chambers was a clear-thinking, if somewhat emotional Dr. Jekyll, consumed with the red menace. To others, including Hiss, Chambers became the deranged Mr. Hyde.[5] Zeligs speculates on the end of the Hiss-Chambers friendship: "Would this parting be sufficient to inspire a lifelong grudge? Not, to be sure, in an ordinary man. But for Chambers, who was so deeply disturbed, so lost in the world of reality, so unsure of his own existence, tormented by the rejection of his homosexual love, it would indeed be sufficient." Nor, as Zeligs writes, was this

---

5. R.L. Stevenson writes: "'God bless me, the man seems hardly human! Something troglodytic, shall we say? or can it be the old story of Dr. Fell? or is it the mere radiance of a foul soul that thus transpires through, and transfigures, its clay continent? The last, I think; for, O my poor old Harry Jekyll, if I read Satan's signature upon a face, it is on that of your new friend!'"

the first time that Chambers, after a passing acquaintance, evidenced—as Stevenson described Hyde—"a sort of murderous mixture of timidity and boldness."

By way of outlining Chambers's personality disorder, Zeligs recounts his brief stay at Williams College in 1920. As a freshman, he spent only the first few days at the school, and then told his roommate that he was quitting and abruptly left for home around midnight. But for Karl Helfrich, Chambers's undoubtedly perplexed roommate, their relationship was just starting. Zeligs writes: "Thereafter, over a period of some six weeks, Helfrich received a number of very long letters from Chambers, written in longhand and running to over twelve pages each. They described peculiar adventures of Chambers which Helfrich thought at the time must have been invented." Then Helfrich received a letter asking his former roommate to collect a letter addressed to a fictitious person at the post office. Alarmed at such intrigue, fearing it might violate postal laws, Helfrich went to the college president, who collected the strange letter and opened it. "The letter in question," writes Zeligs, "was one written by Whittaker to himself. Helfrich remembered it as 'a weird recital.' It dealt, as he recalled, with some mystic communion between Chambers and the Devil." No doubt by this time Helfrich was happy to be living alone.

A psychoanalyst, Zeligs puts the incident in the context of Chambers's later accusations against those from his past, including college friends and some he knew casually, like Hiss:

> The incident of the self-addressed letter is indeed significant, for it heralds in form and plot the schemes

he later designed to protect himself from his persecutory fears. The use of this particular device—the "mail drop"—recurs many times in Chambers' activities. This manipulation by which he hoped to outwit Helfrich and the postal authorities gave Chambers a feeling of omnipotence. Similarly, his romantic letter to Helfrich purported to demonstrate his worldly experiences and personal strength. His colorful fabrication, a composite of play-acting, and writing-out, of wishful fantasies, had all the merits of producing excitement and intrigue, a façade to cover the emptiness inside him.

In his award-winning biography of Chambers, Tanenhaus covers Whittaker's stay at Williams, in its entirety, as follows:

> The next month he arrived as a member of the freshman class but felt instantly out of place, repelled by the postcard-pretty campus. Lost amid the mass of "young collegiate faces," he shunned all the orientation events. Skipping a freshman dinner, he stayed behind to read the Bible. When his roommate returned, Chambers announced that a "great light had come to him." After three days at Williams, he took the night train to New York—and Columbia University.

Light on the road to Damascus, if not North Adams, is as far as Tanenhaus takes the Williams story. In *Witness*, Chambers is even more cryptic: "But one or two days on that beautiful and expensive campus told me that Williams was not the place for me, that my parents could never stand the costs of that little Harvard. I saw I had a quick and difficult decision to make. I took a night train for New York."

EVEN CHAMBERS'S CAREER as a self-professed Communist spy has the same aspects of "play-acting" and "wishful fantasies." He had joined the Party in 1924, and, by his version, he was recruited into an underground apparatus in the early 1930s. There he was a courier who moved stolen documents between Washington offices, including that of Hiss, and Party photographers, who copied the papers for transmission to Moscow. But was Chambers really a spy?

Certainly Chambers wanted his friends to think the underground he was frequenting was that of espionage. But as a spy he shared more traits with Austin Powers or Maxwell Smart than with James Bond. For example, on a trip to Russia allegedly to study at the Lenin School, he sent postcards to his friends, although that trip may never have happened and the cards were to cover up the mythical debarkation at the Finland Station. Even Weinstein writes:

> During trips to New York he also continued to visit his non-Communist friends and kept in touch with them, in addition, by mail, discussing mainly personal or family news. One letter confided to the Meyer Shapiros that he (Chambers) had just been awarded a "high honor" by the Soviet government for his services as an agent, an award he later identified to Herbert Solow as "the Lenin Order." Despite peculiarities as an underground operative, Chambers—that most un-secret agent—had apparently earned the respect of his colleagues and superiors.

As a spy, Chambers was always taking breaks from the cold. Zeligs writes: "There is no shortage of anecdotes;

Chambers cut a memorable figure. Lionel Trilling and others have pointed out that despite the danger he always seemed to be in, Chambers was always reminding everyone that he was a secret Communist agent by going around behaving like a spy. It was enough of an open secret, to those who knew Chambers in the thirties, to enable Trilling to base the main character of a novel on Chambers' bizarre behavior." Later at *Time* magazine, on some occasions when he would have lunch with a colleague, he would first lead the bewildered co-worker on and off a few subway trains, as though his every move was being watched. He also kept furtive notebooks on many of his colleagues, and a loaded gun in his desk.

Whether Chambers was a freelance spy or a just freelance writer, he proved adept at collecting stacks of documents from the Washington bureaucracy. Government in the 1930s was a small town, and anyone inclined to collect papers could have come across open stacks, unguarded archives, and accommodating officials. (Another State Department official, Julian Wadleigh, admitted to having given Chambers more than 500 documents.) In such an environment, it is not surprising that Chambers would have later turned up with papers that had crossed Hiss's desk. His motivation, however, for collecting such documents is less clear. No search of the Russian intelligence archive has ever indicated that Chambers was a Soviet agent. In addition, several retired Russian intelligence officers have dismissed such a proposition, arguing that spies were not recruited among party members, especially among those, like Chambers, who maintained links with Trotsky-ites—then Stalin's great enemy.

According to Zeligs, Chambers had psychological reasons for squirreling papers of all description. These were his so-called "life-preservers":

His mind was a compendium of fact and fantasy. He kept dossiers of facts and foibles on his friends, colleagues, and many of those with whom, at any time, he had any dealings. These were his "life-savers." Some of them he actually hid or asked others to hide for him. But he filed in the unwritten archives of his mind, a private storehouse of facts, ideas, real and fictional plots, gathered from readings, translations, and actual experience for future use.... In his inner struggle, the stealing, copying (by typewriter or microfilm), withholding, hiding, and timely production of documents provided a "life-preserver" useful to any eventuality. Chambers' actions were equivocal. He had need to deceive almost everyone he dealt with, because he had need to always deceive himself. Chambers' sense of his own identity was so tenuous and unrealistic he required a "life-preserver" at all times to sustain him.

Concerning Hiss in 1948, Chambers at first testified that Hiss had only been a card-carrying Communist. He denied that Hiss had been a secret agent. Nevertheless, Hiss sued Chambers for libel—a case Chambers's lawyers thought he would lose unless he "had something" on Hiss. In response, Chambers produced a collection of typewritten documents and 35mm film—some of which he stored in a pumpkin, for safekeeping, at the last moment. He said Hiss had removed these materials from the State Department and typed copies of them for the purpose of having them photographed. Hiss made it clear that he could not type, so Chambers covered his errant tracks to say that Hiss's wife, Priscilla, had typed the documents, which Chambers collected directly from the Hiss household over many months.

Before the perjury trials, 1949 to 1950, a search of

Washington turned up a Woodstock typewriter that, it was inferred in court, had belonged to Hiss and that had been used to type the purloined State Department letters and documents. Its typefaces, as well, were said to match those contained in several letters once typed by Hiss's wife. At the trial Hiss had no explanation for how the documents Chambers produced were typed on his machine. His closing statement, often quoted, contained: "I want only to add that I am confident that in the future the full facts of how Whittaker Chambers was able to carry out forgery by typewriter will be disclosed."[6]

Since 1950, many hypotheses have been advanced to answer this riddle. It has been proved that the Woodstock typewriter in court was not the one that had belonged to Hiss. Another analysis concluded that two typists, not one, had typed the so-called Baltimore documents (Chambers took them to Baltimore, he said). Other historians have pointed out that Mrs. Hiss herself wasn't much of a typist, and certainly could not easily have typed sixty single-spaced pages. Plus the documents themselves passed over many desks, not just Hiss's, and the logical question has been raised why Hiss would circulate documents in the underground that could

---

6. Only later could he write: "Nixon called Woodstock number 230,099 "the key 'witness' in the case." But it was a false witness. It was not Priscilla's old typewriter. The fact was known to the prosecution but was withheld at the time of the trials. Its disclosure at that time would have destroyed the government's case." Priscilla's typewriter had been acquired by her father in 1927, when the serial numbers ranged between 145,000 and 204,500. Chester Lane, a defense attorney, went further in his analysis of the machine: "A Woodstock typewriter bearing the serial number N230099 would have been manufactured in or around August 1929, and certainly no earlier than the first week of July 1929. At the same time the best available information indicates that the typeface style on our machine (N230099) was a style used by the Woodstock Company only in typewriters manufactured in 1926, 1927, and 1928, and possibly the early part of 1929. These inconsistencies point to the conclusion that N230099 is a fabricated machine."

have been so easily traced to him? But anyone convinced of Hiss's guilt has to accept the world according to Chambers, because at the trials no other witnesses testified that Hiss had stolen State Department documents.

No ONE IS more accommodating to Chambers's outline of history than Allen Weinstein, who has transmuted his book, *Perjury: The Hiss–Chambers Case*, into the last word on Alger's guilt. Talk with anyone who has only a passing interest in the matter, and after a while they will say: "Wasn't there some book that proved he was guilty?" The "some book" is that of Weinstein, who taught at Smith College in Massachusetts and later founded The Center for Democracy in Washington. More recently his nomination to become the archivist of the United States touched off a storm of protests among those who believe his scholarship, instead of proving Hiss guilty, proved only that academics can tailor their views to political and career expedience. In Weinstein's case, his Hiss bashing credentials gave him cachet with the Reagan administration, for whom Whittaker Chambers was one of the patron saints. (Reagan awarded Chambers the Medal of Freedom.)

If *Witness* is a rewrite of FBI documents produced on the case, *Perjury* is a rewrite of *Witness*. The book shares the assumption of Senator Joseph McCarthy that Communists lay under many government beds and that Hiss was foremost among those who had infiltrated the State Department. As history, *Perjury* reads like a Walter Winchell column on the red menace. One reviewer noted: "Weinstein has aligned himself with those Cold-War intellectuals who presumably sleep better at night secure in the knowledge that there was an internal Communist espionage menace ." But Weinstein's genius wasn't to decipher the intricacies of the Hiss case so much as to claim that, when he had begun his research, he believed Hiss innocent and that, when he was done looking at the files, he believed him guilty. Thus the conclusion is that if anyone bothers to sift the body of evidence, they, too, will conclude Hiss guilty.[7]

For someone nominated to preside over the government archives, Weinstein's use of original material is surprisingly slipshod. The editor of the *Nation* magazine, Victor Navasky, tried to follow a footnote in *Perjury*, only to conclude that in backing up a point made by Chambers, the source was none other than Chambers himself: "He was being used to corroborate himself." On another occasion, Weinstein offered to open up his research materials to Navasky or to donate them to the Harry Truman Library. Not only did he not give them to the presidential collection, he canceled the meeting with Navasky to review the source material—not exactly the qualities sought in the national archivist. Dismissing Weinstein's objectivity, Navasky wrote:

> Professor Weinstein is now an embattled partisan, hopelessly mired in the perspective of one side, his narrative obfuscatory, his interpretations improbable, his omissions strategic, his vocabulary manipulative, his standards double, his "corroborations" circular and suspect, his reporting astonishingly erratic (brilliantly enterprising where it serves, nonexistent where it complicates, and frequently unreliable).

---

7. At times Weinstein's prose makes his hero look like Chance the Gardner, aka Chauncy Gardiner, in the film *Being There*: "Chambers taught himself to write and speak several languages, including German, Russian, Spanish, and—according to his friends—more difficult ones such as Hungarian and Chinese. Julian Wadleigh, who later confessed to passing State Department documents to Chambers from 1937 to 1938, described a dinner with "Karl" in a Washington restaurant when the latter read the entire menu aloud in what appeared to be Chinese." Unless, of course, the restaurant printed its menus in Hungarian.

Independent filmmaker John Lowenthal, who was also my friend, had his own encounters with Weinstein, who later collaborated with Alexander Vassiliev in publishing a book about Soviet espionage in America, *The Haunted Wood*. Vassiliev sued a magazine in which Lowenthal challenged the book's sources. Among the points Lowenthal made was that the footnotes in the new book simply referred readers to *Perjury*—which, as Navasky demonstrates, is an annotated black hole. The English court held for Lowenthal, who had written as follows about *The Haunted Wood*:

> The co-authors' references and their own narrative statements cannot be checked or verified by anyone else, because they derive from excerpts "quoted" out of context from KGB files closed to other researches. The co-authors' publisher, Random House, paid undisclosed sums (reportedly more than a million dollars) to an association of retired KGB agents for "exclusive" access to KGB files for Weinstein and Vassiliev.

Not that paying the Russians a million dollars for their archives would have guaranteed the application of sound scholarship to their interpretation. Elsewhere Lowenthal writes: "Six of Weinstein's most important interviewees for *Perjury* protested that they had been misquoted or otherwise misrepresented in the book, and one of them sued for libel, demanding that Weinstein produce the interview tapes he claimed to have. Unwilling or unable to produce them, Weinstein paid a substantial five-figure sum in damages and published a retraction and apology." But the jacket for *The Haunted Wood* has praise for *Perjury* from Alfred Kazin, Gary Wills, William F. Buckley, Jr., and Arthur Schlesinger, Jr.

The latter called it "the most objective and convincing account we have of the most dramatic court case of the century."

WHAT IS LACKING on the Hiss side of the bookshelf is the definitive volume of vindication. That may be forthcoming when the late William A. Reuben's history of the case is published. I am told the manuscript runs more than a thousand pages. For years before he died in 2004, every time he was asked to submit it to a publisher, he found new leads to pursue. But some of the chapters have been posted on the Internet, and from those passages, the book promises to set numerous records straight. Reuben studied the case for fifty years. He even interviewed Chambers's high school principal, who described his celebrated alumni as "some kind of a nut." He looked into Chambers's charge that he had been dismissed from his job at the New York Public Library "because he was a Communist," and ascertained that he was fired because he had stolen sixty-three library books. He was run out of Columbia for the same reason. As for his various testimony that eventually convicted Hiss, Reuben writes:

> Chambers had been shown to be inaccurate about almost every detail of his personal life, from when and how he left Columbia University and the New York Public Library to how he made a living, to whether his mother worked, to when he got married and how old his brother was when he committed suicide. More important, he had contradicted his earlier testimony given to the Committee on numerous crucial subjects, from when he joined and left the Communist Party and how long he was in it, to whether he had known Harold Ware, to how and when he first met Alger Hiss. Since he had testified under oath

in both instances, it was clear that either he had willfully perjured himself or that he was a man incapable of differentiating truth from fiction.

Reuben also reports that, during the time Chambers claims to have been a Russian spy, he was busy translating eighteen books, including *Bambi*. (Chambers testified he had only translated a few books.) Reuben also documents that in 1937, prior to the date Chambers claimed to have left the underground, he was working, under his real name, at the WPA in Washington—not exactly a place where spies go to hide. But Reuben's book has yet to be published, and other important books on the case are out of print and hard to find.

To find a book by The Earl Jowett, an English barrister, I remember hunting among New York City's used bookstores. I eventually located *The Strange Case of Alger Hiss* at Argosy on East 58th, the kind of shop where they wrap all sales in brown paper and tie the books up with string. Jowett served as Lord Chancellor in England and only knew the Hiss case from reading the transcripts of the trials. He read them as a judge might, and published his opinion in 1953. "That brings me naturally to another remarkable feature of this case," he writes,

> —namely, that Alger Hiss himself, by bringing libel action, caused Chambers to produce the incriminating documents. It is an interesting problem of psychology to consider whether a man who had treacherously handed over secret papers typed on his own typewriter or written in his own handwriting would have sued for libel the agent to whom he had handed them because that agent called him a Communist.

Jowett is scathing on the lack of corroboration for Chambers's testimony: "There was, as I see it, no such corroboration, except such as could be deduced from the documents themselves, and no such deduction could be made in the case of the documents which had been photographed." Lastly he brings common sense to the matter, as when he writes about Hiss's next door neighbor on 30ᵗʰ Street in Georgetown: "He never saw Chambers, nor did he hear typewriting going on in the Hisses' house. After Hiss moved from 30ᵗʰ Street, that house was occupied by a newspaper columnist. He noticed the change, because then he did hear the typewriter a great deal." As it happens a good friend of mine, who, by chance, knew (and liked) Chambers at *Time* and is now in his eighties, lives in this house that was next door to the Hisses. I visit him often, and try to imagine the sound if sixty single-spaced paged had been typed on the other side of the wooden walls.

Such a commonsense approach to the case also informs the writing of William Howard Moore, a lapsed Dominican priest who published a monograph at his own expense to poke holes in Weinstein's thesis. Bill sent me *Two Foolish Men: The True Story of the Friendship Between Alger Hiss and Whittaker Chambers* for Christmas, 1987. He knew Moore as a correspondent and admired his deconstruction of Chambers and Weinstein. Better than any professional historian, Moore reveals the absurdity of how Chambers purported to collect documents from Hiss in Washington,[8] and have them photographed in Baltimore:

---

8. "After photographing the documents, I would return them on the same night to Alger Hiss in Washington. I usually traveled between Washington and Baltimore by Pennsylvania Railroad."

In the story at hand, one puzzled investigator did think to ask Chambers how he journeyed from Baltimore, where he lived, to the Hiss domicile in Washington. Chambers replied that he took the train. Simple, isn't it? Just take the train. But think what is involved here as compared to the painless Wadleigh method [that of photographing the original documents]. Poor Chambers, after a weary day of gumshoeing, had to hoist himself out of the easy chair after dinner, walk down to the streetcar line, wait for a car, take it to the station, walk to the train station, wait for a train, walk to the streetcar, take it to the Hiss neighborhood and then walk to the Hiss home. But this was only the beginning of a truly exhausting night. For Chambers, when he got himself into this preposterous adventure, forgot that Hiss would have brought the documents home that day. There wouldn't be time for Mrs. Hiss to type them up, surely a trying frustration to her. So Chambers took the documents along with the typed pages to Carpenter's studio in Baltimore. But then the documents would have to be returned that night so that Hiss could put them back in the files the next morning. So Chambers was forced to relate that he made *two* round trips the same night. Four trains, eight streetcars and sixteen walks, plus the waiting periods for trains and street cars, were involved in this fantastic journey that was rendered totally useless by the Wadleigh method.

By his testimony, Chambers made twenty to thirty such excursions, always at night, but no neighbor of the Hisses ever remember seeing him coming or going, leading Moore to conclude that "Chambers had the documents typed up [professionally] to incriminate an innocent Hiss." But there was one witness to the events on 30th Street who testimony at the trials was never heard.

LIVING AT THE time with Alger and Priscilla Hiss was Timothy Hobson, Priscilla's son by a previous marriage, who was ten-years-old when Chambers was the alleged night caller. Hobson served in the Navy at the end of World War II, but had been discharged after what is called in some histories as a "homosexual incident." John Lowenthal, who was a legal researcher at the two Hiss trials, describes the FBI's conduct:

> At the time of the trials (1949–50), Timothy Hobson was twenty-three and twenty-four years old, and he had wished to testify on his stepfather's behalf. But the FBI, questioning Hobson and some of his friends before the first trial began, made it unmistakably clear—Hobson called it 'polite blackmail'—that, if the defense called Hobson as a witness, the prosecution would discredit him by revealing homosexual incidents in his life. So Hiss told one of his lawyers that "I'd sooner go to jail than have them embarrass Timmy on the stand."

It has also been suggested that Alger's lawyers may not have wanted Timmy on the stand, fear, as Hobson himself says, "it would have hurt Alger to have it brought in front of the jury that he had a homosexual son."

Witness has a maudlin description of the last meeting between Chambers and Hiss. By his account, in 1938, Chambers informs Hiss that he has left the Party and urges Alger also to quit. Ever the die-hard Marxist, Hiss refuses, but cries on their parting. Timothy makes a cameo appearance in the story, in which Chambers describes Hiss as "his closest friend in the Communist party."

In *The View From Alger's Window*, Tony Hiss says that he never saw his father cry, even when he went to prison. But more to the point, he spoke with his stepbrother about what he had seen around the house in the days when Chambers claimed he was coming by or his mother was furiously typing documents. Tony writes:

> My brother, who is the final living eyewitness in the Hiss case (as well as the only one who didn't testify at the trials), had been seven—my son's age now—when, according to Chambers, he and Alger first met; and Tim had been twelve when, again according to Chambers, he had paid his last call on the Hisses. Tim... had been ten and eleven during the time when, according to Chambers again, Alger had brought home State Department papers; Prossy had stayed up late to retype them; Chambers had arrived to collect them.
>
> Tim assured me that maybe about 1 percent of this was either real or based on something real.... Nobody in the family knew them [Chambers and his wife] well or had any other connection with them, and none of the Chamberses ever came back.... Any typing would have resounded through the small 30th Street house—it was flimsily built, with insubstantial walls. Prossy was a poor typist; typing was always a chore for her, not a pleasure.

Of the final Hiss-Chambers meeting, Tony writes: "Tim told me: No 1938 encounter ever took place. It was fabricated without even a seed of truth."

Hobson is now a retired doctor and living in California. He still regrets that he was not able to testify at the trials:

I have never understood Alger's reticence to use legal fire to fight fire as far as that case went. Alger always thought that it was not only more dignified, but absolutely demanded that everything be done in a completely justifiable, honorable way, and the fact that he felt the opponents were using other techniques did not influence his judgement.

He has also said:

I have never quite forgiven [Lloyd Paul] Stryker [Hiss's attorney in the first trial] for not once turning to Chambers and saying, "Are you now or have you ever been a homosexual?" because that would have blown the whole case out of the water.

Unlike Professor White, I know and like Tony Hiss and admire his writing, which flows as gracefully as Alger would speak. He is now a man in his sixties, with interests other than the case. But he returns to his father's conviction, as if to clear a family curse. And he doesn't give up. His Web site about the case is a model of how the Internet can keep history alive. I have never met Timothy Hobson, but his sentiments about Alger's need to be "honorable" echo remarks I have heard from others who knew Hiss well. White writes that Hiss was "prepared to betray the trust of loyal friends, and family members" to help foster "the ideals of Communism." But, in my view, Hiss went to jail rather than see his stepson humiliated.

LIKE SO MUCH else in American politics, the issues in the Hiss case have moved overseas. Among Hiss supporters, there remains the hope that FBI archives may someday shed light on intricacies of the case—for example, the tangled history of the typewriter. But for now research into the case has moved to Russian files, where both sides are looking for proof to support their positions.

I, myself, have chased some of these white whales. In 1991, for my work in Switzerland, I began traveling to Russia, and noticed the breakdown in central authority. The KGB was in disarray, and many of the old Soviet bodies were being wound up or privatized. In such a climate, I was among those, including Alger himself, who encouraged John Lowenthal to visit Moscow. He returned with an interview with General Dmitri Volkogonov, an official with top clearance to the archives, who spoke eloquently in front of a camera: "I have been able to establish that Alger Hiss was never recruited by the intelligence services…he was never a spy for the Soviet Union." Of Chambers, he reported that he "could have had party contacts but not intelligence contacts." Hiss critics dismissed Lowenthal's findings, arguing that the Russians would never admit to having spied against the United States Or, they said, Volkogonov had not searched the complete Russian archive. Lowenthal responded: "Volkogonov, however, in Washington a few weeks after delivering his report in Moscow, said that he had searched the KGB, GRU (military intelligence), and Presidential archives and that he would have found something if Hiss had been a spy."

Not to be outdone in the business of Russian sources, Weinstein and Vassiliev, or at least their publishers, paid the huge advance to a group of retired intelligence agents in exchange for exclusive access to other archives. Normally, in Russia, ex-government officials buy up natural resources at insider prices, and then sell them to the West for staggering gains. But the deal with Random House may have been the first management buy-out of KGB files. Alas, nothing in the expensive cache of documents proved that Hiss had been a Russian spy. Nor did they shed any light on Chambers's Soviet activities in the United States. So Weinstein and Vassiliev pinned their advance money on transcripts of the so-called Venona project, an effort during and after World War II to decode Russian diplomatic and intelligence cable traffic.

Lowenthal writes: "A widely-circulated but erroneous view is that Venona confirms Hiss's guilt because a 1945 Soviet cablegram describes an espionage agent cover named 'ALES' whom the Federal Bureau of Investigation (FBI) tentatively identified as Alger Hiss." The identification is based on speculation, at a time when Hiss was dominating the news. In the article over which he was sued, Lowenthal exposes the folly of assuming ALES to be Hiss: "Ales conducted espionage throughout the 11 years 1935–45 whereas Hiss was accused, and in effect convicted, of having conducted espionage only in the mid-1930s and not later than 1938." He goes on, calling the so-called ALES proof against Hiss "mutton dressed as lamb":

> It is a fact that Chambers did denounce Hiss to the US government in 1939, and he continued to do so over the next dozen years. Thus the GRU, and Hiss himself, would have been reckless beyond belief to continue for seven years after 1938 the alleged espionage activities that the penitent Chambers could be expected to expose.... In reality, the FBI began investigating Hiss in 1941 and kept at it for half a century...without ever finding what they were looking for.

IN AN EFFORT to clear his father's name and to identify ALES, who has probably been dead for more than fifty years, and thus end the confusion between ALES and Hiss, I helped Tony Hiss contact some senior Russian officials. I did not know them directly, but friends of mine had a connection to former Prime Minister Evgeniy Primakov, who then had responsibility over intelligence archives. Eventually, in response to letter from Tony, a letter was sent to Primakov by Major General V. Federov, chief of the Main International Relations Directorate of the Defense Ministry of the Russian Federation:

> Dear Evgeniy Maksimovitch,
>
> With reference to your letter IIP/89, dated 12 March, 2002, please be informed that the Ministry of Defense of the Russian Federation possesses no material on Alger Hiss's involvement of any nature in the activities of the Soviet military intelligence.
>
> > Yours sincerely.
> > V. Federov
> > Head of Department

Only Orwellian logic dictates how information received from Russia in the Hiss case is processed. Letters clearing Hiss are always denounced as suspect, filed under: "Well, what did you expect them to say?" In this instance, it wasn't enough for just Russian military intelligence to confirm what Volkogonov had said about foreign intelligence: that Alger Hiss had never been a spy for the Soviet Union. Hence Tony Hiss went back another time to the chief archivist, asking if the Russians could identify ALES, or at least say he wasn't Hiss. If ALES was identified as someone who was not Alger Hiss, then Hiss, by extension, would be proven innocent.

A weary Federov responds to Hiss on January 21, 2003:

Dear Mr. T Hiss,

I am expressing again my admiration of the great work you have undertaken to restore the good name of your father - Alger Hiss.

Regretfully, I have to confirm the information outlined in my letter from November 6, 2002, that the Department of Defense of the Russian Federation does not have available any information on the question of interest to you. This conclusion was made after a thorough examination of all archival materials, and later on I would have felt myself very uncomfortable to once again bother our archivists with this problem.

With best wishes for you and your family in the New Year.

Sincerely,

Although I found the letters convincing, Tony sought additional confirmation, and thus arranged through a researcher for an interview with Lieutenant General Vitaly Pavlov. Now retired, in the 1930s he had been deputy chief of the American section in the service of foreign intelligence. He was not responsible for military intelligence, and many of those keen to believe that Hiss was a spy will say he was in the GRU (military intelligence), despite Federov saying he was not. Nevertheless, in the 1930s and 1940s, Pavlov had agents in the United States, and he has studied the case in his retirement, much the way The Earl Jowett read the transcripts in England.

Pavlov begins the interview: "At the time when I first read in the press of the charges against State Department official Hiss I had an immediate question: could he really be involved? And I do remember exactly that on all the lines, including operational, I was told clearly: he has nothing to do with foreign intelligence." Nor does Pavlov think Hiss, as a diplomat, would have been an agent of military intelligence: "They were more interested in officials of the Department of Defense in people dealing military problems."

In the interview Pavlov begins with his assessment that the Baltimore documents were of little importance. He says that even to type up the documents, Priscilla Hiss would have needed certification as a Russian agent—something she never had. He doubts Chambers was a spy, because he remained in contact with Trotskyites while purportedly in the intelligence underground. Pavlov says agents could never pass on documents with their name attached to it, whereas the Baltimore documents include notes taken in Hiss's handwriting and many indicate they were routed through his office. He doubts Hiss was ALES (*I can say with much certainty that it could not be used as an agent's pseudonym.*) but goes on to say that even if Hiss had been ALES, he would never have received an award while passing through Moscow. He derides the concept of a spy giving another spy a gift, as in the rug that Chambers gave to Hiss in the 1930s. He says it was forbidden for agents to fraternize (Chambers says the Hisses were his best friends) and that agents had to leave the Party to join the underground, something Chambers did not do. He chides Weinstein's *The Haunted Wood* (*Any of Weinstein's allegations and guesses have nothing to do with reality*"). Pavlov heaps the most scorn on Chambers's description of carrying documents from Hiss's house to Baltimore, in language not unlike William Howard Moore. He concludes: "From an intelligence point of view it would never stand.... Such a thing would never happen. Not a single more or less trained intelligence officer would allow such a situation."

AFTER BRINGING THE reader such a long distance, it is only fair at the end to say what I think happened in the case. Such a conclusion is only based on what I have heard, read, and seen in the last thirty years. Unlike Weinstein, I make no claim to have had access to inside information. Nor did I ever hear from Alger "what really happened." (I think the great myth of the case is that anything "happened.") But I have visited many of the principal locales of the case—Georgetown, Baltimore, Lewisburg, the Eastern Shore, Brooklyn, Long Island, Moscow, and Ukraine. Plus I have seen or met a number of principals involved, read nearly all the books on the case, and perused the documents as much as is possible for someone not living in Washington. From that I don't claim omniscience, just curiosity.

I think Whittaker Chambers was *Jekyll and Hyde*, a gifted storyteller and writer, but also someone who needed to fictionalize his own life, and the lives of those he came across casually. As Dr. Jekyll, he impressed those like Richard Nixon and William Buckley, Jr. As Mr. Hyde, he may have dabbled in revolution, but I don't think he was a *bona fide* Russian spy. To my mind, the underground he frequented was that of homosexuality, and to those curious about his absences or his presence in the back of movie theatres, he used the excuse of his commissar's secret service. I believe Chambers passed himself off to Alger Hiss as a freelance writer, George Crosley, and as such he was forever gathering documents in Washington. Sometimes he may have passed such documents to other Communists, but I don't think Russian intelligence would have hired someone as erratic as Chambers or someone with his links to Trotskyites, however informal. After quitting the party, he now saw that his cloak-and-dagger pantomime could be interpreted as treason. Or, in his paranoia, he believed he was under threat from the Russians themselves. Thus, he climbed aboard his life raft, and denounced a slew of government officials as fellow travelers, including Hiss and Woodrow Wilson's son-in-law.[9]

Meanwhile Hiss, working in various New Deal offices, had acquired friends and enemies, like anyone in politics. But he overplayed his hand in 1934 when he wrote a memo arguing that FBI director J. Edgar Hoover be fired for stalling the progress of the New Deal. After Chambers first made his charges against Hiss in 1939, no one took them seriously. But during the early 1940s, Hoover and the FBI paid more and more attention to Hiss. The FBI tapped Hiss's phone during 1944 to 1945, but heard nothing suspicious. In 1948, after Chambers and Hiss appeared before HUAC, the FBI again entered the witch-hunt, at Hoover's insistence. At one point the case involved nearly every field office, although a dragnet produced no evidence independent of Chambers's. The FBI's most damaging contribution against Hiss, however, was to withhold key information in both trials, notably

---

9. Chambers could well have been a character in Thornton Wilder's *The Bridge of San Luis Rey*: "He possessed the six attributes of the adventurer—a memory for names and faces, with the aptitude for altering his own; the gift of tongues; inexhaustible invention; secrecy; the talent for falling into conversation with strangers; and that freedom from conscience that springs from contempt for the dozing rich he preyed upon."

the background on the typewriter that was assumed to have belonged to Hiss.

The FBI also brushed up Chambers in front of the jury by not revealing that he had cruised the homosexual underground, and they may have kept a key witness, Timothy Hobson, from discrediting what Chambers had to say. The FBI also suppressed the fact that Chambers tried to kill himself on the eve of this first trial.

It is impossible for me to believe that Alger or Priscilla Hiss typed the so-called Baltimore documents. I believe Chambers, a journalist who had typed articles and books all his life, and lived with typewriters, either typed them himself or had them typed as part of his obsession to collect so-called life preservers. He might also have had help later from the FBI or HUAC, but no proof of that exists. The so-called Pumpkin Papers were nothing more than Nixon-staged Agitprop, exhibits worthy only of a purge.[10] These documents, never given by Hiss to Chambers, had little intelligence value, but were priceless to secure Hiss's indictment during the red scare.

In the meantime, Hiss, who had no experience with litigation, organized his defense as if preparing for a debate, and not a street fight. His defense team found a typewriter he thought was his old one, and they let it sit there in court—

---

10. A post at amazon.com contains a succinct summary of what was found in the pumpkin: "The original State Department files were rated 'classified' to 'secret.' Most consisted of trade agreements, which were of commercial, not political importance. When Chambers learned that Alger Hiss could not type, he then claimed Priscilla did it! (Did writer and translator Chambers assume that men had this skill?) The most telling fact about these documents is that most had never been routed through sections where either Alger or Donald Hiss had worked! This discrepancy has never been explained. When the contents of the three rolls of microfilm were released in 1975, they were found to be Navy Department instructions on how to use life rafts, fire extinguishers, and chest parachutes. Where did they come from?"

without ever challenging its authenticity. The FBI expert at the trial testified that the same typewriter had typed both some of Priscilla's letters and later the Baltimore documents. Case closed. But the smoking-gun typewriter in court turned out not to have been the Hiss machine. At the second trial, Hiss appointed as his attorney a corporate lawyer from Boston, someone who had never tried a criminal case. It was further bad luck that his case was tried during a period of Communist hysteria. Eastern Europe had just fallen to the Soviets. The Russians had the bomb. Hiss was the perfect symbol for all that had supposedly gone wrong because of Yalta and the New Deal. In the meantime, Chambers had sequestered himself for months with the FBI, and together they cut-and-pasted a story line to fit with elements of Chambers's invented lives. Later, re-write man Chambers took these FBI field dispatches, as he had done for years at *Time*, and rewrote history.[11] He became an icon of the Cold War, the Dostoyevsky of Washington, someone who broke literary form with a novel in which the author, as protagonist, returns from the house of the dead.

Coda

WE KNOW FROM the views of Frankel, White, Weinstein and others that the majority of those interested in the case think I am wrong. But I hold to my beliefs, not just because they

---

11. From *Witness*: "In the first months of the new year, I continued my testimony before the new Grand Jury. I had already begun with the F.B.I. what amounted to a total recall of my life. It amassed all that I could remember about Communism and Communists in the United States and elsewhere. In report-form it made a fair-sized book."

are mine, formed over thirty years, but also to maintain the bonds of friendship formed with Bill Rodgers during that first conversation on the Hiss case. For whatever reasons, I have come to think of Bill, Alger and John Lowenthal as family, and in that sense I want to see a family injustice righted. In a larger sense I think that one way the health of a democracy can be measured is by its ability to correct unwarranted prosecutions.

Alger Hiss died in 1996, at the age of ninety-two. At the end of his life, he was frail, and suffered from macular degeneration, which limited his vision. Thus he had friends read to him aloud, much as he once read to Oliver Wendell Holmes. In his lifetime he never found the vindication in the courts that he had sought. In the 1980s the Supreme Court refused to hear an appeal for *coram nobis*, which would have wiped out the conviction. The judge who wrote the opinion against Hiss in a lower court was a Nixon appointee. Nor did the requests under the Freedom of Information Act unearth all FBI documents in the case, notably about the typewriter, leading me to speculate that some of these files were destroyed at the time of Hoover's death. Throughout these disappointments, Hiss maintained himself with the same dignity that was his trademark. He gave interviews to researchers, wrote a second volume of his memoirs, taped interviews for oral history projects and films, and lectured at universities. Asked if his case had been tragedy, he responded: "In some ways, it was a personal tragedy for me, mostly in terms of my marriage. This did have tragic results. Tragedy of history in some over-all Spengelerian sense? No, I think that's more of Chambers's self-inflation." On the idea of ostracism, Nathaniel Hawthorne wrote of the effect of *The Scarlet Letter*: "It had the effect of a spell, taking her out of the ordinary relations with humanity, and inclosing her in a sphere by herself." But Hiss never felt its presence.

Bill Rodgers died in 1997 in Chestertown, Maryland, up the road from Centreville. He was eighty-four. I was in Tokyo when the nursing home called me to say that he was failing, and he died a few days later, with his devoted nurse, Michele Francis, at his bedside. I organized his funeral in the Centreville graveyard, where he and I had once picked out a plot. About fifteen friends were present. My parents were among those who spoke words of farewell—my father remembering the lonely courage that it took to fight on the cruel seas in the Atlantic during WW II. In my own eulogy, I remembered Bill's love for the Eastern Shore, where the winter sky comes alive with migrating Canada geese. I also recalled his friendship with a local coach, Appy Middleton, who by chance had known Alger Hiss, from his summers by the Chesapeake. Bill and Appy were men of similar age and habits of mind, and once Bill interviewed his friend about the Hiss case. Before the trials, the FBI had come to question Appy and had asked a series of leading questions, ones presupposing Hiss's guilt. After a while Middleton asked one of the agents: "Don't you want to hear any nice things about Mr. Hiss? I know him as a fine man, incapable of what you suggest." To which the agent replied: "We'll tell you what we want." I still visit the Eastern Shore, and even stay in the old railroad station that Bill converted into his last house. But there's a sadness to sit at his dining room table and not to hear Bill, in that lively, humorous, and exasperated voice, intone something to the effect that they had targeted Hiss "for a variation of the Soviet show trials."

John Lowenthal died in 2003 at age seventy-eight. He

had a difficult form of stomach cancer, and it required ghastly treatments at Sloan-Kettering hospital. At the time John was editing the transcript of his film, *The Trials of Alger Hiss*, for posting on the Internet. During the final illness, he would work at his computer on the footnotes, take a break to bicycle across New York to the hospital, endure his treatment, and then, when feeling better, return to his computer, adding to his annotated Hiss bibliography. To anyone who asks me how to begin deconstructing the case, I refer them first to John's documentary, which made its debut in 1980. Filmed in the late 1970s, the movie captures on tape many of the principal actors in the case. A few like Richard Nixon refused to co-operate in this project. But many others, both for and against Hiss, agreed to interviews. Using newsreels from the period, the film captures the communist hysteria of 1950, when Hiss was convicted.[12] It also gives voice to Chambers's existential words (*"I am a man who, reluctantly, grudgingly step by step, is destroying himself that this country and the faith by which it lives may continue to exist"*)—something valuable to have in mind when later reading *Witness*. What the film shows is how the jurors in the second trial were misled into thinking that the typewriter in the courthouse had both belonged to Hiss and had been used to type the Baltimore documents. Lowenthal shows that the courtroom Woodstock had never belonged to Hiss. But it comes thirty years too late to save him. As Gussie Feinstein, a juror, says on camera: "The typewriter

---

12. Alice Roosevelt Longworth and Mrs. Theodore Roosevelt, Jr., were fixtures at the Hiss trial. Hiss remembers: "There they sat, directly facing the jury, for all the world like *les tricoteuses* of the French Revolution, who knitted on their balconies as the tumbrels rolled beneath them on the way to the guillotine. Though ladylike in their decorum, they made no secret of which side they were on. Their expressions of approval and satisfaction when the prosecution scored a point were matched by their scornful attitude toward my witnesses."

was in the courtroom, and blown-up exhibits of the documents that were supposed to have been typed on it showing the defects in the letter, and matched exactly to the defects in the typewriter.... That's what convicted him." She adds that she would not now vote for conviction.

A British film service sells the rights to stream the movie over the Internet, and it remains the best introduction to the case and includes long conversations with Hiss himself. My own favorite characters in the documentary are Claudie Catlett and her son, Raymond, to whom the Hisses gave the original Woodstock typewriter. Claudie was the Hisses' cook in the 1930s, and she remembers Chambers exactly as I could imagine him to have been, a skulking acquaintance:

> A guy named Crosby (sic) used to come up there all the time. I don't know who he was, nothing like that, but he used to come there all the time. And I never cared much for him. I used to watch him, because I didn't think much of him.

Like Timothy Hobson, Claudie Catlett was present during the friendship between Alger Hiss and George Crosley. Unlike Hiss, Claudie senses that Chambers is up to no good. At the trials, Claudie tried to identify Chambers by the alias, George Crosley, but black maids from pre-war Washington were not considered reliable character witnesses—although she seems to have understood the witness best of all.[13] So

---

13. At the trials only Claudie Catlett and Priscilla confirmed that Chambers had used the alias Crosley, and neither was believed, although in his lifetime Chambers used dozens of phony names. Another possible witness who did know Chambers as Crosley was a pornographic publisher to whom Crosley had submitted homoerotic stories. He did not testify. Chambers name at birth was Jay Vivian Chambers, which may account for his attraction to aliases.

too did her son, Raymond, understand the geopolitics of the case better than many academics. He talks on film about how the Hiss typewriter never worked and how he finally junked it. But as an aside in his account of the typewriter, he observes: "If Roosevelt was living, Hiss would not have been prosecuted. But when he passed, Hiss and the rest of the officials were doomed."

I was asked to speak at John Lowenthal's memorial service, held in the chapel of Columbia University. Many of those still following the Hiss case were there. I met William A. Reuben, a man then in his late eighties who walked slowly with a cane. (A friend said he died in 2004 while reading White's description of Alger, which doesn't surprise me.) Tony Hiss spoke in remembrance of John, an act of forgiveness and compassion, as John wasn't always the easiest of friends to Tony. Tony spoke of John's devotion to Alger, and how Alger and Priscilla had known John's father, Max, in the 1920s. John once remembered: "The statement that Hiss read to the House Un-American Activities Committee on 25 August 1948 had been written a few days earlier at my parents' Connecticut country house; I was there at the time."

I myself had known John for almost twenty-five years; we met the year his film was released. In turn I introduced him to Bill Rodgers, who added John to his expansive list of correspondents. Whether in New York or London, where he later lived, John and I met regularly for lunch, tea or dinner, and swapped notes on the case. I would often proofread his writing, and I helped him defend the London libel case. In return, John would fax me his findings at all hours. Like Bill, he was one of those friends who was always there for me, with either a letter or a phone call. I still recall how when I once lost my job, he rallied to my side. It so happens that our continuing conversation was the injustice done to Alger Hiss, but it could also have been music or history, and we would still have been lifelong friends.

In saying good-bye to John, I quoted the last lines in Alger's *Recollection of a Life*. They are a postscript not just for John and Alger, but others, like Bill, who found their lives altered by the case. Alger sums up his life: "My goals still seem to me bright and attainable. In any event, I subscribe to the view that the way the journey is traveled counts for more than the goals reached. In the words of Job, I have pursued my goals 'in mine own ways.' In that I am content." But for Alger, as with John and Bill, the road ended short of their collective destination—a legal vindication for Hiss.

In another celebrated spy case, the so-called Dreyfus Affair, ten years after Captain Alfred Dreyfus was stripped of his rank and almost executed, France awarded him the Cross of the Legion of Honor. Dreyfus called it an "extraordinary effort at rehabilitation" and hoped his case would lead to "an era of immense progress for the ideas of freedom, justice, and social solidarity." Alas, it led more to the trenches of World War I than it did toward Utopia. Like Hiss, Captain Dreyfus rarely showed bitterness at his sufferings, the closest being when he stated: "My life belongs to my country; my honor does not"—sentiments that Alger would well have understood. Dreyfus hoped his "Affair" would "serve humanity," which, for better or for worse, is all that now can be expected in the Hiss case.

Vindication may come from some unexpected quarter, or the case may continue to drift on the tide of guilty judgment, books always received as "the last word." On the question of clearing his name, Alger himself balanced his familiar optimism with a dose of realism, once admitting that he had learned "the hard lesson that not every miscarriage of justice can be set right." Maybe so, but he might also have quoted, as does Meyer Zeligs, from the martyred heroine in *The Chalk Garden*: "What I have been listening to in Court is not my life. It is the share and shadow of my life with the accidents of Truth taken out of it."

Remember the Mesopotamia

(2006)

IN RECENT WEEKS much noise has been raised over the CIA
detainee flights that crisscrossed the world to deliver Islamic
prisoners of war into jurisdictions where torture had some
local flavor. In response to these allegations, Secretary of State
Condoleezza Rice has tried to argue that the United States
is not a torturing country. That said, anyone who has seen
those orange-clad jihadists in Guantanamo Bay, kneeling on
their chains in what look like dog kennels, knows that most
American citizens have one definition of what constitutes
torture while the Bush administration has printed up its own
set of rules, using small type unfamiliar to anyone attending
to Geneva Conventions.

In most cases, I suspect, those languishing in Polish or
Australian no-man's land prisons tend to be abducted from
terrorism's enlisted army—cell members snatched from Ham-
burg study groups or Muslim brothers deported from Egypt.
Already the United States is exempt from the International
Court in the Hague, and at the time that the anonymous
CIA charter flights were delivering their passengers to places

like Bulgaria, the Bush administration was threatening to veto U.S. legislation that would outlaw "cruel, inhuman, and degrading treatment or punishment," as such amenities were the principal attractions of the CIA package tours.

I have my doubts that the torture underground has yielded much in the way of useful information. Most of those grabbed from half-lit rooms in Karachi probably know little about the whereabouts of Osama bin Laden or al-Qaida's command and control centers, for the reason that those flying Blindfold Class are recruits for a nebulous set of ideas—Allah, eternity, those seventy two virgins, the purity of Mecca, etc.—not German general staff officers of 1914, getting ready to unleash the von Schlieffen Plan against Belgium.

In my view, modestly proposed, the Bush administration would get more bonus miles out of its night flights if it were to kidnap Arabic scholars from around the world and make them deliver lectures on Middle Eastern nationalism or the history of Iraq to another set of detainees—ones hustled from the corridors of power around the White House and Capitol Hill. Alas I am not sure those in power ever do much reading or listening, but even a short history of Mesopotamia makes it clear why the Bush administration is not having much luck with its fortified sand castles.

For the most part, we can thank the messianic President Woodrow Wilson for the modern idea of Iraq. After the war to end all wars, Wilson pounded the peace conference tables of Paris in 1919 to reapportion Ottoman Mesopotamia into a single nation, initially run under a British mandate.

Forgive me for not having a higher view of Wilson, but I have always thought him a pedantic, self-righteous academic who made judgments about the world not so much to achieve peace in our time, but to prove the Princeton faculty wrong for scoffing at his mojo. In Paris, he held forth on European and Near Eastern borders as if he were lecturing freshman seminarians on the Treaty of Westphalia, although his world experience consisted mainly of a few parades through the streets of London and Paris. In Iraq, he thought that Basra, Baghdad, and Mosul should be "regarded as a single unit for administrative purposes." Then, presumably, he adjourned for lunch, although probably not with the French president, Georges Clemenceau, who confessed to Wilson's friend, Colonel House: "I understand you but talking to Wilson is something like talking to Jesus Christ."

In the past year, I have spent a lot of pleasurable time reading and rereading *Peacemakers* by Margaret MacMillan, an account of the Paris Peace Conference. Many modern problems, from the Balkans to Iraq, have their origins in the settlements often lumped together under the Treaty of Versailles, although in the Paris peace accords, there were also treaties named for the palaces of Trianon, St. Germain, Neuilly, and Sèvres. My paperback edition of the book identifies MacMillan as a Canadian professor and provost with a doctorate from Oxford, but more than that, she is an excellent writer and researcher, and the 574-page history has flashes of wit and humor. I learned subsequently that she is also the great-granddaughter of David Lloyd George, the British prime minister, although she writes about him without fear or favor.

In *Peacemakers*, MacMillan writes eloquently about Wilson's ignorance in Mesopotamia:

> In 1919 there was no Iraqi people; history, religion, geography pulled the people apart, not together. Basra looked southwards toward India and the Gulf; Baghdad

had strong links with Persia; and Mosul had closer ties with Turkey and Syria. Putting together the three Ottoman provinces and expecting to create a nation was, in European terms, like hoping to have Bosnian Muslims, Croats, and Serbs make one country. As in the Balkans, the clash of empires and civilizations had left deep fissures. The population was about half Shia Muslim and a quarter Sunni, with other minorities from Jews to Christians, but another division ran across the religious one: while half the inhabitants were Arab, the rest were Kurds (mainly in Mosul), Persians or Assyrians....There was no Iraqi nationalism, only Arab.

Wilson's ally in Paris was Lloyd George, who came to the peace conference with the idea of "making the Hun pay" and keeping the French out of the colonial Middle East possessions of the British empire. He also showed up in Paris with his mistress, Miss Frances Stevenson, which Clemenceau or another wag compared to "bringing a sandwich to a banquet." Lloyd George's dream of a Pax Britannia washing over the tribes of the Middle East forecasts the same mirages seen shimmering in the Bush White House. As MacMillan writes: "Lloyd George, a Liberal turned land-grabber, made it worse. Like Napoleon, he was intoxicated by the possibilities of the Middle East: a restored Hellenic world in Asia Minor; a new Jewish civilization in Palestine; Suez and all the links to India safe from threat; loyal and obedient Arab states along the Fertile Crescent and the valley on the Tigris and Euphrates; protection for British oil supplies from Persia and the possibility of new sources under British control; the Americans taking mandates here and there; the French doing what they were told."

Enter Winston Churchill. During World War I he was

cashiered from the Admiralty and the war cabinet for the fiasco at Gallipoli. Subsequently he had done time in the trenches of France and written memoirs, but in the 1920s he was again in the cabinet, first as minister of colonial affairs and later as Chancellor of the Exchequer. Under his colonial ministerial hat, Churchill had taken Gertrude Bell and T.E. Lawrence to Cairo, and there drawn lines in the sands of the British Arab mandates, including those around Mesopotamia. But a history of Churchill's gambit, *Winston's Folly* by Christopher Catherwood, echoes MacMillan's thesis that Iraq has never been a country: "Iraq was created out of three Ottoman vilayets that had previously been quite separate. The Kurds are Sunni, like the Arabs in the middle of the country, but ethnically they are Indo-European, like the Iranians. The Shiite majority in the south might be Arabs, but religiously they are the same branch of Islam as Iran—Shiite—and therefore have loyalties that are distinct from those of the rest of Iraq's people."

Arab nationalists who had supported the Allies and read Wilson's Fourteen Points felt betrayed when the Paris Peace Conference divided up the Middle East into European spheres of influence. That anger lingers to this day, in the politics of those like Osama bin Laden or the Palestinians. In Iraq, Churchill adopted the similar strategy of divide and rule, hoping to keep larger Arab blocs from uniting against Western colonial interests, if not their shares in local oil companies. A Hashemite, Feisal, was anointed king, and he presided over an Iraq that gave disproportionate influence to the mid-country Sunnis and limited autonomy to the Kurds. (Through the rule of Saddam Hussein, that same coalition, in varying forms, ran the country.) Not that such gerrymandering ended that era's war on terror. As Churchill noted: "It is an extraordinary thing that the British civil administration should have succeeded in such a short time in alienating the whole country to such an extent that the Arabs have laid aside the blood feuds that they have nursed for centuries." I have read that I. Lewis "Scooter" Libby is a great Churchill admirer, although I have to doubt that he recalled these words during his entangling moments with the *Times'* Judith Miller.

Winston's problems in Iraq were a lot like those of Donald Rumsfeld today: those of bleeding an imperial treasury to win hearts and minds in places like Falluja. As minister for colonial affairs, Churchill had sympathy for the navy's craving for Kurdish oil ("the greatest oil field in the world extends all the way up to Mosul and beyond"), but as the Exchequer, he needed to prove he could balance a postwar budget that was then under pressure to ditch the gold standard. He confessed: "The cost of the military establishment in Mesopotamia appears to me to be out of all proportion to any advantage we can ever expect to reap from that country." Churchill wrote: "We are at wits' end to find a single soldier." His novel solution was to replace the depleted British infantry in Iraq with squadrons from the newly founded air forces. Whenever rebels infiltrated a village, cost-efficient bombers were sent to rain even more terror on the local population. Even before the war in Vietnam, bombers were destroying villages to save them.

Over the next thirty years, without redrawing the country's internal or external borders, the British Empire muddled its way in and out of Iraq. King Feisal ruled until 1933, when his son, described by MacMillan as "a cheerful playboy," succeeded him. The king died in a car accident in 1939. His son ruled Iraq until a coup in 1958 declared the country a republic. A year later Saddam Hussein made his political debut, participating in an attempted assassination of the country's prime minister. In 1968, Hussein's Ba'athist party finally ousted the country's republican government, with Saddam assuming the position of Vice-Chairman of the Revolution Command Council. In 1979 he was 'elected' president.

The next year Saddam ordered the invasion of Iran, a war that lasted until 1988 (thanks, in part, to U.S. military assistance), because he despised the same Islamic fundamentalism that the Bush administration so opposes in Arabia. Hussein also feared Iranian support for Iraq's Kurds and the Shiites in the south (another current American preoccupation). In 1990, citing disputed oil reservoirs, Saddam invaded Kuwait. The occupation that lasted five months liberated most of that country's luxury cars and color televisions: conspicuous jihadist consumption. The Allied coalition that drove Iraq out of Kuwait, however, left Hussein in power to run Iraq. During the next decade, as was said of King Feisal's father, the sharif of Mecca, Saddam proved "interested more in the fortunes of his own family than Arab self-determination." But after September 11, 2001, the Bush administration needed 'a good, safe menace' for its war on terrorism, and it selected Hussein for the photograph under the Hearst headline: "You furnish the pictures and I'll furnish the war."

The Bush dilemma is that of Churchill or, ironically, that of Saddam Hussein, who knew that the only way to hold together the artificial construct of Wilson's Iraq was to brutalize the population, gas the Kurds, and declare war on Iran. As Catherwood writes: "Churchill and Lloyd George were wrestling with the same issues the U.S. administration is facing in 2004: how to have a genuinely democratic Iraq that did not at the same time deliver the nightmare scenario of a clericalist and theocratic Shiite regime on the Iranian model."

In time for the sound bites of the 2006 mid-term election, Bush could declare victory in the Sunni triangle, 'Vietnam-ize' Iraqi forces into the front lines, and head for the exit. But disintegration in Iraq might leave Iranian mullahs as the dominant Middle East power, not to mention a newly declared republic of Kurdistan at war with its neighbors, led by Turkey. As they say in commodity markets, the Bush administration would like to be long on oil and short on political turmoil. But because President Bush got his invasion orders from God and is in Iraq, as Wilson would understand, "to rid the world of evil," most of the those contracts are out-of-the-money.

When faced with the prospect of Iraqi civil war, whether the United States stays or departs from Mesopotamia, Bush recently cleared the decks of the Oval Office to receive many of the former secretaries of defense and state, stretching back to the Kennedy administration. Posing for the photo-op later in front of the president's desk (Maureen Dowd called the picture "a mesmerizing blend of 'Sunset Boulevard,' 'The Last Supper' and a 'Sopranos' ad") are the likes of Robert McNamara, Mel Laird, James Schlesinger, Alexander Haig, Madeleine Albright, Lawrence Eagleburger, James Baker, Colin Powell, Donald Rumsfeld, Dick Cheney, and George Schultz, all of whom fought savage wars of peace as ill-defined as the current Iraqi mandate.

Even if everyone around the desk had wandered through the same fogs of war, conversation during the old-timers' day was perfunctory, as deferential to authority today as it was when they were giving warrior counsel to earlier presidents. Clearly a smiling President Bush was happy for the company, as if to reverse President's Kennedy observation, after the Bay of Pigs, that while success has a number of fathers, "failure is an orphan." This gathering looked like a paternity clinic, hosting the fathers of so many splendid little wars. But here also was a roomful of individuals who, although wily in the ways of Washington power, often found the world a confusing abstraction—in the manner of Lloyd George, who asked in 1916: "Who are the Slovaks? I can't seem to place them." Looking at the photo—and then recalling the white men's burdens in Vietnam, Cambodia, Grenada, Panama, Kosovo, and Iraq—I couldn't help but think of the assembled best and brightest as just another group of CIA detainees. They had flown the world on unmarked government planes, landed during the night in places like Shannon and Geneva, and ordered fanatical death on symbolic battlefields. But when later questioned in the press or before Congress, they could no more explain their leaders' actions or goals than could your average al-Qaida suspect getting blasted with rap music in Abu Ghraib. Nor do I think the secretaries would have grown more eloquent if they had been chained to a Guantanamo fence or piled up in front of Lyndie England.

I do think, however, that all of them would have been comfortable seconding Woodrow Wilson in Paris, dividing up the world or briskly showing him maps of Wallachia or Bessarabia. ("No, sir, it's near the Ukraine, not Baghdad. With respect, sir.") At the same time they probably would have run afoul of the old Tiger, Georges Clemenceau, who one day during the Paris Conference asked: "Who is Pichon?" The answer came back that Stéphen Pichon was his foreign minister, to which Clemenceau replied: "So he is. I had forgotten it."

War's End:
From Okinawa to Nagasaki
(2004)

"Nothing except a battle lost can be half so melancholy as a battle won."

—The Duke of Wellington, 1815

AT DAWN I departed the new Hong Kong airport at Chek Lap Kok. Before the 1999 changeover, the British Empire ran up $8 billion in construction costs—to leave China a terminal that feels like a shopping mall with runways, not to mention the invoices. Spacious gates, long avenues of escalators and endless duty-free shopping speak of Hong Kong's business-class future. By contrast, the old airport at Kowloon had the narrow confines of a sweat shop—a juxtaposition that says more about Hong Kong's evolution than did the changing of the guard to Chinese landlords.

I made my connection in Taipei, and then flew northeast toward Naha, the capital of Okinawa, the largest island in the Ryukyu chain that, like beads of coral, stretches between shoulders of the Chinese and Japanese imperial dominions. In the Pacific war, they were the last islands to hop before the Americans would land in Japan. Breakfast was raw fish, rice, and green tea, served on plastic trays not much larger than the airplane's seats. Around me were what the Japanese call "salary men," getting ready for another day on the road.

I had a long weekend to travel between the financial centers of Hong Kong and Tokyo, which is normally a four-hour direct flight. My plan was first to visit Okinawa and then to fly another hour north to Kagoshima, Japan's southernmost city, on the island of Kyushu. In driving from Kagoshima to Kumamoto, I wanted to see those beaches that, had the invasion of Japan gone forward, would have become Asia's Normandy coast. By ending my trip in Nagasaki and afterwards Tokyo, which was also claimed in a firestorm, I wanted to judge for myself whether Winston Churchill was correct when he described the atomic bomb as "the miracle of deliverance."

Landing in Naha: *"The great Spanish Armada would have been run over and never sighted."*

AS THE PLANE descended into Naha, it passed over Ie Shima, the small island where, several weeks into the campaign that began on April 1, 1945, the war correspondent Ernie Pyle was killed. Before he was struck by a Japanese machine-gun bullet, he wrote: "In Europe, we felt that our enemies, horrible and deadly as they were, were still people. But out here I soon gathered that the Japanese were looked upon as something subhuman or repulsive; the way some people feel about cockroaches or mice." The battle for Okinawa lasted for two months after Pyle was killed. During the eighty-two days of fighting, an average of almost three thousand soldiers and civilians were killed daily.

The airport at Naha is inland from the blue waters of the East China Sea, where the largest naval task force in history landed an American army of almost 600,000 men. As a marine in the invasion forces, Russell Davis, recalls: "We were going 'up' again...we were outbound for Okinawa by way of Ulithi," where he saw "the greatest gathering of ships in the history of the world....In such an army, the great Spanish Armada would have been run over and never sighted." But despite the size and power of the American fleet, the seas turned red wherever the waves of kamikaze planes washed over the American bows.

For the past fifteen years, I have been collecting books about the battle of Okinawa and reading chapters about the fighting in longer histories of the Pacific war. I have also heard many stories set among its ridges. From before war and into the occupation, my father served as a combat infantry officer in the Marine Corps, commanding C Company, 1st Marines, through some of the worst campaigns, including Guadalcanal. Before the 1st Marine Regiment landed on Okinawa, however, he was "sent stateside," along with others who had fought three earlier campaigns. But many of his stories about the war touch on Okinawa, where, in particular, his close friend, Robert Fowler, was killed and many other 1st Marines were killed or wounded.

Before leaving for Okinawa, I asked a number of C Company marines about the fighting, receiving answers about the face of battle that suggest its portrait is best painted in the agonies brushed by Goya. "I saw one of my men fall," wrote John Wilkerson. "I missed him later that day and I never learned his fate." He also recalled a close encounter with the enemy: "We were about three feet apart. He looked me dead in the eyes for a split second. My first bullet hit him two inches above his right eye." Also serving with C Company, John Pido remembered: "I'm 75 now and 55 years ago, June 9,

1945, I was shot through the face, jaw, and neck while with the First Marine Division." Emil Buff spoke for many when he recalled randomly:

> My mind is more a sea bag than a filing cabinet....As kamikaze pilots continued to introduce their god to our fleet, we who knew him would soon take refuge in ours....The lead teams, stretched far too thin for the ground they covered, were pinned and bleeding....Smoke was thick, could find no one...the smoke drifted and stung eyes... trail now slick with mud...was on a hospital ship that night.

In my luggage, I had several books about the war's end, notably *Downfall* by Richard Frank, and several articles about the atomic bomb by my friend Murray Sayle, whom I planned to meet in Kagoshima. I also had a fifteen-page memoir, dictated by my father, titled: "Life in a Conquered Land," in which he recounted his military service after the 1944 battle at Peleliu through the occupation of Japan in 1946. In winter 1945, he was G-3 at Camp Pendleton, in charge of the training given to recruits who would later serve on Okinawa. But he could have been sent back overseas at a moment's notice. Had he been among the invasion forces landing in Japan, he feels, as do most, that his luck might have run out. "Based on years of experience," he writes in the memoir, "veterans knew only too bitterly of Japanese willingness to fight to the death for the Emperor, even during campaigns in which their case had become hopeless."

Nearly every Pacific veteran I have spoken with credits the bomb with saving their lives. So too do soldiers who were being transferred from the European theater for the last assault against Japan. On one such troop ship was Paul Fussell, who writes on behalf of many when he concludes: "You think of the lives which would have been lost in an invasion of Japan's home islands—a staggering number of Americans but millions more of Japanese—and you thank God for the atomic bomb."

My father arrived in Nagasaki two months after the second atomic bomb destroyed parts of that city. Perhaps because he lived briefly in its wake, he has never been among the bomb's champions—skeptical of the direct equation between so many civilian deaths and the war's end. That may be an infantry officer's view of the air forces, which Murray Sayle captures well in his *New Yorker* article, "Did the Bomb End the War?": "If there is such a process as military leaders being cowed into submission by air attacks, nuclear or otherwise, history has no clear example of it." But the road to Nagasaki runs through Okinawa.

One Quarter of Okinawa: *"a standing army"*

THANKS TO AN introduction by my friend George Feifer, whose book, *Tennozan*, is one of the best histories of the battle on Okinawa, I was met at the airport by Alex Kishaba, a man in his early forties, the president of the Ryukyu-American Historical Research Society. Landing at Naha has the feel of stepping into the Hawaiian sunshine, and Alex's round, warm countenance, dark hair and complexion, made other connections between these islanders and those of Polynesia. Walking to his parked car, we formed an immediate bond— sharing a mutual admiration for George and his history, and discussing that day's tour of battle.

Beginning on April 1, 1945, the battle for Okinawa was fought along a ten-mile front, with Naha the western anchor of a fortified Japanese line that cut across the island to the east coast. With the marines on the right and army divisions to the left, the American 10th army attacked from the north, encountering about 100,000 Japanese entrenched between low, razor-back hills that line the Okinawan landscape. By the end of June, the 600,000-man American force drove the last Japanese soldiers into the sea off the southern coast. But first they had to gain the Japanese trenches and fortifications east of Naha, and that was a struggle of World War I desperation played out with World War II weaponry.

Leaving the airport to head toward the Peace Museum, Alex and I drove south on Highway 7, along a stretch of urban sprawl which suggests that one way that Okinawans tried to forget the war was to cover the front lines with nondescript apartment blocks and stores selling motorbikes. Once clear of the congestion, we drove on narrow roads through land Feifer describes as "an ancient patchwork of tiny fields, sparely inhabited mountains and thousands of sharp ridges and rises." The cliffs break the landscape as though whales of granite, and as we drove south, Alex associated many of the humpbacks with desperate battles. Often we passed small Shinto burial shrines, which in the fighting became Japanese pillboxes that poured fire against the Americans, who, in response, laid waste to many sacred family treasures.

Driving through small fields of sugarcane, Alex described an economy that had yet to shake the chains of colonialism. Sugar is one of the cash crops, but much of the best farmland is locked behind the perimeters of the thirty-eight American bases, which cover almost a quarter of the island. Tourism is of the package variety, and mostly just enriches the airlines. Tokyo subsidizes both local industry and the American occupation, which, Alex implied, helps the Japanese maintain their own imperial claim over islands that were an independent kingdom until late in the nineteenth century. To host a G-8 summit, which included the flying visit of President Bill Clinton, Tokyo fertilized $180 million into local fields of dreams, but, to hear Alex read the accounts, they yielded only pork.

We stopped the car near a wooded knoll where the American ground commander, General Simon Bolivar Buckner, was killed—the highest ranking U.S. general to die in combat in World War II. According to H.C. Merillat, a family friend and a Marine Corps correspondent who served throughout the battle in his headquarters, Buckner was a "handsome" general who believed in tactics that pushed forward, each day, on one long extended front. Toward the end of the battle, he had gone forward to observe a marine regiment, was marked by his entourage as an important officer, and killed by a mortar fragment, which, I have read, prompted a massacre of nearby Japanese prisoners.

About 225,000 people died in the fight for Okinawa, of which some 120,000 were civilians. Many were Okinawans impressed as laborers into the Japanese lines; others were squeezed between two industrial armies. A few committed suicide. Feifer writes: "Still, the majority of civilians did not choose death but were killed by starvation, disease, individual Japanese cruelty and, most of all, indiscriminate American firing."

Near the Buckner memorial we peered into one of Okinawa's many caves, deep crevices that hid well-armed Japanese soldiers, camouflaged gun emplacements and, often, cowering Okinawan civilians. It prompted Alex to tell the story of his mother's family, which during the battle hid in one such cave. In their advance south, Americans sealed hundreds of caves; sometimes after warnings shouted in Japanese, sometimes not. In this instance, the cave was attacked with satchel bombs and smoke, and, miraculously, Alex's mother (then a child) survived. Her eight brothers and sisters and parents did not, which may explain the cliff-side we passed later where Okinawan nurses chose suicide over American captivity.

All war memorials in Japan are called peace parks, and this one, near the island's southern cape, is surrounded with concentric circles of marble, where the names of dead American or Japanese soldiers and Okinawan civilians are engraved, in the manner of Washington's Vietnam Memorial. To Alex's discomfort, the peace museum and shrines cost $25 million—more grist for the pork mill. Inside are galleries of political correctness, arranged to wean the samurai inheritance from innocent school children, plus some more conventional cabinets of battle. We had tea with the director, Mr. Seiji Hokama, a man of simple elegance, and then wandered through an exhibition of the American occupation (1945–72), in which the portraits of the U.S. military governors had the impassive expressions of Roman proconsuls.

The best history of Okinawa in English, *Okinawa*, was written in 1958 by George Kerr, whom Feifer quotes on the postwar years: "Washington virtually lost sight of the Ryukyus....An appalling indifference blanketed [Okinawa].... The island became an immense, neglected military dump."

Under the protectorate of the American military, Okinawa was a Gibraltar of the Cold War, a forward base of operations near the Russian Far East, Korea, China, and Vietnam, for which it was a principle staging area. Okinawan cars carried U.S.-style license plates, but as Feifer writes: "The real business of Okinawa's governors was to run America's defense installations, not to care for the natives." In 1972, looking to shed the imperialist epithet, President Richard Nixon restored Japanese rule to the islands—one hundred years after another disgraced president, Ulysses S. Grant, tried to mediate rival claims from Japan and China to the independent kingdom of the Ryukyus.

Twenty-five thousand American troops remain on Okinawa, and from my short-tour impression, most seem either to be standing guard duty behind barbed wire or cruising Naha's neon strips in oversized American sedans. Months before I was there, several soldiers had been convicted of raping a young girl. As much as the brutality incensed the local population, so did the remark of the base commander that rape was unnecessary when the supply of local women so exceeded the demand. Okinawa seems a long way from Thomas Jefferson's sentiment, expressed in a letter in 1799: "I am not for a standing army in a time of peace which may overawe the public sentiment."

Before leaving the museum, Alex and I hiked up a long hillside, which was lined on both sides with oriental gardens and shrines, dedicated by each of the Japanese prefectures that lost men in the battle. Each has delicate shrubbery, rock gardens, or altars of Shinto elegance. A steady line of tourists, all Japanese or Okinawan, were paying their respects to the departed spirits. Farther on, we came to the southern coast of the island and looked down on a necklace of rocky, forbidding beaches. In earlier times, American whaling ships plied the waters off these shores, where the last survivors of the Japanese 32nd Army died from their own despair or at the hands of American riflemen. In a cave that overlooks the sweep of the Pacific, General Mitsuru Ushijima, the Japanese commander, and his second, General Isamu Cho, committed ritual suicide—faithful to Melville's expression in *Moby-Dick* about the "impenetrable Japans."

Shuri Castle: *"straight ahead into the sausage machine"*

NORMALLY ON MY trips I arrive with a good map of the destination. But in this instance I was reduced to carrying an airport brochure called "Paradise of the Sun." Instead of showing the Shuri Line or Yuka-daze, where C Company lost half its men, the map highlighted the Palm Hills Golf Course and the Naha and Nanzan country clubs, much as in Normandy the signs lead the way to the Omaha Beach Golf Club. Despite the billions in Pentagon procurement that has sunk into the Okinawa soil, only a handful of monuments and directional signs recall the deeds of the 10th Army, and nearly all require a guide to find them.

In the car Alex had an official army history, complete with regimental maps. During the day we were trying to retrace the steps of the two marine divisions, the 1st and the 6th, and those of Robert Fowler. But only a visit to the Shuri Line brings into focus the relentless American tactics on Okinawa, as one quote recalls in *Tennozan*: "There was no other way for Buckner but straight ahead into the sausage machine."

The Japanese strategy was to allow an American landing but then to defend a fortified line across the island from Naha to Shuri Castle, and then to the eastern coast. A Colonel Yahara devised the interlocking fields of fire and fortifications. As Feifer describes: "The Japanese had carved the limestone and coral of each commanding hill there into a kind of land battleship.... A network of trenches, galleries, caves and tunnels—some complexes almost two miles long—featured the added advantage of exits at both ends and sometimes flanks of the hills." The objective was not victory, but to bleed the Americans, who might then waver in their determination to invade the home islands or lose heart for the war.

At the center of the line was Shuri Castle, which was rebuilt after the war, although the independent kingdom of the Ryukyus has never been restored. Alex and I parked near the imperial grounds, where ponds, lily pads, and cherry blossoms cover battle works as formidable as anything that plugged the line at Verdun. The castle is now part of a local university, and it brought to mind not just the heart of the Okinawa battle, but the comedy of errors that was the mission of Commodore Matthew Perry to push the Japanese door open.

As recounted in Kerr, Perry used the port at Naha as a staging area for his visit to Yokahama. But he was the first in a long line of Americans for whom the inscrutable East would remain as confusing as chopsticks. For starters, Perry's translator at Shuri spoke only Chinese, not Japanese or Okinawan. Nor did the admiral ever grasp that the Ryukyus were a kingdom independent of its imperial suitors in Japan and China. He was incredulous that Okinawa did not circulate currency or coins. Ever the organizational man, Perry decided not to return home empty-handed. Before leaving, he signed a treaty of friendship that, devoid of substantive issues, at least capped the price of a barrel of water that would be paid by subsequent merchantmen calling at Naha.

The next delegation of Americans to call at Shuri was the 1st Marine Division, in May 1945, and on that occasion it, too, remained a remote kingdom. Russell Davis, serving in the 1st Regiment, describes an early glimpse of the castle: "Beyond the edge of the wall, the ridge ended. There was a long roll into the valley below. Far across the valley, beyond low hills and one east-west escarpment, was Shuri itself. ....Off beyond a coastal flat near the China Sea, Naha—largest city on the island—smoldered like a city dump."

In the same attack, E.B. Sledge, a marine infantryman whose memoirs Fussell describes as "one of the finest to emerge from any war," remembers the Shuri Line as: "the worst area I ever saw on a battlefield.... I shudder at the memory of it.... Each time we went up, I felt the sickening dread of fear itself and the revulsion at the ghastly scenes of pain and suffering among comrades that a survivor must witness." It echoes a line in Davis: "The thought of dying in the mud was a terrible one that haunted my dreams," if not a line from Siegfried Sassoon's "Suicide in the Trenches": "The hell where youth and laughter go."[1]

Despite the large number of marines and soldiers on Okinawa, the sharp end of the battle was seen by relatively few frontline infantrymen. Feifer writes: "It was only within rifle range of the enemy where the world went mad, where life was so unlike anything previously known, that those just a quarter of a mile behind could not easily imagine it." But the numbers of dead and wounded along that battle line were some of the highest in World War II.

---

1. Sledge made the analogy between Okinawa and the trench warfare of World War I when he wrote me a letter on September 14, 1982, shortly after *With the Old Breed* was published: "In writing W.T.O.B., I often thought how similar much of the experience around Shuri, Okinawa, was to that which I had read in Sassoon, Frank Richards, Owen, and Blunden of their World War I experience. These conditions on Okinawa, some of the most awful imaginable, resulted from the rain, mud, and near-impregnable Jap defensive positions we faced. Unless our tanks could support and move with us (and they *could not* in that mud), those Jap defenses simply stopped us, and resulted in the Shuri Stalemate. Thus it resembled the Western Front in WW I. This has rarely been mentioned as far as I know, because journalists and war correspondents or photographers never came anywhere near the front line during that period on Okinawa."

American casualties at Okinawa were 7,613 killed and 31,807 wounded. Another 26,221 left the lines at some point with battle fatigue, most in the assault against Shuri. In Sledge's unit, 485 marines served at some point with K Company, 5th Marines, and only a handful walked off the island without wounds. 107,539 Japanese soldiers and impressed laborers were also killed. A marine captain who served under Robert Fowler, Robert Sherer, told Feifer: "The only glory was in surviving, in staying alive."

Sugar Loaf: *"hell's cesspool"*

TOWARD DUSK ALEX and I drove the short distance from Shuri to the hill known as Sugar Loaf, which, in the currency of blood, was the most expensive piece of real estate acquired during World War II. We had to park in a field off the side of the road, and gazed into the darkness at a low hill that is now covered with a water tank. It felt more like a New Jersey suburb than a Pacific island. As James Hallas, the author of *Killing Ground on Okinawa: The Battle for Sugar Loaf*, a vivid account of the encounter, writes: "The remote spots men died for fifty years ago are now—preposterously—covered with McDonald's hamburger franchises, Dairy Queens, Kentucky Fried Chicken outlets, pawn shops and used car lots." Later I complained to a marine veteran of Okinawa, Richard Whitaker, about such a desecration. But he was more philosophical:

> Yes, I agree, the water tank on Sugar Loaf Hill is disturbing. However, one must remember that as far as the Japanese and Okinawans are concerned, the events of the spring of

1945 are bitter memories that are best left forgotten. The Japanese gave Sugar Loaf their best shot and so did the Sixth Marine Division. We prevailed. The water tank is understandable.

Feifer estimates that the battle for Sugar Loaf ranged over an area the size of "six football fields." One veteran recalled: "What made Sugar Loaf such a stunner was its seeming insignificance.... It wasn't a mountain, it wasn't even a hill." Another called it "a little lump in the ground... it looked like a plowed field." But it was one of many little round tops the marines and the army had to take, and each time they took one slope, they came under raking fire from interlocked positions, such was the genius of the Yahara defensive system. In less than a week, almost 3,000 marines were dead or wounded on ground that today is paved with the paradise of convenience.

In the gloaming Alex spoke at length of his friendship with General James Day, who fought as a marine corporal at Sugar Loaf and years later returned to Okinawa as the commander of the American forces. Alex mentioned that when in recent years Day had visited Okinawa, he often stayed in a hotel that, by chance or design, overlooks the foxholes that he had manned during the fighting. Day told Hallas that it was the approach to Sugar Loaf that claimed most of the casualties: "Now the killing zone on Sugar Loaf wasn't really to our front and it wasn't actually on top of Sugar Loaf. It was to our rear. It was about a 300 x 300 area back there—300 yards by 300 yards—that the marines had to cross in order to reach Sugar Loaf Hill. And that's where the majority of them were killed or wounded."

By one calculation, the marines made eleven concentrated

attacks against Sugar Loaf. But rarely did they see the enemy, which fired machine guns and mortars from concealed positions. "They were almost shapeless forms," a veteran recalled. Another remembered: "Men were clinging to the hill as men would cling to a reef in a heavy surf." As Sledge describes: "The place was choked with the putrefaction of death, decay and destruction.... Every crater was half full of water, and many of them held a Marine corpse.... Men struggled and fought and bled in an environment so degrading I believed we had been flung into hell's cesspool."

Sledge recounts the world of the 1st Marine Division, in the line to the east of the 6th Marine Division. My father's comrades-at-arms, C Company of the 1st Marines, were hard against the ramparts of Shuri Castle. In the marine regiments given the luckless task of directly attacking Sugar Loaf, the newly formed 22nd and 29th, my father's former lieutenants commanded several of the frontline companies.

Captain Maurice F. Ahearn led F Company, 22nd Marines into the jaws of Sugar Loaf, was wounded, but refused to be evacuated. "Yes, that sounds like Mike," was my father's remark when he heard this account. They had served together on Guadalcanal and Cape Gloucester, as each had with Robert Fowler, who during the struggle for the Shuri line moved up from command of F Company, 29th Marines, to S-3 of the 2nd Battalion. The 29th eventually seized Sugar Loaf on May 19, and Captain Sherer credits Fowler for devising the strategy that allowed the marines to envelope that and the surrounding hills: "The strategies that enabled the 2nd Battalion to seize and hold Sugar Loaf were undoubtedly formulated by Captain Fowler."

Another member of the 2nd Battalion at Sugar Loaf was

William Manchester, whose memoir of the Pacific war, *Goodbye, Darkness,* must be among the most controversial of the war. In an article I wrote about Guadalcanal, I complimented Manchester's writing, echoing later sentiments expressed by Feifer: "The book's puzzling inaccuracies do not invalidate some of the best descriptions in English of the fighting on Okinawa and in other Pacific campaigns." But in response, I received a number of letters from other veterans, dismissing Manchester's accounts as war stories. Still, he can write graphically, as when he describes Sugar Loaf: "I realized that something within me, long ailing, had expired. Although I would continue to do the job, performing as the hired gun, I knew that banners and swords, ruffles and flourishes, bugles and drums, the whole rigmarole, eventually ended in squalor. Goethe said: 'There is no man so dangerous as the disillusioned idealist.'"

Robert Fowler: *"the USMC never had a better officer"*

NEVERTHELESS, IT WAS largely to track down a passage in Manchester's memoir that I had gone to Okinawa. He had known my father's close friend Robert Fowler. But his account of Fowler's death on Okinawa had drawn angry responses from other historians, Feifer among them. In his descriptions of Sugar Loaf, Manchester writes:

> My father had warned me that war is grisly beyond imagining. Now I believed him. Bob Fowler, F Company's popular, towheaded commander, had bled to death after being hit in the spleen. His orderly, who adored him, snatched up a submachine gun and unforgivably massacred a line of unarmed Japanese soldiers who had just surrendered.

Until the book was published in 1980, my father had never known how his close friend had died.[2] It pained him further to imagine his death as the cause of a massacre. Many of my father's regrets about the war focus on the loss of Robert Fowler. "I always thought," he says, "that if he had stayed with me, I could have gotten him through." He also speaks of war as a lottery. After four years of the worst combat in the war, Fowler's luck ran out—in the last engagement his battalion fought, in its last battle of the war.

After the war, my father paid his respects by visiting Fowler's parents in Hartford. They were undecided whether to have their son's body returned to the United States or to leave him overseas. Wanting to spare his parents further grief, my father told them that "Bob would have wanted to be buried in the Pacific." His grave was later moved to the Punch Bowl war cemetery near Honolulu. On my first trip to Hawaii, to pay tribute to my father's lost friend, I found Fowler's headstone in a tranquil, volcanic valley that sits among that island's tropical peaks.

From Colonel Jon Hoffman, a Marine Corps historian with access to the archives, I had with me on Okinawa a sketch of Robert Fowler's life and military career. In my father's recollection he graduated from Dartmouth College with the class of 1941, having grown up in Hartford. Then Hoffman's notes pick up the story:

---

2. Nor had other members of C Company known the story, as is reflected in a letter that I received from Guadalcanal veteran Ed Foley: "That part of your letter that really hit me, where it hurts, was your recounting the of the death of Lt. Fowler. I had asked repeatedly about his death and they answered: 'Oh, he got killed in one of the battles.' He was my platoon lieutenant, who had earned my lasting respect, as had your dad. He emulated your dad with his style of command. He was a leader, but still one of the troops."

He was a reserve captain whose "date of appt/enl" in the Corps was 7 February 1942, in Philadelphia, PA. It says he had prior service, so he may have enlisted before that and was merely commissioned in 1942. He was born 16 April 1920 in Milwaukee, Wisconsin. He was married and his legal residence in 1945 was in West Hartford, CT. He was wounded by shrapnel on 15 April 1945 and returned to duty the same day. (It says wounded in the spine, but obviously it was not very serious.) He died of a gun shot wound to the chest on 12 June 1945, and was initially buried in the 6th Marine Division cemetery on 13 June. A Navy chaplain wrote the condolence letter to his family. In March 1948, Fowler's foster father authorized his interment in the Punch Bowl cemetery in Hawaii. (His wife may have remarried since 1945.)

To retrace Robert Fowler's last steps, I had several sources, in addition to Manchester and several official Marine Corps histories. I had letters from marines in the two companies in which he had served during the war, including correspondence from Robert Sherer, who was with him when he died. I also had Feifer's history, in which one of the narrators is Richard Whitaker, who, by chance, served in Fowler's F Company, 29th Marines. Whitaker was with Charles Oates, Fowler's orderly, when the alleged massacre occurred.

From Manchester, I had thought Fowler died at Sugar Loaf. But a letter from Sherer places his death almost a month later, on the Oruku peninsula. Marines from the 6th Division, including Fowler's 29th Regiment, made an amphibious landing onto that peninsula—on a small scale opening a second front on the Japanese flank that Buckner's critics wanted sooner and with more troops. Certain army and marine officers believed that a marine landing below the Shuri line could have rolled up the Japanese from the rear, breaking the stalemate. But Buckner was reluctant to divide his forces, and the landings on the peninsula only leapfrogged along the coast and flanked a portion of the Japanese lines.

The fighting at Oruku (where the Naha airport is now located) lasted little more than a week but still cost almost 2000 casualties. An official Marine Corps history of Okinawa describes the fighting around Easy Hill:

> During the day the 29th Marines broke through the hard core of the enemy defense that had been holding it up for a week....By 15:40, 1/29 had overrun the center of resistance, permitting 2/29 to move up on the left. Company F moved out from Oruku to seize Easy Hill, immediately south of the village—the last strong point in the zone of the 29th Marines.

Sherer's letter to me picks up the story:

> The death of Captain Bob Fowler, S-3, 2nd Battalion, 29th Marine Regiment, 6th Marine Division, on June 12th, 1945, to this day lacks cogent explanation as to the reason for his presence at Easy Hill on Oruku Peninsula, Okinawa.

He continued:

> I do not know the reason that Captain Fowler approached Easy Hill as the mopping up was in progress....He did not wear a steel helmet but a fatigue cloth baseball cap. He was armed only with a shoulder-holstered .38 caliber

pistol, not a Marine issue weapon. At a distance of about fifty yards from the base of Easy Hill he was observed to have been hit by either rifle or machine gun fire.

Why was he forward with hostile action in progress, particularly since he was so easily identified as a leader by his dress and arms? I doubt that Bob had been ordered forward and can therefore only reason that his motivation was of the highest desire known to a Marine—that of being with the men of the Company that he formed, trained and led into combat until he was ordered to a greater responsibility, the S-3 Operations Officer of the 2nd Battalion.

Of Manchester's account of a massacre, Sherer adds dryly: "I cannot confirm his version in *Goodbye, Darkness*."

Three versions of a massacre that followed Bob Fowler's death have circulated, each involving his runner, Charles Oates, who in most accounts had gone "a little Asiatic" in his pursuit of a Japanese kill. Manchester's account implies that the slaughter happened immediately after Fowler's death. Feifer and Whitaker describe another incident, but it happened several nights later and may or may not have related to Fowler's death. Sherer wrote me that on the day that Fowler died, Oates had killed a prisoner who was trying to escape:

This incident may have been the source of Bill Manchester's account but based on hearsay it grew in numbers and actuality. I do not deny that there was a company-wide passion of anger and grief from the death of Captain Fowler. Bob was all that your father knew him to be. Fox Company, under his leadership, was a family.

After the fighting on Okinawa, Sherer wrote letters to both Fowler's widow Mary and his parents, to the latter praising the way that Fowler had been devoted to Oates. Sherer describes Oates at length: "He was so grief stricken over Bob's death that he was determined to have vengeance on every Jap he could find and sought to go on every patrol for this reason." Oates was found dead a week after Fowler was killed. No one was with him when he died.

By all accounts, Captain Fowler had acted as a father figure to the troubled Oates. Their bond included a pact that each would get the other's personal effects should they die in the combat zone. To Oates then went Fowler's revolver, with its Western holster, probably similar to the one my father wore. According to Whitaker, as recounted in Feifer, Oates had Fowler's weapon at his side when several days later he and Whitaker were on watch together. Three Japanese approached a hut where they were alternatively sleeping and standing guard. Wearing only loincloths, the Japanese could have been soldiers out of uniform, trying to slip through American lines as civilians. They also could have been on a suicide mission. Or they could have been unarmed. Oates waited until the Japanese were within a range that was point blank, and shot down all three. Whether he was a brave marine fulfilling his mission or whether this was Manchester's massacre, in memory of his lost friend, are questions of war and revenge as old as the stories of Achilles and Patroclus. Homer tells us:

> *Achilles led them now in a throbbing chant of sorrow,*
> *laying his man-killing hands on his great friend's chest:*
> *"Farewell, Patroclus, even there in the House of Death!*
> *Look—all that I promised once I am performing now:*

I've dragged Hector here for the dogs to rip him raw—
and here in front of your flaming pyre I'll cut the throats
of a dozen sons of Troy in all their shining glory,
venting my rage on them for your destruction!"

In *Master and Commander*, Patrick O'Brian writes that "a serving officer in an active war has an intense rather than a lasting grief." But I sense it might have been the opposite for my father. After returning from Okinawa, I mailed to my father the letters about the death of Bob Fowler, and he responded:

> The correspondence you sent, as to the details of Bob Fowler's death, shed final clarity on a matter that had troubled and eluded me all these years. From it, I see that he died exactly as I would have imagined could well have happened, having seen him act with similar, spontaneous bravery quite often on Guadalcanal and Gloucester. The USMC never had a better officer!

Okinawa's Legacy: *"invasion was too high a price to pay"*

LEAVING SUGAR LOAF, I asked Alex if we could drive past the memorial known as the Garden of Remembrance. I had remembered a newspaper article that described its dedication, and how some of the U.S. veterans present had refused to mix with their Japanese counterparts, fifty years after the peace.

We lacked base clearance to visit the 6th Marine Division memorial. All we could do was peer through a chain-link fence at the low obelisk, similar to those that remember the Civil War in New England village centers. Alex made the point that the few U.S. monuments rest on borrowed ground, and perhaps on borrowed time—implying that when the bases reverted to Okinawa, the monuments would be returned to America.

We ate dinner in a small restaurant, exchanging stories of our families and work. Alex spoke of his campaign to repatriate Okinawan artifacts that during the war were stolen or liberated as "souvenirs." One American officer in the occupation had "plundered copiously," to use Herman Goering's phrase, and, as a bridge between the United States and the Ryukyus, Alex was pursuing suspect treasures in museums and private collections. I sensed his cause was a lonely vigil, against the same interests that keep the Elgin Marbles in London. But I admired his good cheer and steadfast courage, which let him see truth on a battlefield that had claimed so much of his family.

I spent a restless night in one of Naha's few commercial hotels, in a windowless room that could well have been one of Okinawa's forgotten caves. Awake at odd hours with jet lag, I flipped through my books and made notes about the day with Alex. Many histories, such as Fussell's and Feifer's, make the connection between the desperate fight in the Ryukyus and the atomic bombs. Feifer has a quote from Ian Gow: "The experience of Okinawa convinced them that invasion was too high a price to pay," implying that the fates of Hiroshima and Nagasaki were sealed along the Shuri Line.

Fussell looks back toward Okinawa from ground zero: "The degree to which Americans register shock and extraordinary shame about the Hiroshima bomb correlates closely with a lack of information about the Pacific war." In much the same spirit, Feifer writes: "It is difficult to comprehend such [casualty] figures and to remember the strains of 1945. Focusing revulsion on the bomb is easier. But if a symbol is needed to help preserve the memory of the Pacific War, Okinawa is the more fitting." The next day, I would be making my own link between Okinawa and the end of the war, flying from Naha to Kagoshima, for the drive to Nagasaki—following the route of the invasion that never was.

Kagoshima: *"God is always on the side of the heaviest battalions."*

THE RUNWAY AT Kagoshima is a shelf carved into the escarpment of Kyushu, Japan's southern island. We circled to land above a landscape of plunging green valleys and great hilltop knobs, lush Oriental terrain that, to American invaders, would have proved a labyrinth of blind alleys, each as deadly as Kasserine Pass.

Had the Pacific war not ended in August 1945, several months later, in November, the largest amphibious assault in history would have come ashore on Kyushu, with the industrial port at Kagoshima as a prime objective. Operation *Olympic* had at its disposal 766,700 men and 1,315 ships, and its mission was to seize the bottom third of Kyushu, which then would have become the staging area for a subsequent operation—*Coronet*—against the plains of Tokyo. Although Napoleon liked to say that "God is always on the side of the heaviest battalions," here they would have come ashore into landscape as turbulent as Smolensk or Borodino.

Estimates as to American casualties can now only be extrapolations, but all speak of a bloodbath. The Navy estimated a casualty rate of 35 percent or about 200,000. Other sources projected 105,000 casualties in the first 90 days of the fighting. Had the invasion of Japan followed the loss ratios of other deadly Pacific battles, such as Iwo Jima or Peleliu, the casualties suffered to seize Tokyo could have exceeded 1 million. Had they tracked the experience in the European theatre, 350,000 Americans would have been killed or wounded—figures that President Harry Truman no doubt considered as he made the decisions to drop the atomic bombs. As a marine in my father's company, Winston Fontaine, wrote to me: "As for my thoughts on the use of the atomic bomb, I can only say that without its use neither you nor I would be here."

In wanting to retrace my father's steps around Japan from 1945 to 1946, I had reserved a rental car at the Kagoshima airport. I also arranged to travel this leg of the journey with my friend Murray Sayle. He is an Australian by birth but has lived the past twenty-five years in Japan, and he was waiting outside customs and immigration wearing his trademark bush gear. We first met in the 1970s when I was a magazine editor and Murray had just moved with his young family from Europe to Japan. He was then beginning to write about Japan, its economy, and the end of the Pacific war. Since that time, he has contributed distinguished essays on those subjects to *The New Yorker*, *The Atlantic*, and the *New York Review of Books*. No stranger to war, he covered the Vietnam struggle for the London *Sunday Times* and is mentioned favorably in the dispatches of Phillip Knightley, who in *The First Casualty* praises Murray for the clarity of his writing and for his personal bravery (he went several times to find the bodies of journalists killed in battle).

On my first visit to Japan in summer 1983, I spent a week in Murray's company, first in Tokyo, where he gave me access to the library at the Foreign Correspondents Club, and later at his home in a small village that is two hours southwest of the capital, on the way to Mount Fuji. His wife, Jenny, also arranged for me to visit the Peace Park in Hiroshima, of which Murray wrote in *The New Yorker*: "No one ever made a positive decision to drop the bomb on Hiroshima, only a negative one: not to interfere with a process that had begun years before, in very different circumstances....Truman never contemplated, or even heard suggested, any delay, or any alternative to the bomb's use on a Japanese city." The official number of dead in the blast was 186,940, and, as I learned in my walk around Hiroshima, the bomb did not fall on military targets buts struck the city's red-light district and neighborhoods of bamboo-and-paper houses.

At the airport in Kagoshima, we found the car rental agency, and I slid into the passenger side with a stack of road maps, assuming that Murray would drive the car across the small roads of Kyushu to Nagasaki. But the pleasure of Murray's company is the witty tenacity of his conversation, which in a short space of time can jump between his extensive knowledge of history, language, and economy. "Hang on," are the words he uses to say: "I'm not finished yet." Now in his seventies, Murray lives for the ideas that come from his reading, travel, and observations, and assumes that, in the meantime, the small details of life will take care of themselves. When, instead of adjusting the rear-view mirror, he was explaining how the theories of Alfred Mahan related to the battle of Okinawa, I decided that I should drive and listen and that he should navigate both the route and the conversation.

Divine Wind: *"not victory but death"*

IT TOOK US more than an hour to drive south through Kagoshima, a deep-water anchorage as strategic as San Francisco, and then across rugged farmland to the small village of Chiran. In that quiet corner of a foreign field, Murray wanted me to see a museum that keeps alive the spirit of the kamikaze. A leaflet in English says that the mission of The Peace Museum for Kamikaze Pilots is "to preserve the true facts of World War II on record and to contribute to eternal peace on earth by collecting, preserving and exhibiting the photographs, relics and correspondence which belonged to the Special Airforce Attack Group members, who are known as Kamikaze pilots." But it is also a place to go to recall with nostalgia the Greater East Asia Co-Prosperity Sphere.

We parked near throngs of tour buses and wandered through a garden of "floating chrysanthemums"—which is what the planes were called—and the small Shinto shrines that remember the pilots whose basic training never covered the elements of landing. The Divine Wind—the *kamikaze*—was a storm that saved Japan from a 13th century Mongol invasion. At Okinawa 2,944 kamikaze missions were flown against the American invasion fleet, accounting for most of the 4,907 naval deaths in the campaign. From Chiran, which had a runway hidden among the remote hills, 1,036 pilots lost their lives.

In Japan, kamikaze pilots are remembered for their romantic souls. As Murray described them, many were second-rate high school students, drawn to the literary rather than the martial arts, and left poetic premonitions of death, much like the verse written in Great War trenches. The museum displays their *haiku*, along with rows of photographs that show smiling young men wearing leather helmets and white scarves. But the packed explosives carried on their wings were deadly. Russell Davis describes one attack: "A kamikaze screamed in under the guns of the picket ships, drove through wallowing transports like a ferret through a henyard, and exploded in a great orange flame against the side of a ship." A pilot defending against kamikaze, Samuel Hynes, now a distinguished war and cultural historian, concluded: "the true end of the war for the men I was fighting against was not victory but death."

Asia's Normandy Beaches: *"vertical cliffs up to three hundred feet"*

AFTER LUNCH IN a noodle house, Murray and I drove toward the western coast of Kyushu to see the 2nd Marine Division invasion beaches where my father might have come ashore. I found driving in Japan easier than I would have expected. Enough signs were in English, and even the back roads had route numbers that I could find on my maps. I drove and listened, while Murray took the high road, explaining American options in 1945 to end the war with Japan.

As he said, one of the greatest battles in 1945 was the U.S. inter-service rivalry to determine which branch could claim credit for winning the war. The navy favored a blockade that would besiege the Japanese home islands. The army saw no other option than an invasion that would eventually seize Tokyo. The newly formed air forces believed they could win the war through incendiary attacks, including nuclear strikes, against Japanese cities. Meanwhile, the Japanese high command was holding out for one more decisive battle—a *tenno-*

zan—that would bloody the Americans and make the peace terms palatable, by which most in Japan meant an armistice that allowed for the emperor to remain on the throne.

In Murray's version of the end game, Japan was already beaten by summer 1945, before the atomic bombs fell on Hiroshima and Nagasaki. American warships and submarines had already isolated movement between the Japanese home islands, Japan's navy had gone to the bottom between the battle of Midway and the sinking of the battleship *Yamato* in spring 1945, and its air force was reduced to suicide missions. The Japanese army remained a force in Manchuria, on the Chinese mainland, on some Pacific islands, and in Japan. But it lacked oil and mobility even for limited defensive engagements. Only the American insistence on unconditional surrender, in which Truman spoke in the voice of U.S. Grant, necessitated an invasion of Japan or the annihilation of its cities with fire bombs.

In Murray's estimation, what ended the war wasn't the two atomic bombs so much as the fear in Japan's ruling circles of a Russian invasion. In the same week that the bombs fell, the Russians attacked Japan's Far East positions with 80 divisions and heavy armor, on a broad front from Mongolia down to the Sea of Japan. Destructive as the bombs were in Hiroshima and Nagasaki, Japan sued for peace because of the breakdown of the Manchurian front, which left Hokkaido, its northern island, vulnerable to a Russian invasion. To continue the war meant for Japan to risk both partition, as it had seen in occupied Germany, and, worse, a communist occupation. As Murray wrote to me later, in his distinctive e-mail prose:

The war ended because the Russkis' entry made borscht of the consensus in the Supreme War Council, to seek

Russian mediation with the US (as a way of postponing the hard decision, hoping something would turn up). Russians in meant Japan would be partitioned as they had just seen Germany partitioned. The one thing more important than the Imperial institution was the integrity of the Japanese home islands.

Near Kushikino City, we parked the car overlooking the East China Sea, which had a heavy swell running against the breakwater, and tried to imagine this stretch of waterfront as Asia's Normandy beaches. Only a few histories have been written about the invasion of Japan, and the best book is Frank's *Downfall*, which I carried in my shoulder bag to help me to locate the beaches. In words I find poignant, Frank writes: "Any solider or Marine infantryman slated for *Olympic* who believed the atomic bomb saved him from death or wounds had solid grounds in this belief."

On occupation duty in Japan with the 2nd Marine Division in 1946, my father visited these invasion beaches and describes them in the memoir that I now carried to Kushikino City:

Like all of Japan's beaches, it is extremely narrow; hills rise sharply close to the waterline. I stared at it for a long time, imaging what it would have been like, thinking of earlier landings on faraway islands: here, in the still silence of an April day, the remembrance of slaughter. Floating off the beach, not yet removed, were concertinas, large wooden sawhorses encircled with barbed wire which, even under intense shelling, would remain lethal barriers to landing craft. The beach itself had been sowed with landmines, covered with barbed wire. On the reverse side of the adjoining hills there lay the mortar pits, artillery redoubts and deep caves for the storage of food and ammunition. It was impossible not to shudder at the carnage which would have inescapably ensued after even the most protracted bombing and shelling.

Much as my father had written when he saw these beaches in 1946, we looked inland at a jagged landscape. As Frank describes: "The continuous terracing of farmlands reinforced these obstacles with rises too steep for tracked vehicles. The corridor to Kagoshima in particular narrowed in places to only one hundred yards, flanked by vertical cliffs up to three hundred feet high—a frontage suitable for less than one rifle company." At Omaha Beach, the dunes were a thousand yards from the water's edge; here the objective, Kagoshima, was sixteen miles inland.

Nor does Frank agree with Murray's conclusion that Japan's army in autumn 1945 was a spent force. According to his research, the home army on Kyushu had fourteen divisions and eleven brigades. On the home islands all together, Japan had 2.9 million men under arms and 27,500 vehicles. The southern command had its headquarters at Hiroshima, one reason that city was targeted, and Frank believes Kyushu could have been resupplied from other islands, despite the blockade. He also concludes that "alternatives to the atomic bombs carried no guarantee that they would end the war or reduce the amount of human death and suffering."

All sides concede that the Americans would have gotten ashore. But what is not clear is whether the invasion would have then followed the course of victory on Okinawa or, for example, the stalemate at Gallipoli, the World War I landing that cost the Allies 256,000 casualties. Compared to Kyushu, Okinawa looks flat and open, accessible to naval support and armored vehicles. But Kyushu can only be described as a tank trap. Feifer concludes his comparisons between Okinawa and the invasions of Japan: "Americans in other units of the occupation force who visited their planned landing sites were silenced by the sight of high sea walls backed by gun-brisling fortifications more formidable than the Shuri Line's."

City of Occupation: *"a farce that was to last many months"*

FROM THE INVASION beaches we drove inland and up the rugged spine of Kyushu, passing through the provincial city of Hitoyoshi, where in winter 1946 my father served in the occupation forces. He writes in the memoir: "I reported for duty as second-in-command of the Third Battalion, 8th Marine Regiment, which was stationed at Hitoyoshi, a former garrison town of about thirty thousand located centrally on Kyushu."

When the war ended, he had sufficient points to resign his commission. But the commandant at Camp Pendleton persuaded him to take overseas a replacement battalion. Thinking all that was involved was a Pacific voyage, he accepted, and arrived in Japan in October 1945, eager to return home to civilian life. But given the shortage of experienced officers in the peacetime Marine Corps, new orders kept him in Japan until the following summer. Much of the time he was stationed in Hitoyoshi—"the cold river stream rushing past the Shinto shrine and the wooden houses clustered against dark green hillsides."

Among my father's responsibilities in that windswept town was to crack down on profiteering. But, unknown to marines in the field, the American occupation actually tolerated the black market, which allowed Japan to horde capital for its subsequent economic miracle. Among those who did not get the word was my father, who found himself cast as a soldier against fortune. He writes:

> Besides the normal duty of maintaining civil order, this infantry battalion had received also the entirely improbable objectives of ferreting out "war criminals" and black marketeers....Thus began a farce that was to last for many months.

The battalion commander had no interest in becoming a district attorney, so he delegated the rules committee to my father, who in turn had to deal with the local police chief, Fumio Wada. Like Claude Raines in wartime Casablanca, Wada found it prudent occasionally to round up the usual suspects:

> From time to time he would advise me that a "suspect" had been apprehended and was waiting for questioning by me.
> Using a Japanese interpreter, thereupon ensued extended excerpts from the theater of the absurd. "Ask him what he did from 1942 through 1945," I would query. On and on and on would the come the answer, cascades of words. When the suspect finally stopped talking, I would ask the interpreter, "What did he say?" The interpreter replied, "He said he was a student."

From Hitoyoshi, we crossed a bleak stretch of mountains to reach Kumamoto, along the western coast, where we had one of those aimless searches for a hotel in a strange city. I would have settled for another windowless room. But despite the late hour, and our fatigue, I was pleased to see Kumamoto, where a family friend, Jim Rogers, who spent most of the war with my father, served in the occupation.[3]

We eventually spotted a Green Hotel, part of a commercial chain and ate dinner at a nearby French restaurant. But in our wanderings around the city, we passed several four-star driving ranges that might have been futuristic cities, maybe part of the Trade Federation that so animates the Jedi Knights. Like baseball stadiums, these golf centers are built on a horseshoe design, with tiered layers of sky boxes, which look like video conference centers. Overhead are stadium lights, which illuminate the fairways and the cascading nets that sweep the perimeter. In the lights, I could see remote figures, many dressed in black, relentlessly hitting buckets of golf balls, no doubt into a rising sun.

Across the Shimabara: *"enormous civilian casualties without flinching"*

To GET TO Nagasaki the following day, we were able to save time and miles by taking a ferry from Kumamoto to the

---

3. He wrote to me: "Did your father ever tell you about our first few weeks in Nagasaki? We had a draft of about one thousand men. Upon our arrival the men would be apportioned to various units. Our camp was a military base that survived the bomb. Your father took a detail to Tokyo. He was confident that I would maintain the high standards of discipline for which he was famous. One night I was awakened by a bell and much shouting. It soon became apparent that something was happening. It was a fire which swept through the camp and leveled all the buildings. The men escaped, the Japanese made a futile try with hand pumps. When morning arrived the division quartermaster sent blankets, no uniforms and the men wrapped themselves in blankets. Several awful days passed and I got word that your Dad would be arriving in Nagasaki by plane. I met him there and he told me all about his adventure—and then the big question: "How is everything at the camp?" "You will soon find out," I said as we climbed a hill and looked down where barracks once stood and men looked like lost Indians.... We separated some days later. I went to Kumamoto and Steve to another battalion."

Shimabara peninsula, from which it is a two-hour drive to Nagasaki. On deck we came across a Norwegian naval architect, who was part of a consortium building eight supertankers in a local shipyard that would be put in service to carry oil from the Persian Gulf to the ravenous petroleum markets in North America. To the unsuspecting, such terms of trade accounted for Japan's economic success. But as Murray explained, once the architect had returned to the car deck, even by charging $70 million per oil tanker, the shipyard was losing money, and the government would subsidize the construction—all to support a local political establishment that looks a lot like the old cronies of police chief Fumio Wada.

As we drove toward Nagasaki along Shimabara's twisting coastal road, lined with American-style car dealers and strip malls, Murray spoke at length about how, throughout World War II, civilians had become legitimate targets of war. Early on in the struggle, the citizens of Berlin, Hamburg, London, Coventry, Dresden, and Tokyo—not to mention Guernica—had been declared strategic targets, a derivative of the notion that terrorized populations end wars. As Murray wrote in *The New Yorker*: "Dresden confirmed one of the best-attested lessons of the Second World War: military leaders, themselves safe in bunkers, can take enormous civilian casualties without flinching."

Hence war planners began targeting something they called "civilian morale," attacks that consumed 25,000 civilian lives in Dresden in the same firestorms that later engulfed many Japanese cities. Referring to the population of Kyushu, the pilot of the Nagasaki bomb wrote in his memoirs: "Thirty-two million civilians—women, children, and the elderly—were being drilled in the art of resistance and guerrilla warfare."

Frank observes that declaring air war on civilians was

making a virtue of necessity, as in 1941 only one-in-five bombs landed within miles of their targets. Even pinpoint bombing missions against select munitions plants involved heavy civilian casualties. Although there was a pretence that both conventional and atomic bombs were to be used against military targets, the reality is that they fell on civilian centers.[4]

Arriving in Nagasaki around mid-day, we decided to head directly to the atomic bomb museum. We had a detailed city map, and Murray had been to Nagasaki on several previous occasions. (He wrote for Conde Nast *Traveler*: "*Nowhere else in Japan will you hear, first thing every morning, the gentle chime of church bells, echoing round its steep hills.*") But the expressway exit ramp dumped us out in a strange suburb, and our run into downtown Nagasaki proved no more successful than that of Major Charles W. Sweeney, the pilot of *Bock's Car*, the B-29 bomber who dropped the second atomic weapon (so called "Fat Man") but missed his target, as I did the museum, by several miles.

Nagasaki: *"Only the dead have seen the end of war."*

IN *THE NEW Yorker*, Murray describes the bomb's descent on Nagasaki:

> Because of the inaccuracies of the radar-directed bomb run, Fat Man widely missed the aiming point over the

---

4. An official responsible for choosing the atomic targets explained: "I had set out as the governing factor that the targets chosen should be places the bombing of which would most adversely affect the will of the Japanese people to continue the war. Beyond that, they should be military in nature." But except for being home to the command structure of the southern armies, including those defending Kyushu, Hiroshima had few military qualities. Another frequently discussed target was Kyoto, which had no military value.

metropolitan center. Instead, it detonated about a mile distant, over the Urakami district, a place that symbolized two facets of the city's history. Near to hand was the Mitsubishi torpedo factory, which manufactured weapons wielded so effectively at Pearl Harbor. But also in proximity was the Urakami Catholic Cathedral, the largest of its kind in eastern Asia and a symbol of Nagasaki's role as Japan's tightly controlled portal to European contact. Fat Man wiped out the cathedral and probably more than half of the fourteen thousand Catholics in Nagasaki.

The bomb fell at 11:02 A.M. on August 9, killing 78,150 civilians, including the Catholics whom Murray described and about 10,000 impressed Korean laborers. We stood at ground zero, which is recalled in a circle of concentric red bricks, which Murray described as "a still, haunted space with a crumpled steel fire tower and a plain black stone marking the actual spot." Inside the museum, we inspected a replica of Fat Man—a Neolithic fish of plutonium, with gills, a squat body and a sharp tail—hanging vertically, as if still on its descent. As well it might be: another exhibit was a three-dimensional map that showed where on earth nuclear bombs have been exploded since 1945. On that globe are more than 2000 points of light.

The port of Kokura was Major Sweeney's primary target, but when it was obscured by clouds he diverted to Nagasaki, which had important steel and shipbuilding plants. Sweeney dropped the bomb using largely visual co-ordinates, but writes confidently in his memoirs: "There was no question in my mind that the two Mitsubishi arms plants at Ohasi, and the Morimachi and Mitsubishi steelworks plants sitting in that valley, were no more." But the Mitsubishi shipyard was spared, and even near the Hypocenter, building walls remained standing.

Ferrying troops to the occupation, my father arrived in Nagasaki two months after the bomb hit. He recalls:

> On a gray October morning, our troop ship sailed into Nagasaki harbor, knowing nothing of what to expect upon arrival in the second city to have experienced a nuclear bomb. As we drew closer, we saw large and substantial buildings still standing on the hillsides outside the city, seemingly undamaged.... The blast had exploded away from the center of the city, with the result that most of the buildings facing it were demolished, while those on the leeward side were largely and strangely untouched.

Like all soldiers of the Japanese occupation, my father found it extraordinary that the surrender had converted a deadly enemy into a warm host. In the first American offensive of the war, on Guadalcanal, my father along with lieutenants Ahearn and Fowler had led his company with bayonets into the Japanese lines. Later an American officer had described the savagery of that battle, at the Tenaru River, which was part of the long reference on the American side that Japan would fight to the last:

> I have never heard or read of this kind of fight. These people refuse to surrender. The wounded would wait until men come up to examine them...and then blow themselves and the other fellow to pieces with a hand grenade.

On the banks of the Tenaru, my father survived one such grenade attack, saved by a warning from Corporal Frank d'Errico. But then, as fate twists, several years later he found himself living amongst the enemy:

> Thus we settled into the surrealist experience of living in a still functioning city which had withstood a nuclear bomb, and this among a pliant population of people who, until a few months before, were enemies of ours until death….How could a people endure such a long and traumatic war with such an overwhelmingly catastrophic climax still act so seemingly normal in the always polite dealings with us, foreign devils, who bestrode their land as conquerors?

Free in autumn 1945 to travel about the city, he decided to visit one of the hospitals treating the victims of the atomic bomb. No one had said he could not, and I am sure that the director of the hospital was as welcoming to him as I was made to feel at the peace museum on Okinawa. But it could not have been easy for someone who believed the bomb had saved his life to then walk among those whose lives were taken in the Darwinian equation. He writes:

> There, in the beds of the long dun-colored wards lay the caricatures of people who had once been whole, flesh torn from limbs, head wounds suppurating under scraps of bandages, and clusters of relatives in bedside vigils. There in those wards lay the answers not revealed to the public of how atomic bombs can, in an instant, sear human lives apart.

To this day, he often recalls a quote from Plato that hangs on the walls of London's Imperial War Museum: "Only the dead have seen the end of war."[5]

Modern American mythology draws heavily on the premise that virtue was in the fallout of the atomic bombs. In this orthodoxy, Sweeney writes: "Any weapon that could bring victory and save American lives was worth trying." His preflight briefing includes a priest's blessing that invokes Thomas Aquinas and the notion of just war. He adds: "Tibbets [who piloted *Enola Gay* to Hiroshima] then closed the briefing by telling us that this bomb would end the war." When the crew of *Bock's Car* returns to Tinian, after an emergency landing on Okinawa, it celebrates the raid with an all-American barbecue. One of Sweeney's conclusions is that "the people of Hiroshima and Nagasaki were the victims of their own warlords." But as Murray writes: "It will be ironical if the defenders of civilization depend for victory upon the most barbaric, and unskilled, way of winning a war that the modern world has seen."

We left the museum in the mid-afternoon and spent a frustrating hour trying to change money or use a debit card at the railway station—incredulous that the local bank market would not circulate coinage. Then, to find our hotel, we

---

5. Of the many letters I received from C Company marines, one from Art Holmberg had this to say about my father and the end of the war: "The reason I am writing you, even though I have not anything to tell you about facts you requested is simply I want to convey my deep pride and respect for a Company Commander that I had the privilege saluting, as one of his people under his command.... Captain Stevenson, as I knew him, is an exceptional-gifted-leader and a Marine that compliments the Marine Corps even to this day, as to my assessment and opinion.... As to the use of the atomic bomb: I thank God for all of the military that was spared because of the bomb. I feel deep compassion for the non-military people of Japan that it affected; but remember too well the men and women who died at Pearl Harbor, and the many non-military personnel on the islands the Japanese bombed and invaded.

had to follow a police car through the narrow streets of the old town. Lastly, I had to return the car to Avis and figure out how to catch the 7:00 A.M. flight on Monday morning to Tokyo. By early evening, I felt like Commodore Perry trying to negotiate at Shuri with a Chinese interpreter and unsure about the cost of a barrel of water.

We revived our spirits with a drink in the restored Dutch *entrepôt*, Dejima, which pinpoints Nagasaki in history as the most Western Japanese city. "It is the path not taken," in Murray's words, "what might have been if Japan had remained open to the world, particularly the Western world." In 1542 Portuguese sailors brought the first firearms to Nagasaki. Catholic missionaries also arrived to stay in the sixteenth century. The Dutch used its free trade zone, now a museum village, to develop business with China and Japan. A Scottish merchant, Thomas Glover, moved to Nagasaki in the nineteenth century, and straddling the worlds of East and West he imported Japan's first steam engine and founded the brewery that is now Kirin. Had Commodore Perry knocked on the door in Nagasaki, instead of Naha and Yokahama, he would have found it had been open for three hundred years.

Murray insisted that our farewell dinner be *champon*, a local soup that at first glance could be steamed aquarium. But I shall remember its delicacy always, as well as the gabled sense of tragedy that pervades the Glover House, which we visited before dinner. We reached the hillside compound above Nagasaki on moving stairs, as though at the mall. The many houses of the Glover family are done in plantation style, with broad verandas, colonial furniture, and hints of Victorian eccentricity: for example, one of the Glovers collected prints of Pacific fish. The story of Madame Butterfly was conceived in these gardens. Among the bronze statues is one of Giacomo Puccini. Directly across the harbor was the Mitsubishi shipyard, which Sweeney's bomb missed. A huge natural-gas tanker was on the skids. Only the entrance to Urakami valley was visible, as a twisting gap between the hills along the river. When the bomb hit with operatic drama, the Glover house suffered only shattered windows, although the patriarch's grandson was a suicide within the month—the family's dream of reconciliation between Japan and the West as stormy as that earlier difficult courtship that blossomed among the family's roses.

Carrying the Fire to Tokyo: *"a silver curtain falling"*

DURING THE WEEK that followed, I had business meetings in Tokyo, which, mired in economic crisis, had a subdued air, as if its zenith was 1969. Between appointments I read in the imperial gardens and drank tea in the lobby of the Imperial Hotel, from which MacArthur ran the occupation. But on my last afternoon, I went looking for the Sumida River. Now it is an industrial waterway running through downtown Tokyo, more a link in the sewage system than a river. But on March 8 and 9, it was one of many ground zeros in the fire bombing that put Tokyo to the torch.

As if a Greek god, General Curtis LeMay carried the fires of Dresden to the skies over Japan in spring 1945. Frank quotes from a Jesuit priest who described the incendiary bombs as: "a silver curtain falling...and where these silver streamers would touch the earth, red fires would spring up." The raid lasted two hours and forty minutes—1,665 tons of incendiaries dropped into an area of ten square miles, which in Frank's words became "burned empty prairie...." Almost sixteen square miles of the city burned, destroying 261,000 houses. One and a half million Japanese became homeless and 79,466 civilians were killed. Those fleeing the flames tried throwing themselves into the Sumida River. But an eyewitness remembered: "The instrument was the tide, which had come and gone since the fire storm passed by, leaving rows of bodies like so much cordwood cast up on the beach."

My father was another witness to the destruction of Tokyo, bringing a company of marines from Nagasaki to the capital in late 1945. He arrived in Yokosuka:

> Across the bay lay Tokyo, immense in its size and devastation, miles of smashed roads, downed telephone wires and charred remains of wooden buildings nearly vaporized by fire. And yet life in the city went on; stores were open, streetcars struggled to negotiate bent rails, impoverished people stood on street corners, offering prize possessions for sale in hopes of earning food.

By current American wisdom, the two atomic bombs sapped Japan of the will to continue the war. Sweeney writes, for example: "They could not fight on after the second atomic strike." But Nagasaki was a provincial port city of 250,000 inhabitants, and many of the victims were slave laborers and Christians. By contrast, after much of the capital was burned to the ground, Japan still had the fortitude to man the lines in Okinawa and prepare the resistance on Kyushu. As Murray argued repeatedly on our drive across Kyushu: just because the war ended after the atomic bombs were dropped does not mean that it ended as a result of their fallout. Would Japan have surrendered in 1942 had an atomic bomb, in that year, wiped out the Urakami valley?

If the fire bombing of Tokyo achieved any military result, it was to convert Emperor Hirohito into what Murray has called "a closet pacifist." He had toured the charred ruins by car and returned stunned to the palace—his first encounter with a war that he had tolerated for the past fourteen years. A biography of Hirohito puts the endgame into personal terms: "Sadly, the war was dragged out for over a year more because of these two obsessions: the need for a military advantage before negotiating, and the need to preserve Tojo as a scapegoat to divert blame from the emperor."

During summer 1945, oblivious that Stalin had promised to join the war effort in the Far East, Japanese envoys tried to induce the Russians to mediate with the Allies. The approach might have been a prelude to armistice talks or, more possibly, authorized by senior military leaders to discredit that faction which wanted terms of peace. In any case, the Russian offensive, launched in early August as the atomic bombs were falling, ended any illusion of continuing peace with the Soviet Union.

Japanese intelligence had estimated Russian forces in the East at three infantry divisions and three tank brigades. Instead the Russians attacked with more than eighty divisions and 2,119 tanks, breaking the Japanese along a thousand-mile front. When Emperor Hirohito was asked by the Supreme Council to break the stalemate between war and peace, he chose peace. The Japanese text of the surrender was a master

of understatement: "the war situation has developed not nec-
essarily to Japan's advantage."[6]

The Yamato Dynasty: *"in neither time nor public memory"*

WANTING TO KNOW more about the role that the imperial
family played in ending the war, I had brought, to read on
the flight home to Switzerland, a biography of the Yamato
dynasty that had come with an inscription from my father:
"Before it all changed in 1945!" Actually, the thesis of the
book, by investigative journalists Sterling and Peggy Seagrove, is that very little has changed in Japan. They believe
that, since the Meiji Restoration in 1868, the royal family has
fronted for an oligarchy that remains in power despite the
holocausts that the war produced. "Today, instead of being
manipulated by Meiji oligarchs, or Hirohito militarists, the
imperial family is window-dressing for financial manipulators
who milk Japan like a cash cow."

The Swiss flight climbed to altitude over the Tokyo Plain,
that which Operation *Coronet*, with the 1st Marine Division,
would have assaulted with one million men and more tanks
than rolled against Berlin. No doubt the capital would have
fallen, but what if, afterwards, the Japanese armies in China

---

6. An intriguing corollary to Murray's thesis is hinted at in a passage written by
Robert Cowley, the former editor of *MHQ*, who implies that Truman also had a
hand in stopping the Russian offensive from crossing the Sea of Japan: "We are
lucky that the Pacific war ended when it did. If the war had gone on for even
a week or two longer, the entire East-West geopolitical situation might have
changed irrevocably. In retrospect, it begins to seem that when Harry S. Truman
warned Stalin to keep away from the Japanese home islands—and the Soviet
dictator reluctantly called off the Hokkaido operation at the eleventh hour—our
accidental president made one of his most important decisions, one that ranks with
his decision to drop the bomb."

and elsewhere had decided to continue the fight, in what one historian calls "a score of Okinawas"?

I had the ideal combination of a window seat and a good book. Before we said goodbye, Murray said that he had not read Sterling Seagrove, but heard he was something of a "rumor monger." But despite the book's sensational prose and sometimes sweeping allegations, I found the biography of the royal family to be a revelation—at least for what it says about how the Pacific war lingers in modern memory.

When Emperor Hirohito died in 1989, he was bid farewell with a funeral that cost $74 million. Among the mourners were the heads of state of nearly all the governments that, as emperor in the 1930s and '40s, Hirohito's military had plundered copiously. Most obituaries described Hirohito's Japan as an economic phoenix that had risen from the ashes of Hiroshima and Nagasaki. If the eulogies quoted from Shakespeare, they were apt to be verses from the divine wind of the sonnets rather than Macbeth, in which it was asked: "What bloody man is that?"

The Seagroves are less forgiving, linking the shy royal family of *People* magazine to some of World War II's worst atrocities, such as the Rape of Nanking in which 300,000 Chinese soldiers and civilians were slaughtered. Prince Asaka, the emperor's brother, was the ranking Japanese commander in Nanking. Under the imperial seal he issued the order: "Kill all the captives." Some 20,000 Chinese prisoners were allegedly used for bayonet practice, and a similar number of women and children were raped. But like the rest of the royal family, Prince Asaka escaped the fate of a war criminal, dying in his bed at the age of ninety-three, after many peaceful years of playing afternoon golf on the imperial course.

Only seven Japanese were hanged for war crimes. Needing Japan as an ally in the emerging Cold War with the Soviet bloc, the United States allowed the emperor to remain on the throne after the war, thus making few changes to a power structure that had spread a plague of death across Asia and, in Japan, created an economy around the black-market principles of oligopoly. The Seagroves write: "MacArthur was in a unique position to inflict reform on a country that urgently needed it, but instead he delivered the Japanese people back into the hands of the same men who led them into the 'dark valley.'" (One of Murray's favorite quotes about the general comes from Dwight Eisenhower, who before the war served as his chief of staff: "*MacArthur?*" said Ike. "I studied drama under him for six years.")

After the war, Germany paid 30 billion dollars in reparations. Japan contributed 2 billion dollars but nothing after 1951, when it unilaterally decided it had paid enough. Moreover, there has never been an accounting of the gold or assets that Japan looted from occupied Southeast Asia. According to the Seagroves, Operation Golden Lily, run by another imperial prince, Chichibu, stockpiled plundered gold in the Philippines, in underground vaults, and even on sunken ships—a new twist to offshore banking that provided the down payment for the Japanese economic miracle.

In Europe, reminders are constant about the tolls of the Nazi holocausts, and of the numbers who vanished into Stalin's death camps. But the casualties of Japanese imperialism from 1931 to 1945 are worth repeating because they are cited so infrequently. According to a number of sources I studied: ten to fifteen million Chinese died in the war with Japan; three million Dutch colonials died in Indonesia; one million prisoners-of-war, in all theatres, disappeared, including those sacrificed in live bayonet practice; 291,000 American soldiers, sailors and marines were casualties in Pacific battles, of whom 100,000 died; the fall of Singapore cost the lives of 15,000 British soldiers, many of whom were executed; and on the Burma-Siam railway line, 82,500 prison laborers were worked to death. Some two million Japanese soldiers also perished in the war, as well as 323,000 civilians in the fire storms.

For the several million American sailors, soldiers, and marines being readied to invade Japan—my father among them—war's end came, as described by Sledge, with silence instead of a nuclear bang:

> We received the news with quiet disbelief coupled with indescribable sense of relief. We thought the Japanese would never surrender. Many refused to believe it. Sitting in silence, we remembered our dead. So many dead. So many maimed. So many bright futures consigned to the ashes of the past. So many dreams lost in the madness that engulfed us. Except for a few widely scattered shouts of joy, the survivors of the abyss sat hollowed-eyed and silent, trying to comprehend a world without war.

Speaking for many who survived, Eric Lomax, in writing about Burma-Siam in *The Railway Man*, confesses: "I regretted that there were not more of them [Japanese military leaders] going to the gallows; I felt that thousands of them were guilty. There was unfinished business between me and the Japanese people."

I thought of these words as my Swiss airliner, describing its long arc to Europe, crossed the empty Manchurian plain, that which the Russians had crossed to close with Japan. Did the war end here or at Nagasaki, in Hypocenter Park? Was the massacre that followed Bob Fowler's death that of the

Japanese shot down by Charles Oates or was it the population of Hiroshima? Does my father owe his life to those he saw in the Nagasaki ward or to his comrades-in-arms in C Company—men like Fowler, Ahearn, d'Errico, Fontaine, Wilkerson, Buff, Rogers and so many others? Did the world gain something by allowing Japan to hide behind its lacquered screens the roll of its dishonor that spread holocausts across Asia?

An oral history about Japan describes the modern memory of its Asian battles as now consigned to the long-ago past. One review of the book is titled: "Collective Amnesia in Tokyo." The authors conclude that "the lost war seems anchored in neither time nor public memory." That detachment may, sadly, apply both to Japanese and to Americans, who each have their own reasons for forgetting the victims of such distant cauldrons as Nanking, Nagasaki, or Okinawa. But as Lincoln said with simple elegance, it is rather for us, the living, to see that they have not died in vain.

Around the World in Fifty Days

(2003)

TWENTY YEARS AGO this month, I was "between engagements." Otherwise it felt like I was out of work. In the spirit of ticker tape, my résumé was floating around New York. While I was awaiting some word, Pan Am's *Clipper* magazine asked me to write a story about the forthcoming Seoul Olympics.

The pay was minimal, but the offer came with a round-trip ticket to Asia. I could have gone to Seoul for a week, checked out the pool for synchronized swimming, and returned to my New York bread lines. Instead I convinced Pan Am to book my return passage via Karachi and London. All I had to do was travel on my own between Hong Kong and Pakistan, the gap in Pan Am's around-the-world service. A week in Korea became a *tour du monde*.

In Seoul, I was assigned a car, driver, and guide. Finding Olympic preparations well in hand, I made side trips to Inchon and the demilitarized zone (where overlooking North Korea I ate cheeseburgers and drank lemonade). Every night, various tourism officials called at my hotel to take me to dinner. Few of my meal companions spoke English, including some of the geisha-like waitresses. But obviously I was an expense-account moment.

I escaped this non-stop hospitality by taking a boat from Korea to Japan, across the Straits of Tsushima, where Japan became a modern nation when it defeated the Russian navy in 1905. The crossing was overnight, which I spent on the floor. I had chosen a stateroom with 'Japanese conveniences,' which were limited to a stack of musty blankets.

From the Japanese port of Shimonoseki, I took a bullet train to Hiroshima, where the Peace Park commemorates the deaths of more than 100,000 civilians. Hiroshima had been headquarters to the Japanese army's southern command, but mostly the first atomic bomb took out the city's downtown and nearby districts of rice-paper houses.

Back on a bullet train, I traveled to the capital, where I checked into the Tokyo Family Hotel, a small inn near the center city where all the guests, including me, took their meals in bathrobes and slippers. (Imagine the coffee shop of a Holiday Inn with all the guests in pajamas.) My room was the size of a steamer trunk and getting up made me feel like Houdini.

Tokyo is a lovely summer city. I was lucky to make new friends—including a couple who had survived the bombing of Hiroshima. I spent a week reading books in the imperial gardens and taking day trips to Kyoto. I even got invited out of town for a weekend, where my hosts invited me to take a Japanese bath. In a borrowed robe and slippers, I was directed to a wooden hut where I was confronted with a cauldron of near-boiling water. Not wanting either to lose face or scorch it, I saw no choice but to lower myself into the stone tub, where I thrashed briefly, lobster-style. Only later was I told that Japanese baths are taken with a bucket, usually the only thing that gets dipped into the broth.

BACK ON PAN Am, I flew from Tokyo to Hong Kong, where I dodged the summer heat and rode the incomparable harbor ferries. I also took a larger boat to the nearby entrepôt of Macau, about which *Vanity Fair* wanted an account of its night life. In the summer of 1983, the city-state was still a Portuguese colony on the Asian mainland, where the dogs were either eaten or raced. Most of the bars had an aquarium-like room, in which young hostesses sat with numbers around their necks—like trout on protected rivers where the rules require catch and release. In the casinos, a popular way of betting was to hurl wads of hundred dollar bills onto the gaming tables, where the dealers, all young women, took in losing bets as if raking up autumn leaves.

I had no business in Bangkok. Monkey business, of course, was an option, but I found the Thai night life a variation on the theme of peep shows. I did have a beer at the famed Oriental Hotel and took a boat ride on the Chao Praya River. But I was happy to push on to Calcutta, where my plan was to see the work of Mother Teresa and then to ride the train across the Indian subcontinent to Bombay and New Delhi, before crossing into Pakistan.

I had the usual visa hassles at the Calcutta airport. (Did they know I was still looking for a job?) Only after a long search did I find a hotel, one run by a Major Smith and his wife, who clearly kept costs down by restricting the flow of water to a trickle. But the hotel had a lovely garden, an oasis in Calcutta's stifling heat, and the eccentric guests had seemingly escaped from an E.M. Forster novel.

I spent some of my Calcutta days with an American lawyer who said he knew President Carter and who traveled
everywhere (in the Indian summer!) in a seersucker suit. We
visited Mother Teresa's hospice and drank beer in the major's
garden. Come evenings I roamed, sometimes by rickshaw,
the underworlds that Winston Churchill called "the city of
dreadful night." At the heart of Calcutta is an imperial British
city, as imposing as Glasgow or Liverpool, to whose scale it
was drawn. But beyond the mall are the labyrinths of urban
cave dwellers where families huddle around primeval fires,
in houses that spill into the narrow streets.

Mostly what I did in Calcutta was buy train tickets. I
wanted a berth on an air-conditioned express to Bombay.
That meant calling on innumerable offices around the city,
manned by impassive clerks, whose lives consisted of ceiling
fans, paper stacks, and milky tea. But when I went with my
bag to Howrah Station in Calcutta—one of Dante's circles
of Hell—I found the train that I had booked was canceled.

When I got this news, I had my bag on a platform that
otherwise looked like a homeless shelter. All around were
motionless figures, wrapped in thin blankets, fast asleep.
Casting for options, I dreaded the thought of returning to
Major Smith's dry cleaning as much as I did the idea of bed-
ding down in Howrah Station. But out of this valley of inde-
cision came a kindly rail conductor who said: "Your train is
canceled, but you can come with me." What he had to offer
was a non-air conditioned train that would traverse the subcontinent in three days, not two, and the berth he proposed
was one of six in a dark compartment—yet another black
hole of Calcutta.

"Never backtrack" was a credo of General Ulysses S.
Grant, and on that basis I climbed aboard the Bombay Mail.

I was assigned a lower berth, more a shelf, but I had none of the sleep sacks that the other passengers brought with them. I rolled a shirt for a pillow and slept in my shorts, into which I jammed my wallet and passport. The train window was without glass, only iron bars, through which, for several days, rolled the frames of an Indian silent movie; one part Bollywood, one part documentary about subsistence farming in scorched earth.

The train had no diner. At intermediate stations some of the other passengers bought prepared meals, which, like prison gruel, were passed through the bars on plastic trays. For a while I resisted 'Chicken Legs Served in Pools of Luke Warm Fat,' living on Thumbs Up—India's answer to Coca-Cola. But when I saw my bunk mates still alive after several days of platform poulet, I took to ordering what I called "room service." But my joke had bad side effects, other than the usual consequences of Indian food. My compartment mates were now convinced that I owned a hotel and restaurant in New York and that I had come to India to find waiters and bus boys—for which I now had five applications.

Our route across India was exactly that of Phileas Fogg, although in the opposite direction. We left the Ganges at Allahabad and crossed central India to Bombay. But the train stopped fifty miles from the city because floods had washed out the tracks. I organized a few of my hotel staff into a taxi, on which we strapped our luggage to the roof in a drenching, monsoon rain. When I finally got to Bombay (and the job interviews had ended), I had the taxi stop at the first decent hotel. My only question to the front desk clerk was whether the room had running water.

The temperature in Bombay was that of a steam room. I got acquainted with friends of friends, who took me to dinner parties and *Passage to India*-like excursions into the Malabar Hills. Forster wrote that Bombay had equal parts of "pathos, piety, and courage." In the monsoon heat of July, it also has a fetid smell. When I departed for Delhi, it was again on the train, but this time I finally had my first-class, air-conditioned berth. But, as only the Indian civil service could manage, I was assigned to a compartment where the other person was a bride on her honeymoon.

I WAS BEGINNING to think Mel Brooks managed the state railways or that at least Gene Wilder was running some of the trains. It should have taken only a brief conversation with the conductor for me to change berths with the perplexed groom. But this was India, where making train reservations is a full-time job. Neither pathos, piety, or courage worked on the conductor. I switched to what Mark Twain called "bucksheesh" and the honeymoon resumed—producing, at a later date, a son they named Matthew, although that was because I left, not because I stayed.

I hated Delhi. The heat was stifling. I stayed in the dreadful Hotel 55, where I argued with the staff and fought with pickpockets. For the only time on my circumnavigation, I called home—waking up my then girlfriend, now wife, with gushing I-miss-you confessions. But traveling into northern India revived me, and I finally crossed from Armritsar into Pakistan on foot, the border being closed to local traffic. A porter carried my bag on his head.

After the din of India—a Sikh friend said it "takes three weeks to adjust"—I found Pakistan tranquil, perhaps because on my first day I paid five dollars for a day at a hotel swimming pool. The amenities at my hotel, Faletti's, were limited to mosquitoes. In Lahore, I bought a carpet, had my hair cut on a roadside chair, and spent several days in the old city, which is dominated by several grand mosques, all of which were cool and peaceful, faces of Islam and Pakistan lost in today's prime-time translations.

My goal in Pakistan was to visit the Afghan refugee camps outside Peshawar. I got there by a combination of bus, taxi, and rental car, and visited the tent villages of Afghans who had fled the Russian invasion of their country. Peshawar is a frontier town. Numerous stores were selling rifles and ammo, as if it were the Wild West, which it was then and remains today.

My Pan Am flight for London left from Karachi at 4:30 A.M. in the morning. I flew there the day before—weary of subcontinental trains. Today Karachi is a poster city for anti-Americanism. Even then it was a city of random street violence and police brutality. I wanted to visit one of the mosques, but my cab driver warned me off. Instead I rode a camel along the Arabian Sea and found an airport hotel where the rooms made those at the Tokyo Family look spacious.

In my mind the trip (which cost less than $2,000), ended late the next morning in London, where I arrived on a crisp, clear August day. England was in the midst of a drought, which gave that day the feel of an American summer. Even the grass in Hyde Park was parched. It felt wonderful to be in a familiar setting, even if the locals were still drinking milky tea. I had mail waiting; one letter was even a job offer. I made plans to see friends and longed to take an endless shower. But first I found a lawn chair in Green Park (surrounded by imperial buildings as grand as the ruins in Calcutta) and fell fast asleep, lost to the world I had just encircled.

Iranamok
(2006)

ASSUMING THAT THE Islamic Republic of Iran does not get
blown off the nuclear map, my sense of recent events is that
Tehran is the clear winner in the war on terrorism. Prior to
September 11, Iran had a revolutionary past, and an uncertain
future. Students—presumably clamoring for blue jeans and
mascara—were rioting against the Persian theocracy. On its
borders it had enemies in Saddam Hussein's Iraq and the
Taliban's Afghanistan, not to mention oil competition from
another traditional foe, Azerbaijan. As always the United
States was hostile, invoking economic sanctions, and the Russian fear of Islam's dry wind blowing sparks across its former
Central Asian republics had Moscow lined up against the
mullahs. But then the enemies of our enemies were reincar-
nated as the coalition of the willing, and Iran found itself
happily being pulled to regional predominance in the wake
of the Great Satan's post-9/11 crusades.

Beginning in November 2001, America stepped up to do
the mullahs' bidding. It pushed the Sunni-rooted Taliban out
of Afghanistan, leaving large portions of that country in the

control of warlords, some of whom are in the pay of Tehran. Next the United States turned on Iraq, overthrew Hussein (who had fought a grisly eight-year war against Iran), and, as it dismantled the Iraqi military, announced that the battlefield objective was to bring democracy to the Sunni triangle. Jefferson had no such illusions when he dealt with Barbary's pirates. But the administration of George W. Bush hoped the idea of a democratic Middle East would play well on sound-bite storyboards. Instead, in Iraq, as the United States removed the minority Sunnis and Baathists from power, it positioned Baghdad either for a Shiite-dominated government (which would be friendlier with Iran) or civil war (also an Iranian interest). As if those gifts were not enough to the heirs of Ayatollah Ruhollah Khomeni, the Bush administration went for an Iran trifecta when it used its swagger to evict the Syrian army from Lebanon—leaving that troubled country more at the mercy of Hezbollah, the Iranian-backed terrorists from whose ranks suicide bombers are routinely recruited. Thus in a few short years, Iran went from fearing a New Age or consumerist counterrevolution to its restoration as the regional great power in the Middle East—all thanks to the theocracy in Washington that, presumably, shares some of its fundamentalist values.

You would have thought that the ayatollahs might have shown some gratitude towards their American soldiers of fortune. After all, al-Qaida's pretensions toward predominance in the Arab world had origins in the Sunni madrassas of Saudi Arabia, not the holy city of Qom. But rather than reward the Americans with some discounted crude oil or invite President Bush to spend New Year's Eve in Persepolis, as the Shah would have done, the mullahs decided to follow up their victories by pushing ahead with plans to enrich uranium and possibly construct nuclear weapons. Seen from Tehran, the choice of atomic energy or a bomb was a no-lose proposition. As follows: once Iran had a nuclear capability, it would no longer fear an invasion from American-occupied Iraq. At the same time it could rally the Arab faithful around the idea of finally having the capacity to "wipe Israel off the map." Yes, the UN could issue sanctions, and the air forces of either the United States or Israel might take out some cooling towers or research laboratories. But those would be minor setbacks and, perversely, might confirm Iran's status as the pre-eminent Middle Eastern power—once again capable of holding the West hostage. Bomb technology might also serve notice on domestic opponents of the mullahs, who in 2005 had banned more than a thousand candidates in regional and national elections and then backed the presidential candidacy of Mahmoud Ahmadinejad, who, to celebrate his victory, decided to win friends and influence allies by announcing the Holocaust a "myth."

Obviously, like anyone who would rather not see Istafan turn into a nuclear Sarajevo, I would like to think the Bush administration is capable of "muddling through" this crisis (as was said of the incompetent Hapsburg government of Franz Joseph). But I am not optimistic. My sense is that the U.S. government needs the idea of a "Mad Fakir" in Tehran just as much as the Iranian government needs to fill the streets with demonstrators rallying against the "Enemy of Islam." Nor do I believe that this nuclear showdown will be easily halted before the brink. Each side has too much invested in its enemy.

JUST A SUMMARY of American-Iran relations should not give anyone reason to hope that Washington has broken the da Vinci code to understanding Iran. Leaving aside 10,000 years of Persian history, let's move the clock to 1953, when British and American intelligence agencies staged a coup against the possibly communist-influenced prime minister, Mohammad Mossadegh, who had nationalized the British-owned Anglo-Iranian Oil Company. Returned to the throne in Iran was Shah Mohammad Reza Pahlavi, whose father—a mid-ranking Iranian military officer—had seized power by a coup in 1925 and proclaimed himself "Shah." In the early 1950s, Iran was seen as a swing vote in the Cold War, and the Truman administration feared that Iran, and its oil, would become another satellite in orbit around the Soviet Union. But the memory of the coup has made the United States an anathema to many Iranians.

Grateful to the Americans for his restoration from exile, the Shah recast the Persian Empire as a modern Western state. In exchange for serving the Americans' security and petroleum interests in the region, he was given carte blanche to skim state profits and crack down on domestic opposition, which included those like the exiled Ayatollah Khomeini, who wanted Iran to became an Islamic state. Neither all the Shah's SAVAK agents nor all the Shah's men, however, could keep a lid on this dissident movement. In January 1979—a year after President and Mrs. Carter had spent New Year's Eve in Tehran and called the Shah "an island of stability"— Pahlavi fled his country. Fearful of reprisal, Carter refused to grant his friend asylum, and the exiled leader wandered the world, as Henry Kissinger put it, like the Flying Dutchman, finding shelter in places like the Bahamas, Panama, and Egypt. When the Shah's cancer worsened in October 1979, he was finally allowed into the United States for treatment. In response, militant students in Tehran stormed the American embassy—taking sixty-six hostages, fifty-one of whom they held from November 1979 to January 1981.

Carter froze Iran's assets in the United States and cut off Iranian petroleum imports, but clearly those holding the American hostages were neither oil traders nor foreign investors. The nightly television news featured bound and gagged American diplomats, who became synonymous with Carter's missing mojo. To recapture his mettle, the President then launched one of the oddest rescue missions in military history, in which a platoon of airborne forces, cruising the Iranian deserts in helicopters, were suppose to liberate the hostages, then held in various locations around a chaotic city of four million residents. Some of the helicopters crashed in a desert sandstorm, the mission was aborted, and the Iranians only released the hostages on the day Ronald Reagan was sworn in as the next president—giving rise to the suspicion that Reagan's campaign had found the hostages as convenient a campaign symbol as did Ayatollah Khomeini.

In the years that followed, the Reagan administration may have thought that it could "do business" with the Imam, who clearly understood the politics of television as well as the Reagan "imagineers." But the Ayatollah proved a spiritual heir to another Persian sect, the assassins of the twelfth and thirteenth centuries, rather than another Middle Eastern potentate eager to jet ski in Cannes. Iran sought to export its Shiite fundamentalism around the Middle East. For example, it backed Hezbollah in the anarchic Lebanese civil war, hoping to secure some missile launch pads near the Israeli border. It may well have plotted the 1983 suicide bombing of the American barracks in Beirut that killed 240 marines. But by that point Iran was involved in trench warfare with Saddam Hussein's Iraq, which enjoyed support, including the ingredients of chemical weapons, from such western powers as Germany, the UK and the United States. (Remember when Reagan sent Donald Rumsfeld on bended knee to Saddam?) Essentially the American strategy in the Iran-Iraq war was to bleed two unpopular regimes, keep an eye out for Israel, and to maintain access to Persian Gulf oil. Iran, however, saw Western trademarks on the incoming canisters of chemical weapons—one reason that today it continues to work so feverishly toward producing an atomic bomb.

Then in the mid-1980s the United States decided to sell weaponry to the mullahs, touching off what came to be known as the Iran-Contra affair, something that suggested that Ronald Reagan had never outgrown his fondness for vaudeville. In this triangular trade, hatched in the mind of Lt. Colonel Oliver North—but backed by everyone in the Reagan administration still in the "loop"—the Americans would sell Iran advanced guided missiles. Israel would act as the middleman, and the proceeds from the arms deals would be sent to the "contras," forces opposed to the ruling Sandinistas in Nicaragua. The reason money for Central American freedom fighters was laundered through Iran was because Congress had outlawed aid to the contras. (A number of Reagan administration officials were later sentenced to jail for lying to Congress over the affair. Bush Senior, however, pardoned them. Bush Junior now has some of them back working in places like the state and defense departments.)

The high-water mark of this deadly burlesque came when Reagan's National Security advisor, Robert C. "Bud" McFarlane, flew to Tehran on an Israeli chartered plane. To confirm his diplomatic bona fides, he had with him a Bible and a chocolate cake. The reason that the United States was doing business at all with Tehran is that the weapon sales were ransom payments for American hostages held in Beirut. For a while these strange dealings prolonged the slaughter in the trenches between Iran and Iraq and topped up the contras' bank accounts. But then Iran realized that hostages were a freely convertible currency, and grabbed a few every time they grew low on ammunition. On November 13, 1986, President Reagan said: "There's been no evidence of Iranian government complicity in acts of terrorism against the United States." Three days later, his Secretary of State, George Shultz, said: "Iran has and continues to pursue a policy of terrorism."

About the time that MacFarlane and his cake were in Tehran, a U.S. guided-missile cruiser, on station in the Persian Gulf (but largely there to protect shipments of Iraqi crude oil), shot down an Iran Air commercial flight, killing some 290 passengers. The USS *Vincennes* had confused the civilian Airbus for an attacking Iranian fighter, and launched its missiles. For that engagement, the Navy decorated the ship's captain. Although it was never proved, as the trail of money and Semtex wove through places like Syria and Libya, it was always suspected that the Iranian government sponsored the 1988 bombing of Pan Am flight 103 over Lockerbie, Scotland, in revenge for the loss of its flight to Bandar-Abbas.

Ayatollah Khomeini died in 1989. At his public funeral, as the body was being carried through Tehran, frenzied mourners rioted and nearly managed to destroy the casket and pitch the dead Imam into the street. Some ten thousand people were injured. Subsequently, during the 1990s, it appeared as though the hard-line relations between Iran and the United States might thaw, especially when so-called reformers occupied more positions of authority within the Iranian government. In the world of Apple computers and Nike sneakers, the Islamic Republic of Iran looked increasingly like Albania or North Korea, countries clothed behind veils of unreality. During the attacks against the Taliban in November 2001, Iran let American forces use certain port facilities. Then, two months later, in his 2002 State of the Union address, President Bush christened the "axis of evil," and included Iran on the list, infuriating Tehran. A year later, not only were American armored forces patrolling the Iraq-Iran border, but also there was talk in the administration and in sympathetic think tanks about how "the road to Tehran lies through Baghdad." So much for reconciliation.

Within the Bush administration, there are two schools of thought with regard to the Islamic Republic of Iran: those who would open a dialogue with the mullahs (sometimes this is called "constructive engagement") and those who would use the American presence in Iraq to launch either an invasion or a pre-emptive strike against the revolutionary council's nuclear facilities. Recently, after an earthquake in Iran, President Bush sent aid to the victims, and spoke of the differences between the Iranian people and those running its government. According to an official quoted in *The New Yorker*, the goal of this kind of engagement is to "talk to them—but with the purpose of overthrowing them." But more hard-liners, notably the circle around Vice President Dick Cheney, see war with Iran over its nuclear capacity as inevitable. They imagine using lightening air strikes to "take out" Iran's uranium enrichment program. As one strategist said: "it could all be done in a single night," which sounds ominously like the refrain in August 1914, that the "troops would be home for Christmas."

IN RECENT WEEKS, while thinking about the coming Iranian-American confrontation over Iran's nuclear capability,

I searched the Internet for a clear statement from President Bush on how he views the Iranian situation. At the same time, I attended a speech in Geneva, Switzerland, given by the Iranian foreign minister on "Iran and the Nuclear Issue." Having now listened to them both, I cling to my belief that this conflict will only end badly—in this sense: I fear that the Americans will first try to set the clock back to 1953 and attempt to overthrow the Iranian government, preferring, in the first stage, covert action to air strikes. But later, especially if the 2006 midterm election looks to be going poorly for the Republicans, I could well imagine that Karl Rove might call the nation to general quarters over Iran's looming nuclear arsenal.

From its side, I sense the Iranians feel their survival as an independent nation is linked to having nuclear weapons, which will give them the opportunity to menace Israel or to take hostages from a distance—and thus keep alive the dream of a theocratic Persian empire. Either way, the two countries seem incapable of rational dialogue.

Let's hear about Iran, first and at length, from President Bush, who recently gave an Iraq set speech to Freedom House in Washington and then took questions from the audience. The point he is trying to make is that Iran needs to hear from many countries, not just the United States, that its pursuit of uranium enrichment, were it to lead toward a weapons capability, is viewed as dangerous and unacceptable. But from the transcript of the President's response, what is most apparent is that his manner of thinking resembles that of some corrupted computer hard drive, broken into a series of partitions, none of which can connect and articulate a coherent position.

Here is what the President said, in answer to a question: THE PRESIDENT: "The Iranian issue is more—in dealing with

Iran, we're dealing with more than just influence into the formation of [Iraq's] national unity government. I happen to believe that ultimately the Iraqis will say, we want to have our own government. We want to be on our own feet. We've had a little problem with Iran in the past and, therefore, let us kind of manage our own affairs. No question right now we're concerned, however, about influencing the formation of the government, but also, obviously, we're deeply concerned about whether or not the Iranians have the wherewithal and/or the knowledge about building a nuclear weapon.

"My negotiation strategy on this issue is that I believe it is better for the Iranians to hear from more than one voice as to whether or not the world accepts them as a viable nation in the international affairs. And so we have asked Germany and France and Great Britain to take the lead, to send a clear message to the Iranian government.

"It's difficult to negotiate with non-transparent societies. It's easier for a non-transparent society to try to negotiate with countries in which there's a free press and a free political opposition and a place where people can express their opinions, because it sometimes causes people to play their cards publicly. In negotiating with non-transparent societies, it's important to keep your counsel.

"But I am pleased with the progress we have made on the diplomatic front. As you know, there are now talks of a presidential letter out of the United Nations, and my Secretary of State, working with Ambassador John Bolton, are constructing such a letter and trying to make sure that there is common consensus, particularly amongst the P5 plus Germany. As a matter of fact, Condi leaves I think today, if not tomorrow, for Europe to sit down with the P5 plus Germany to continue keeping people knitted up on our strategy. Obviously, there's some cross pressures to some members of the P5. There's a lot of politics in Europe—which is a good thing, by the way, that people are questioning whether or not it's worth it to try to stop the Iranians from having a nuclear weapon. I just believe strongly it's worth it. Now is the time to deal with these problems before they become acute.

"I'm troubled by a non-transparent regime having a weapon which could be used to blackmail freedom-loving nations. I'm troubled by a president who has declared his intentions to destroy our ally Israel. And we need to take these admonitions and these threats very seriously in order to keep the peace."

Not long after the President made these stream-of-unconscious remarks, Seymour Hersh reported in *The New Yorker* that U.S. military planners had "not ruled out" using tactical nuclear weapons on various Iranian nuclear facilities. Under the administration's Orwellian logic, this phrase does not mean the United States had decided to use tactical nuclear weapons against Iranian reprocessing laboratories buried underground; only that it had not eliminated tactical nuclear weapons in the arsenal of any possible attack against Iran. But when it comes to confront Iran on the nuclear issue, the United States will discover that it is more isolated than it thinks in the Middle East, and that the region's system of alliances more resembles the anarchy of the Balkans in 1914 than the system of checks and balances that lead to stability in Europe after the 1815 Congress of Vienna.

Here's a brief update on who is friends with whom in the Middle East:

—The United States has Britain and Israel as firm friends and allies of convenience in Afghanistan and Pakistan—so long as the money keeps rolling in. In the oil states of the

Persian Gulf, the U.S. has suppliers, or customers, but not really allies.

—Russia, wary of American encroachments in Central Asia, has looked to expand its relations with Turkey, and renew those with Syria. Plus it would like to be the "honest broker" in solving the Iranian standoff, and thus capture that rich market for itself. Both Russia and Iran oppose American efforts to siphon Caspian Sea oil west through Georgia and Turkey.

—Turkey, which would like to be closer to the European Union, failed to support the American invasion of Iraq, fearing it could lead to an independent Kurdistan, which would threaten Turkey's territorial integrity. In recent years, its ties with Israel have waned, as it seeks Syrian support on the Kurdish question and thus it has developed more ties with Russia and, by extension, Iran.

—India, fretful about all the American aid pouring into Pakistan, demanded, and received, commercial nuclear technology from the Bush administration, despite the fact that India has steadfastly refused to sign the Nuclear Non-Proliferation Agreement (NPT), a treaty that even Iran has signed. Presumably, the Americans let India have more nuclear genies, thinking some help may be required in a face-off between war-headed Iran and (in a worst case) a more fundamentalist regime in Pakistan.

—If Iraq dissolves into civil war, neither the Americans nor its coalition allies will know whom to support. Support the Shiite majority, and you help Iran. Help the Kurds achieve independence, and you start a war with Turkey. Restore the Sunnis or the Baathists, and you will have fought a war both to topple Saddam Hussein and then another to restore his followers to power.

—In Iran, the confrontation with the Great Satan continues to solidify the power of the mullahs, at a time when they could have been marginalized. Meanwhile, Iran is well positioned in Lebanon to press the campaign against Israel, has some Russian support (at least for its commercial nuclear intentions), has less to fear from Afghanistan, is well-positioned in southern (Shiite) Iraq, and now is coming to the table with nuclear cards.

THE FOREIGN MINISTER of Iran is Dr. Manouchehr Mottaki, who addressed, in good English, the Geneva Centre for Security Policy. He appeared behind the lectern wearing a black suit and a high white collar, making me think I was listening to an Iranian Woodrow Wilson. To get to his position, he has risen through the ranks at the ministry of foreign affairs. I find his academic background odd, at least for someone hired by the revolutionary council to justify to the West Iran's nuclear strategy. He received his undergraduate degree in Bangalore, India, and most of his academic writings have focused on Iran's relations with Japan. Maybe he's there to keep a big client happy? Often overlooked is the fact that Japan would have the most to lose if UN sanctions were voted against Iran. The Islamic Republic supplies 15 percent of Japan's energy needs, and no one needs a reminder as to what happened the last time Japan's oil trade was cut off.

In defending Iran's nuclear option, Dr. Mottaki invited many atomic chickens, first hatched by the United States, to come home to roost. On the matter of national security, he invoked the specter of 9/11 to argue that all countries have the right of self-defense. He aligned Iran with "multilateralism" and the ideas of collective security, in contrast to the "unilateral" approach taken by the Bush administration in Iraq. He made the point that Iran has been a member of the IAEA (International Atomic Energy Agency) for thirty-six years but now asked: "Why can't we enjoy the privileges of membership?" (It made the bomb sound like an American Express card.) He equated Iran with environmentalism: "Why can't we have clean nuclear energy?" Of course, he attacked Israel: "The nuclear program of the Zionist regime and its nuclear weapons, which are outside the safeguard regime, are a threat against regional peace and security." But the sophistry reached its height when Dr. Mottaki invoked the spirit of Thomas Jefferson, citing Iran's "inalienable right under international law to peaceful use of nuclear energy" and "a natural right of the Islamic Republic of Iran" for uranium enrichment. It reminded me of George Orwell's observation that: "War is peace. Freedom is slavery. Ignorance is strength." In that sense, I suppose the Declaration of Independence justifies going nuclear.

Of course, Dr. Mottaki is a professional diplomat, not unlike the Japanese foreign minister who in 1933 walked out of the League of Nations rather than answer questions about his country's invasion of Manchuria. But he preferred to score rhetorical points—"How can we trust a country that has already used atomic weapons on Hiroshima and Nagasaki?"—rather than explain how Iran has gotten as far has it has with its nuclear program. Several other countries, not unlike Iran in world politics—Brazil, South Korea, and Argentina—all undertook independent nuclear development, and each gave up before being able to process weapons-grade plutonium or to test-fire an accurate intercontinental ballistic missile. But no matter what it says in world forums, Iran is far down the road toward atomic independence, be it for clean energy or dirty bombs, although not for reasons that will ever appear in one of President Bush's press conferences.

In order to understand how we are approaching the nuclear precipice with Iran, I would suggest reading a two-part series that appeared in *The Atlantic* in the last year. The author is William Langewiesche, and the first part is entitled "The Wrath of Khan." It is a profile of a Pakistani atomic scientist, Dr. Abdu Quadeer Khan, who effectively stole nuclear technology from the West and coordinated Pakistan's development of nuclear weapons. The second essay has the title "The Point of No Return," and it describes how Dr. Kahn, undoubtedly with the knowledge and support of the Pakistani government, sold turnkey nuclear programs to a variety of rogue states, including North Korea, Libya, and Iran. In one of the series' more damning sentences, Langewiesche writes: "Though it would be politically inconvenient to admit this now, the United States was aware not only of Khan's peddling of nuclear wares to Iran but also of the likely involvement of the army and the government of Pakistan." He also concludes: "Indeed, Iran was Pakistan's longest-standing customer."

How it was possible for Pakistan, the American linchpin in the war on terror, to have sold nuclear technology to Iran makes compelling reading. Initially, Langewiesche writes, Kahn assisted the effort to build a Pakistani bomb out of fear and loathing for India: "He believed, as many Pakistanis still do, that India had never accepted the Subcontinent's partition, and (as he told his friends) that Hindus were tricksters with hegemonic designs." In the 1970s, India tested nuclear weapons not far from the border with Pakistan.

By 1982, thanks to Kahn, Pakistan had the capacity to make weapons-grade uranium. By 1984, "it was producing enough fissionable material to build several bombs a year." But once Kahn had developed a domestic nuclear capacity he needed missile technology for its delivery system, and that led him into business with North Korea, which traded information about its NoDang missile in exchange for some of Pakistan's enrichment components. Later, either for money or the glory of fathering a "Muslim bomb," Kahn started doing business with the likes of Saudi Arabia, Iran, and Libya. Pakistan became the Wal-Mart of the atomic bomb: a place to go for do-it-yourselfers.

Why the United States turned a blind eye to Pakistan's atomic warehouse is a mystery of criminal negligence. During the 1980s, the United States needed the support of Islamabad to fight its Afghan proxy war against the Russians. In the 1990s, it may also have tolerated a Pakistani bomb as a way to establish a balance of power on the Subcontinent; India had proven maddeningly non-aligned. After 9/11 the Bush administration bet all on finding Osama bin Laden, fighting the Taliban in Afghanistan, and launching its invasion of Iraq. For those enterprises, Pakistan was an indispensable, if shaky ally, and by all accounts the United States chose to ignore the signs that Dr. Kahn was wholesaling the country's atomic secrets.

Langewiesche is most scathing about the Bush administration's delay in releasing, until October 2002 (by which time Congress had authorized the invasion of Iraq), the intelligence information that Pakistan had supplied nuclear technology to North Korea. He continues: "The blundering of that fall defies belief: while dragging the United States into a disastrous war in the pursuit of phantom weapons programs in Iraq, the United States condoned the tangible actions of

Pakistan—which…was delivering nuclear-weapons capabilities into the hands of America's most significant enemies, including regimes with overt connections to Islamist terrorists." When the news broke that Pakistan, via Khan, was running an atomic chop shop, the government in Islamabad quietly pensioned off the scientist, confined him to a form of house arrest, and continued to round up the usual al-Qaida suspects. The United States did not react. Clearly someone left the yellowcake out in the rain.

WHAT WILL HAPPEN next in the nuclear showdown could well be the following: the United States will push the European Union to take the lead in confronting Iran's successful enrichment program, and there could be forms of so-called "smart sanctions" enforced against the Islamic Republic. In response, Iran will hole up in its nuclear bunkers, and then occasionally fire off some test ballistic missiles, to make the point that it has the capability to reach Tel Aviv or the West. More locally, it will increase the funding of subversion in southern Iraq, not to mention turning up the heat on Lebanese anarchy—both of which serve to undermine American interests in the Middle East.

From its side, the Bush administration will seize on the Iranian nuclear capability as the ideal midterm campaign issue, one both to justify the presence of American forces in Iraq and to make the electorate forget about Scooter Libby, the various deficits, and Jack Abramoff's Indians. Rove is also a big believer in the permanent state of war. I doubt, however, the Bush-Cheney war lobby will mobilize against Iran before the election, for the simple reason that it is thought to be years, not months, away from having the bomb. But, facing ruinous budget figures brought on by the splendid little war in

Baghdad, the administration will put its energies into covert operations against the mullahs. It will seem a cost-efficient front to open, and already the Deputy Assistant Secretary of State of Near Eastern Affairs has vastly increased the budget to besiege Tehran with what might be called Radio Free Iran. That Secretary also happens to be Elizabeth Cheney, Dr. Evil's daughter.

IN THINKING ABOUT the coming crisis with Iran, I can't help but be reminded of the Cuban Missile Crisis, those thirteen days in October 1962, when the world perched on the nuclear brink. At the time I was eight-years-old and watched with my parents on a black-and-white television as President John F. Kennedy announced that he was placing Cuba (it always sounded like "Cuber") under quarantine. Even in the third grade, I was obsessed with what the teacher called "current events," and every day I brought clippings to class to indicate where the American Navy was stationed and how long it would take the Russian missile ships to reach the blockade. I had enormous admiration, as well, for President Kennedy. I had seen him during the 1960 campaign and knew intimately the story of PT 109, which had seen service among the same Pacific islands where my own father's infantry battles had taken place. But during the Missile Crisis, school children spent a lot of time under their desk or in the halls, hands covering our heads, drilling for deliverance.

What I learned later was that Soviet Premier Nikita Khrushchev had acted from weakness, rather than strength, in sending Russian missiles to Cuba. He had seen the gap widening between American and Soviet atomic capabilities, and figured a few intercontinental ballistic missiles off the Florida Keys might narrow the divide. He withdrew his missiles in exchange for guarantees that the United States would not invade Cuba and for dismantling NATO missiles in Turkey. Could Iran's supreme council be arming for the same reasons of weakness, fearful of American troops on their border and nuclear weapons held by Pakistan and Israel, both in America's pocket?

The differences between the Cuban Missile Crisis and today's Iranian nuclear standoff are many, but perhaps most striking is the incongruous background of the respective leadership in the U.S. and Iran from those, in 1962, who were running America and the Soviet Union. Kennedy had seen war among the bloody waters of the Solomon Islands, in some stretches known then and now as Iron Bottom Sound, for all the ships sunk at a cost of thousands of lives. Khrushchev had served in World War II as the commissar with Russian forces holding the desperate line at Stalingrad, where more than a million lives were lost between the German and Russian armies in a campaign that unfolded as the Americans were clinging to the beachhead at Guadalcanal. I sense that by 1962 both leaders had seen enough war to last them a lifetime.

In their place today, in both the United States and Iran, are men comfortable with the chants of religious fundamentalism, for whom Armageddon is more a promised land than a mine field to be avoided. The current Bush administration places great faith in a military in which few of them served while the mullahs, not to mention the country's new president, owe their tenuous political legitimacy to the halcyon days when Iran held America hostage. Sadly, President George W. Bush may be "no Jack Kennedy." My fear is that he will confront Iran much the way, after 9/11, he reduced the complicated history of Iraq and the Middle East to the simplistic plots of a Clint Eastwood movie ("We're taking that fucker out."). But this time he will be confronting an enemy of religious zealots for whom martyrdom—yours and theirs—is one of the recommended paths to salvation.

An Easter in Serbia

(2005)

DURING WINTER'S DISCONTENT, that stretch of dark no-man's land between New Year and springtime, I asked the children at dinner one night if they had any ideas for an Easter vacation. Although we live in secular Switzerland, where the churches look like chalets and everyone skis on Sundays, Easter merits an important school break—from the Wednesday before Good Friday through Easter and the following week, making it a good time to travel. As always in these conversations, the children quickly put into nomination such familiar candidates as the Maldives, the Caribbean, and the Mediterranean, standbys in their travel dreams. Ours is a family that dreams of warm water more than did the Russian tsars. In gentle opposition, I suggested that this might be the time for us to take the train around the contours of ex-Yugoslavia. What little family we have in Europe lives in Belgrade, and I sketched out a journey that, in addition to Easter in Serbia, included stops in Venice and Budapest, destinations I thought might at least swing my wife's vote.

Needless to say, Serbia did not pass by acclamation. Subtle questions were raised about the plumbing that might be encountered. A few of the geopoliticians around the table discussed the recent wars. The teenage girls announced flatly: "We are not going," as if in support of a United Nations resolution. My wife rolled her eyes when saying, "but we just went to Croatia," referring to a summer trip in 1999 down the Dalmatian coastline. The boys, 8 and 11, and younger than their sisters, were tempted by the idea of overnight train travel (*"Remember how much we love the upper berths?"* one of them recalled), but I could sense that the political machine was moving in on their votes. "Do you know what the food is going to be like?" the boys were asked. "Remember the hot dogs we had for breakfast in Croatia?" When the polls closed, the vote followed the lines of one of President Lincoln's cabinet meetings, of which he observed: "There were seven nays and one yea—the yeas carried it."

The reason I insisted on Serbia had less to do with wanting the family to encounter suspect plumbing or to drag them through what had been a war zone than to continue a family connection that dates to 1970, when my parents took their three children to Yugoslavia. Since that trip, our family had retained close ties to the children of my father's cousin, men now in their sixties, whom we call Stasha and Boba. After we moved from New York to Switzerland, they became our European family, and we would see them, when we could, during Christmas and other holidays. But my children had never been to Belgrade nor seen Koprivnica, the Serbian village where my grandfather, Milivoy Stanoyevich, was born. In addition, Stasha, who has lived in Paris since the 1960s, had married a Frenchwoman, and she had never seen the house where he had grown up. Similarly, my sister's husband had never been to Slovenia, which his own grandfather left during World War I. There were thus many reasons to visit Serbia, and the occasion became the dedication of the small Koprivnica church, to which my father and I had contributed money in 2003 to help with a restoration.

At the Geneva railroad station, some weeks before we departed, I booked a series of overnight sleepers: from Geneva to Venice, and then from Ljubljana to Belgrade. On the way home, we would take day trains to Budapest and Vienna, and then an overnight sleeper to Geneva. In between we would spend a day in Venice, a week in Serbia, and then a few days in the remnants of the Austro-Hungarian Empire, where it was said that, among his many palaces, Emperor Franz Josef had ten thousand rooms. I only needed two of them, for the nights we would not be on a train. Via the Internet I had no trouble booking accommodation in hotels along our route. I even decided to surprise my wife with a suite in Belgrade. Her initial enthusiasm for that luxury faded when she found out that many of the overnight trains arrived at 6:30 in the morning. (*"You call that a vacation?"* she asked on several occasions.)

Not even the amplification that the Venice train would arrive "at 7:36 A.M." provoked much revelry among the children, who, the day we left, joylessly assembled backpacks in the hall. My wife came downstairs carrying her bag and some odd pieces of wire. A plumber working at the house that day had heard of our trip "east" and launched into a long story about how thieves on Balkan trains used sleeping gas to knock out travelers and then loot their luggage. Only wire on the compartment door could thwart these gangs, he had explained, although my wife was packing what looked like picture wire, perhaps thinking that we would be fooling art thieves. Wired, perhaps in several ways, we parked at the station, hauled the backpacks to the train, bought soda and wine in the station, and, once aboard our sleeper, headed east on a long gentle arc around the western shores of Lake Geneva.

Venice: *"with the elation of Byron"*

WE AWOKE AS the train crossed the long bridge that connects Venice to the mainland. I poked my head out of the car window and spotted a freight train sporting the label "U.S. Steel Serbia," perhaps one of the spoils of war. We checked our luggage, passed on the idea of station showers, and bought day passes for the *vaporetto*, the Venetian water buses. In early sunshine, some of the best on the trip, we caught the boat heading to St. Mark's Square. Although we were tired from a restless night, needed breakfast, and were squeezed among morning commuters, I still sailed the Grand Canal with the elation of Byron.

I first saw Venice in 1970, on a family trip similar to the one I was now leading. We passed three days in Venice, although the pleasures of a go-cart track, set up near Harry's Bar, proved more alluring to those American children than did the splendors of St Mark's or the Doge's Palace. (Maybe Byron had this in mind when he despaired: *"This is a veritable school of disillusion."*) To make up for that earlier dilettantism, as we glided along, I pointed out various palaces, including Palazzo Mocenigo, that was inhabited by Byron himself. In *Byron's Travels*, a book I greatly admire, the historian Alan Massie describes the muse's household:

In addition to the Swiss mongrel Mutz and the bulldog Moretto, the Palazzo soon accommodated numerous birds, including crows and at one point an eagle, many other dogs, cats, monkeys, a fox and wolf. Many were transients, but they contributed to the atmosphere of negligent and disorganized splendour that Byron radiated.

It was pretty early for the romantic poets (*"I stood in Venice, on the Bridge of Sighs/A Palace and Prison on each hand"*), but also for the tourists, and with the sun coming up we had St. Mark's Square to ourselves. The cathedral and the campanile were still closed, so we continued along the seafront, peeked into the stately Danieli Hotel (Was this Byron's *"Holy Alliance of obscurantism and privilege"*?), and ate morning ice cream while waiting for the Naval Museum to open. Looking out on the Venetian seascape, I was reminded of a line in one of my guide books "that in Venice, more than anywhere else, the whole is greater than the sum of the parts." Then I tried to tell the children that the city was unchanged since 1970, except for the absence of go-carts. But I was corrected. One of the children knew from *National Geographic* that Venice had sunk twenty-three centimeters in the last century. So much for paternal omniscience.

In fact, another changing of the generational guard came during our day in Venice; my oldest daughter, Helen, now sixteen, took command of the tour. She first saw the city when she was nine, together with her mother and grandmother, and by all accounts she threw as many tantrums as there were Barbie dolls in her luggage. My wife remembers her tears when she entered a restaurant reeking of fresh fish and, more appropriately, on the Bridge of Sighs. But since then, she has studied Venice's history and architecture, spent time on the canals with several classes, and now knew her way around far-flung ferry stops. (*"No, Daddy, you go to the left here."*) Thanks to her guiding, we walked around the Arsenal, found glass blowers on Murano, and had a perfect tired-traveler's lunch near the Accademia. I have noticed that parents give up their authority with great reluctance. With my own parents I can still feel, at times, fourteen. At least here the power sharing took place in a setting worthy of Turner.

Slovenia: all aboard the *Casanova*

THE TRAIN TO Ljubljana operated under the name *Casanova*, although instead of reclining sofas and dim lighting, the interior was brightly lit and the seats more resembled those of a Metroliner than the dingy Balkan compartments of my childhood. Despite my wad of train tickets, I lacked reservations for this express. Fortunately, the train had spare seats, and the conductor was cheerful, especially after I paid an additional € 48 for reservations. The trip to the Slovenian capital took four hours. I read while my wife dosed. The children slept against their backpacks, nibbled on chocolate bars, and read magazines. But after the train left the Italian vineyards and flatlands, all of us became fascinated, knowing that Slovenia was new to the European Union.

When Bismarck said that politics was not an exact science, he could well have been referring to the lands around Trieste. In the last hundred years, the governments there have been Austrian, Italian, Yugoslav, German, Yugoslav, and Slovenian. In earlier times, they were Venetian and French. At the Paris Peace Conference in 1919, President Wilson was under the mistaken assumption that Trieste was a German city. That didn't stop him from drawing a line that divided

Istria between Italy and the Kingdom of Serbs, Croats and Slovenes. In 1991 Slovenia was the first of the former Yugoslav republics to declare independence. Its departure from Tito's federation triggered little fighting, as that republic had neither Serbian nor Croatian minorities. More recently Slovenia became the first of the former Yugoslav republics to join the European Union. Indeed, as the train snaked among the mountain passes that connect Ljubljana to the coastline, it felt more like we were approaching Salzburg than a Balkan capital. The houses were clean and modern, with roofs of red tile. A late spring snowstorm had covered the high ground and muddied the roads. The journey was remarkable for the prosperity of the villages.

My sister Nanette and her husband, Joe, surrounded by three weeks' worth of luggage, met us at the central Ljubljana station. By now it was cold and dark, and we needed dinner before boarding the night train to Belgrade. For whatever reason, the only station restaurant closed at 8:00 P.M., and a nearby McDonald's appealed only to the children, who immediately mastered enough Slovenian to order Happy Meals. My wife and Joe, neither of whom grew up idling on Balkan railway platforms, looked a bit skeptical in the station half-light. But my sister and I both knew the situation called for a railway Stevenson picnic. With the briefest discussion we crossed the street to a small supermarket and bought two grilled chickens, fresh bread, cheese, red wine, chocolate, and mineral water. After our train departed at 9:05 P.M., we spread out the picnic on a lower berth, where we ate chicken with our fingers and toasted each other with wine in plastic cups.

Although my sister and I had once taken a night train from Venice to Belgrade, made memorable by the heating

217

failure in the car, this evening, in particular, evoked one we had shared in 1965 with my father in Mexico.

We were, respectively, ages ten and twelve, and he had taken us on a business trip that started in New York and ended in Oaxaca, entirely by train. (For the last night, as a reward, we flew to Acapulco and swam in the Pacific Ocean.) On the overnight train from Mexico City to Oaxaca, my father discovered that the train had no dining car. At the last minute he had sprinted into the station maelstrom to secure dinner. Seconds before the train departed—at least in my mind, which feared a fatherless exile on the Mexican railways—he returned with grilled chickens, indistinguishable from those I was now eating with my own family, in a similarly worn third-world sleeping car.

Needless to say, not many tourists go to Belgrade, and few who do choose a night train from Ljubljana. *Cook's European Timetable* lists the train as the *Olympus*, which implies God-like service from Slovenia to Thessalonika. During the recent Balkan wars this service was cut and has only recently been restored. The sleeping car was tired, if not dirty, and the *Olympus* ran local for much of the night, forever shunting cars and stopping to take on border guards. We were crossing Slovenia, Croatia, and Serbia, and, as we were to discover, the Balkans remain a land of uneasy frontiers.

By 10:30 P.M. everyone was in bed. Three of the children were in one compartment. With one child, my wife and I were in another. The rooms were not connected. We could, however, tap to each other on the compartment walls, and after a while worked out codes familiar to anyone who has watched prison movies.

Around 11:00 P.M., just after we had fallen asleep, came the first border crossing, that between Slovenia and Croatia.

We were stamped out of Slovenia and then into Croatia. No one asked if we had anything to declare. We did have five hundred dollars worth of household gifts for relatives in Belgrade, but I decided this wasn't the forum to review either family or Yugoslav history. After a little wall tapping, we all went back to sleep. At 4:00 A.M., the train stopped at the Croatian-Serbian frontier, and everyone's mood reflected the uncomfortable time and place. Police, immigration, and customs officers, from both countries, stormed through the car, rapping on the doors with their keys, shouting what sounded like *"Policia, Policia."* It was the martial sound of angry republics. Only slowly did it dawn on me that much of this commotion was in front of the children's door.

Apparently neither Croatian nor Serbian border guards have ever tried to wake up a sleeping teenage girl, because they failed to rouse either one of ours, or their eight-year-old brother. Despite a lot of knocking, their door remained steadfastly closed. The guards summoned the sleeping-car porter, either to open the door or to explain who was inside. He retrieved a manifest of the passengers, but then confronted an inexplicable aspect of modern American families: that mothers do not always share the last name of their children. Both my wife and my sister kept their maiden names after marrying. Thus the porter decided that the mother of the slumbering children was my sister, who bears the name Stevenson, as do the children. With a flashlight the guards pounded on her compartment—no doubt still redolent of chicken—and demanded to know if the children were hers? Who knows what they thought when she answered no or if it mattered who was sharing Father Stevenson's compartment? By then, however, my younger daughter, Laura, had opened the door and flashed the passports, much the way her sleepy hand can snap off an alarm clock. I joined the commotion only at the end, but long enough to glimpse the heavy boots on the border guards, their expressions of angry officialdom, their lineage to the recent civil wars. Ten years ago people had vanished off trains similar to this one.

A Yugoslav reader: *"history of an idea"*

LYING AWAKE ON my bunk, listening to the metal keys rap against the metal doors, I thought often of Yugoslavia's demise. My grandfather, whose village we were on the way to visit, left Serbia in 1908, never to return. One reason he was exiled was because he believed in the Yugoslav ideal, the union of South Slavs as an alternative to the domination either of Vienna or Istanbul. In the hundred years since his departure for America, the Yugoslav ideal has come and gone. Since 1991, the republics of the former Yugoslavia have divided into six countries—Slovenia, Croatia, Bosnia-Herzegovina, Serbia, Montenegro, and Macedonia. Within Serbia, Kosovo has declared independence, and while Bosnia-Herzegovina is considered one country, it could easily fracture along the lines of its ethnic frontiers—those separating Serbs, Croats, and Muslims.

Since the fall of Yugoslavia, I have spent a lot of time reading about its demise, just as I have traveled to each of its former republics. Beginning in the early 1990s, on a trip to Montenegro, I read Alex Dragnich's concise *Serbs and Croats: The Struggle in Yugoslavia*, which makes the point that Tito's artificial internal borders made war inevitable after Slovenia, Croatia and finally Bosnia declared independence. Once they became national boundaries, large minority populations—Serbs, Croats, and Muslims—found themselves living in countries not of their liking or choosing.

In the mid-1990s, I admired Mihailo Crnobrnja's *The Yugoslav Drama*, which concludes: "The crucial issue in both the constructions and destruction of Yugoslavia has been the fact that many Serbs live outside Serbia." A former Yugoslav ambassador to the European Union, Crnobrnja—despite writing during the worse of the civil wars—ends optimistically: "The encouraging fact is that Serbia, though it appears today to be an authoritarian, even brutal state, also has a deeply ingrained liberal democratic tradition, perhaps more of one than have the other nationalities or newly created independent states of former Yugoslavia."

In Zagreb in May 1999, I finished Laura Silber's and Allan Little's *The Death of Yugoslavia*, an account of the 1990s Balkan wars by two articulate and brave British journalists. Among their sad conclusions they noted: "The march to war in Bosnia-Herzegovina was a terrible doomed procession. It gathered speed when war erupted in neighboring Croatia, but might have been prevented if the European Community had not recognized Croatia as an independent state in January 1992. Bosnia's President Alija Izetbegovic then faced a stark choice—either to seek recognition or remain in Serb-dominated Yugoslavia." He achieved independence, but only after some 90,000 people were killed in battles that sought ethnic purity in lands that had been mixed for centuries.

On our family vacation along the Dalmatian coast in summer 1999, just after the war ended in Kosovo, I finished John R. Lampe's *Yugoslavia as History: Twice There Was a Country*, an examination of the country's dissolution in 1941 and 1991. "Now, after seventy years of two Yugoslavias, created by two world wars and their survivors," he writes nostalgically, "another war has incinerated even the identity. Perhaps the saddest of the present survivors are those for whom the ashes still glow. For they were Yugoslavs, and once, or twice, they had a country."

On a drive around the Former Yugoslav Republic of Macedonia in 2003, I found a poignant quote in Mark Mazower's *The Balkans*: "In one sense, a race in Macedonia is merely a political party." On that same trip, I read an account of the Balkan wars:

> The burning of villages and the exodus of the defeated population is a normal and traditional incident of all Balkan wars and insurrections. It is the habit of all these people. What they have suffered themselves, they inflict in turn upon others.

That paragraph was written about fighting in 1912 to 1913. It could well have described the years 1992 to 1995.

On this journey my literary tour guide was Stevan K. Pavlowitch, an emeritus professor of history at Southampton University in England. New York University Press published his book *Serbia: The History of an Idea* in 2002. My friend Tom Leonard, who lives in Pennsylvania, sent it to me with a short cover note: "I found this book at a splendid book store that just opened in Harrisburg, run by a couple of local professors. Do you know the author?" I did not, but during my long stretches of reading, as the trains worked their way around the Balkans, I came to admire the clarity of his insight into the rise and fall of Yugoslavia, as well as the history of Serbia. His introduction captures well the changing iconography of what it means to be a Serb or live in Serbia:

In modern times, Serbia and the Serbs have been noticed during the Eastern Crisis of 1875–8, when the insurgents of Herzegovina and Bosnia had a good press; in 1903, when the gruesome murder of King Alexander Obrenovic and Queen Draga shocked the courts and foreign ministries of the more conservative powers; in 1914–16, when gallant little Serbia stood up to, and was crushed by, the Central Powers, and when its cause was a good one, to be explained in schools and prayed for in churches; in 1941, when the Serbs were said to have done the same again by standing up to Hitler; and after Yugoslavia collapsed in 1991, when they were collectively seen as faceless war criminals, lookalikes of mispronounced President Milosevic, Dr Karadzic and General Mladic.

The train was pulling into the old Belgrade station, that which my grandfather left from when he went abroad. Along the tracks were abandoned cars and vacant lots of garbage, and the fences in the fields were made with fallen branches. But my mind was stuck on the Yugoslav question. When had it begun? What was the difference between Croatia and Serbia? Why had there been a civil war?

From Serbia to Yugoslavia: *"more realism than idealism"*

IN THE NINETEENTH century, the Yugoslav ideal developed as it presented both Serbs and Croats with an alternative to imperial servitude. Croatia was then one of the captive nations of Austro-Hungary, ruled from Budapest. Likewise, nineteenth-century Serbia, although nominally independent, feared an Ottoman restoration. Austria's 1908 annexation of Bosnia-Herzegovina had shown both Serbs and Croats that the great powers still wanted to divide and conquer the Balkans. Hence federation became a lesser evil than colonialism.

As a country, the Kingdom of Serbs, Croats, and Slovenes declared its independence in December 1918, thus presenting itself to the Paris Peace Conference as a *fait accompli*. A historian of that conference writes:

> On December 1, 1918, Prince Alexander of Serbia proclaimed the Kingdom of Serbs, Croats, and Slovenes. The name itself was a problem; non-Serbians generally preferred Yugoslavia because it implied a true union of equals. Serbians wanted a name that enshrined the central importance of Serbia.

As Pavlowitch writes, the idea of a union of South Slavs had gained momentum during World War I. The Western powers floated the notion to recruit allies in the fight against Austria and that "to pose publicly the Yugoslav question— the creation of a state of all Serbs, Croats and Slovenes— was at least a way of weakening the enemy, perhaps even guaranteeing the future."

In 1918, for both Croats and Serbs, union was the best of several bad choices. "The National Council in Zagreb," Pavlowitch writes, "faced the option of a Yugoslav union at any price, or partition of the formerly Hapsburg southern Slavs between Italy, Serbia, Austria, and Hungary, with a residual Croatia not unlike Albania." Croatia chose alliance with Serbia over dismemberment.

For Serbia, with its populations scattered across the Balkan Peninsula, the choice was either the Yugoslav federation or trying to make a go of Serbia as an independent country, sometimes called Greater Serbia. Pavlowitch writes: "But any solution except a Yugoslav one would have left ethnic Serbs outside Serbia, however much extended, and any addition to its territory would have taken in more non-Serbs." No matter how great Serbia would have been in 1918, it would still have left Serbs beyond the pale and absorbed unwarranted minorities. Plus it was easier for non-Serb minorities to accept Yugoslavia than it was to accept Serbia. Pavlowitch concludes: "The fact remains that Serbia's leaders, for motives of realism and idealism (probably more realism than idealism), went for Yugoslavia."

By the 1920s, both Austro-Hungary and the Ottoman Empire had vanished. Without mutual fears of imperial encroachment, the partnership between Serbs and Croats became tenuous. No outside forces held it in place. Forty percent of Yugoslavs were Serbs. Serbian politicians wanted to incorporate all Serbs into a single state, and in the 1920s they made little distinction between Yugoslavia and Serbia. Croatia rebelled against what it perceived as second-class status in the governing coalition. The kingdom of Yugoslavia came under pressure in 1929, after a Montenegrin representative assassinated several Croatian deputies on the floor of the Parliament. After that, King Alexander suspended the unworkable constitution.

Yugoslavia limped into the 1930s as a frail monarchy. In 1931 Alexander had re-established parliament but remained the "guardian of the unity of the nation and of the integrity of the state." In 1934, Croatian fascists assassinated him. Later in the decade, his brother Paul, as regent, flirted with fascism, hoping such sentiment might avoid or delay the outbreak of war. In March 1941, the military toppled Paul in a coup, and then reaffirmed Yugoslavia's western alliances. In response, Hitler bombed Belgrade on Easter Sunday 1941 and overran the country. "After the Belgrade coup of 27 March 1941," Pavlowitch writes, "Hitler had decided to destroy for ever the 'Versailles' construct that was Yugoslavia. He was angry that his immediate plans had been upset, and wanted to punish the Serbs, whom he saw as the main disturbers of the European order." In those sentiments Hitler was true to his Hapsburg origins.

From Tito to Milosevic: *"the issue of borders"*

DURING WORLD WAR II, Yugoslavia lost a fifth of its population and was occupied by armies from Germany, Italy, Albania, and Bulgaria until liberated by Tito's Partisans and the Russian army. "The outcome of the Second World War thus led again to a united Yugoslavia, this time under Communist rule," Pavlowitch summarizes. But the challenge for Tito, as it was for King Alexander, was to gerrymander Yugoslavia's ethnic mix so that no one nationality felt aggrieved in a federal structure. As Pavlowitch writes, it was not an easy task: "Yugoslavia's Communist leaders, just like their Soviet mentors, had exploited nationalism as a tactical device. They had always denounced 'greater-Serbian hegemony,' and they did not want a Serbia that dwarfed the other federated units. At the same time they utilized a structure to acquire and hold on to power that was largely manned by Serbs from Croatia and Bosnia." To weaken Serbia within Yugoslavia, Kosovo and Voivodina were declared autonomous regions, and Serbia's internal borders relegated many Serbs to other republics—not an issue so long as the republics maintained their feelings of fraternal solidarity.

I have never agreed with those who believe that Tito was the key to holding Yugoslavia together. Late in his life, Josef Broz, aka Tito, lived more like an Austrian squire than a Comintern revolutionary. He had summer and winter palaces, and entertained visiting movie stars, like Sophia Loren, on speed boats. As a swing vote in the Cold War, he collected tribute from both the American and Russian camps. He drained profits from places like Slovenia and Dubrovnik to subsidize failed industries in Bosnia and Kosovo. As a champion of non-alignment, he brought the Olympics to Sarajevo—which celebrated circuses over bread. By 1985 the country's foreign debt was $20 billion, and aggregate inflation since 1979 had exceeded 1,000 percent. Yugoslavia could survive as long as the Americans or the Russians would rollover Tito's interest payments. But that foreign aid ended with the fall of the Berlin Wall, when Yugoslavia's worker councils became an expense as frivolous as chamois shoots—something Tito exercised with passion. Within Yugoslavia, none of the constituent republics wanted to be stuck with the invoices of socialism. Rather than pay a share of what they owed on the $20 billion, they headed for the exits.

The problem with dismembering Yugoslavia was that its internal borders were drawn to prop up the Communist coalition, not to outline national boundaries. Pavlowitch concludes: "Serbia could not at present be a 'state' like the other republics, because of the way in which it had been fragmented." He explains: "By 1981 a little under 2 million Serbs lived in other republics, with another 1.3 million in Serbia's two autonomous provinces, as against inner Serbia's 4.9 million Serbs. Serbs were still the most numerous national group at around 40 percent of the total population. The territorial division of Yugoslavia had been acceptable to them as an administrative structure. The issue of borders began to arise as the republics came close to being sovereign states, and nation-states at that."

Yugoslavia was abandoned, Pavlowitch writes, because it was "identified with centralism, and perceived in Slovenia and Croatia as a mask for Serbia's predominance." The secession of Croatia and Bosnia, with large Serbian minorities, raised intractable problems, leading to war in Bosnia, where Serbs and Muslims, of roughly equal numbers, and, with 16 percent of the population which was Croatian, lived in communities that had mixed nationalities for centuries. It matched the emotions of earlier ages, when it was said of Sarajevo: "Only the poets and revolutionaries are awake."

On trial in The Hague is the question whether the wars in ex-Yugoslavia were solely a result of Slobodan Milosevic's aggression. As presented by the prosecutors, Milosevic and his henchmen directed wars and genocide in Croatia, Bosnia, and Kosovo, in order to create Greater Serbia—the analogy being Hitler's wish for *lebensraum* in claiming the Sudetenland and Danzig. I have no brief for Milosevic, whose record in leading Yugoslavia includes looting its banks, ruining the economy, imprisoning dissidents, and colluding with the president of Croatia, Franjo Tudjman, in trying to carve up Bosnia into spheres of influence. At the same time, Serbia did not lend itself to independent statehood as easily as Slovenia or Croatia, whose internal borders enclosed much of their populations. When the wars of the Yugoslav succession began in 1991, and later when they ended with the 1999 NATO attacks, Serbs were scattered across four Balkan countries. Milosevic was unable to save an imperfect union. Nor was he ever sure if he was fighting for Greater Serbia or a Yugoslav Risorgimento. In the Balkan wars, as was said of the Treaty of Versailles, "Some nations were more successful in their self-determination than others."

Belgrade: *"the man who would be king"*

OUR MERRY BAND of tired travelers checked into the Hotel Moskva, on one of Belgrade's main squares. Under gray skies, the city appeared monochromatic, as colorless as the street cars that shuttle about on undulating, worn track. Belgrade is one of the few capitals of Europe that came together as a city during the Bauhaus and Communist eras of architecture. Until the 1920s, the population was less than 100,000. A few neighborhoods have trees overhanging the sidewalks, and elegant buildings, but much of Belgrade is lined with office blocks and worker housing of little distinction. My cousin Boba, who is an architect and expert in urban planning, for which he has won prizes, once said to me, "We had no money to do anything," in explaining the fading cement-and-glass buildings that dominate the city. Our $200-a-night suite, however, had a loft sleeping corner, a small kitchen, a soaring living room, and enough heavy furniture to fill the quota of a five-year plan. We sank into the easy chairs, ordered coffee from room service, and watched the sofas fill up with relatives and friends, some of whom seemed surprised that we did not want to begin our day with plum brandy.

Actually the plan for the day was a walk to Kalemegdan Fortress, overlooking the Danube, a family lunch at Boba's home, and then an afternoon visit at the Royal Palace, where we had an invitation from the man who would be king, Prince Alexander Karageorgevich. Packs of friendly stray dogs walked with us to Kalemegdan, breaking my son Henry's heart. We overlooked the dramatic confluence of the Danube and Sava rivers. Near here the Austrians attacked in 1915, and here the Nazi bombers struck in 1941. We toured the Serbian Military Museum, which with displays of bayonets and pistols tells the story of Serbia as a succession of pitched battles, many of them fought against the Turks.

Through a light drizzle we walked to the family lunch, a procession of salads, bread, side dishes, soup, and meat— enough to feed several large families. I warned the children that just when they thought they were full, a large platter of meat would be put on the table. Around 4:00 P.M., the palace staff sent three cars to the apartment to take all of us to the prince. We hardly merited such royal treatment, but they insisted. I didn't know Prince Alexander well; I first met him in passing at a wedding in Canada in 2000. Then a man in his fifties, he was working in London, with few prospects of returning to Yugoslavia, which his family had fled in 1941 after the Nazi invasion.

After the fall of Milosevic, the government of Zoran Djindjic had returned Belgrade's two palaces to the Karageorgevich line, and Prince Alexander had assumed semi-official royal duties. Alexander and his wife, Princess Katherine, had taken up both the residences and the mantle of monarchy. They attended state functions, worked for charitable causes, and gently pressed the case that Serbia should officially restore its monarchy, something that would require an act of parliament and a referendum. In the meantime, they were freelance royalty.

Our group of fifteen was ushered into a palace parlor, and we sat in a large circle, nibbling on crustless sandwiches. Prince Alexander told the story of having been born in Claridge's Hotel in London. For his birth, Winston Churchill had declared the hotel suite property of Yugoslavia, so it could be said that an heir to the throne would be born in Yugoslavia. Princess Katherine described her charitable work for Serbia. On Easter Sunday, for example, she had organized a day-long party at the palace for 2000 orphans from the recent civil wars. A woman of Greek origin, she seemed thrilled at the prospect of the palace overrun with noisy children. She also spoke about a fire that had damaged the Serbian monastery on Mt. Athos in her native Greece. Both the Prince and Princess are people of learning, culture, energy, and empathy—qualities not often found in Serbian or Yugoslav leaders. Before taking a tour of the two palaces, we stood for pictures with the royal family. The prince passed out ceremonial pens, and the princess distributed literature about her foundation, Lifeline Humanitarian Organization. Proving that even monarchy can adapt, they gave us their Web site, www.royalfamily.org, although there was no hint that anyone in the palace was posting a blog.

As we toured the Royal and Old palaces—one of which has a Moorish billiard room as you might find in a London club—I wondered whether Serbia needs the services of a king. Prince Alexander believes that a monarchy would lend stability to Serbia's otherwise fractured political landscape— that which had to endure Hitler, Tito, and Milosevic in the last sixty years. He could well be right, and his habits of leadership reflect well on his military education at Sandhurst in the UK. At the same time not even the monarchy was able to save Serbia or Yugoslavia from itself in the last hundred years—a point that struck me as I looked at the tragic expressions on many of the royal portraits that line the palace walls.

Serbian Monarchy: *all the king's ancestors*

PRIOR TO THE founding of Yugoslavia, Serbia had two royal families—those descended from Karageorge, who led the first revolt against the Turks in 1804, and those whose ancestor was Milosh Obrenevic, who also confronted the Turks and led Serbia in the nineteenth century. In 1903, the last of the Obrenevic line literally fell away when King Alexander Obrenevic was thrown from a Belgrade window, together with his wife, Queen Draga. The finest moment of the Serbian monarchy came during World War I, when Prince Alexander— the present prince's grandfather—led the long Serbian retreat to Corfu. Many contemporary accounts applauded his courage. The author of *With Serbia Into Exile*, Fortier Jones, describes seeing that prince during the 1915 retreat:

> He seemed like a young American lawyer, clean-cut, with suppressed energy in every movement as he walked down the street, followed at some ten paces by a single Serbian major. His inheritance was dwindling to the vanishing point, scarcely one third of the fine army of which he was commander-in-chief remain, and in all probability he was about as hungry as the rest of us, but one would have thought from his face that he was going to a dress parade.

After the war, Alexander sat on the throne of the short-lived Kingdom of Serbs, Croats, and Slovenes, dissolved the Parliament in 1934, and then was assassinated by Italian and Croatian fascists in Marseilles. Rebecca West writes: "Mussolini had believed that with the King's death the country would fall to pieces and be an easy prey to a foreign invader." Actually, the shock of his killing briefly restored unity to Yugoslavia, which lasted until 1941.

As regent for Prince Peter—King Alexander's son and the current Prince Alexander's father—his uncle, Prince Paul, flirted with Hitler, hoping to keep the wolf of war away from Yugoslavia's door. But the military coup dispatched Paul. (A few of his relatives wouldn't mind having a Belgrade palace.) During World War II Prince Peter, then in exile, proved a steadfast ally of the British, although the government of Winston Churchill supported Tito's Partisans rather than the royalist forces that were fighting inside Yugoslavia. The man who helped influence Churchill was Fitzroy Maclean, a British officer who was operating behind the lines in Yugoslavia during World War II. His memoirs, *Eastern Approaches*, describe the British tilt toward the Communists, another cruel defeat for the Karageorgevich family:

> But there was one aspect of the situation which was still disturbing Mr. Churchill. In 1941, after Prince Paul had come to terms with the Germans, King Peter of Jugoslavia, still in his teens, had headed the revolt which threw out the Regent and his Government and brought the country into the war on the side of Great Britain, at that time fighting alone against the Axis. Then, when the German invasion and occupation had forced him to fly, he had taken refuge in Great Britain where he had formed a Government in Exile. This government had from the outset backed Mihajlovic [head of royalist forces fighting inside Yugoslavia] and shown a correspondent hostility towards Tito, whom they regard as a dangerous revolutionary upstart.

After the war, Tito abolished the monarchy, having already executed many of its officers. The Karageorgevich became yet another royal family in London exile, where at least Prince Alexander could enjoy the support and patronage of his godmother, Queen Elizabeth II.

It is not clear that, were Prince Alexander declared king of Serbia, whether he would also wish to become king of Montenegro, the sister republic in what was officially called The State Union of Serbia and Montenegro. Montenegro was the last partner in Yugoslavia. But even that government had doubts about its alliance with Serbia and voted its independence.

Nevertheless, Prince Alexander would have some claim on the throne of Montenegro, as his great grandfather, King Peter, married a daughter of King Nikola, the last Montenegrin king, who was also known as the "father-in-law of Europe." Nikola ruled Montenegro from 1860 until he fled during World War I. In addition to the daughter who married King Peter, two other daughters married Russian grand-princes, and another married the King of Italy, Victor Emmanuel III. Another of Nikola's sons married a descendant of Obrenevic line. On this trip, I had hoped to persuade everyone to make a side trip to Cetinje, Montenegro's ancient capital. But even I knew that pressing such a claim would make it risky for me to stand near open windows. I contented myself by reading a passage aloud to my wife from a book I was reading about the old king and his court:

> There was a whiff of the middle ages about King Nicholas: his insistence on leading his own troops into battle, his dispensing of justice from his seat under an ancient tree, even the magnificent capital, Cetinje, was merely a large village, the Bank of Montenegro a small cottage, and the Grand Hotel a boarding-house. The Biljarda, his old palace,

was named after the much prized English billiard table, which had been hauled up the mountainside, and looked like an English country inn. His new palace was more like a German pension, with the royal children in folk costume doing their lessons with their Swiss tutor and the king sitting on the front steps waiting for visitors. Franz Lehar used Montenegro as the model for *The Merry Widow*.

Another historian compared his war record with that of his Serbian counterpart: "Instead of following King Peter's heroic example in retreating over snow-capped mountains to fight another day, Nicholas fled into exile with his camarilla and empty dreams of a postwar restoration. Peter shared the privations of his troops on Corfu and in Salonica, while Nicholas languished in Italy and on the French Riviera, where he eventually died at Cap d'Antibes in 1921."

At the moment, Serbia does not appear in much of a hurry to re-establish the monarchy. None of the post-Milosevic governments has felt comfortable promoting a restoration. Criminal elements of the far right, heirs to Milosevic, assassinated Djindjic, who of recent prime ministers was most sympathetic to Prince Alexander. Nor have his successors thought it opportune to share power with a monarchy. Clearly many admire the Prince's good intentions and generosity of spirit although others in Serbia may share the views of Tacitus, who said: "Had he never been emperor, no one would have doubted his ability to reign."

Bombing Around Belgrade: *"singing telegrams"*

BEFORE LEAVING BELGRADE the next morning for Koprivnica, the village where my grandfather was born, the traveling central committee decided that we should make a tour of the buildings bombed in Belgrade during the 1999 NATO blitz. Those air raids began after the government of Slobodan Milosevic sent troops against the Kosovo Liberation Army that was then operating in the mountainous shadows between Albania and Yugoslavia. For seventy-eight days NATO-allied bombers attacked Serb positions, both within Serbia's Kosovo province and in other areas of Serbia. To press for a Yugoslav army withdrawal from Kosovo—despite it being an autonomous region within Serbia—NATO planes even took out civilian targets, including a Belgrade television tower and cigarette plant in Nish. Eventually the Yugoslav army withdrew from Kosovo, but the war ended with Milosevic still in power and Serbia's economy in ruins. The bombs may have been smart, but the logic behind the war suggested a lack of precision.

What is amazing about the missiles that fell on Belgrade is how accurate was their targeting. Clearly Pentagon planners had mapped out the back rooms of the Milosevic government, and down the elevator shafts at the police, army, and party headquarters came an assortment of sophisticated weaponry. Either because Serbia has no money to clean up the damage or because the government is comfortable in the role of a NATO victim, the buildings remain as they were when hit. In some cases the bombs exploded only after they had penetrated the buildings, which left the outline of the ministry intact but destroyed the interior. During the Vietnam War, Robert McNamara's Pentagon spoke of bomb-o-grams being delivered to Hanoi. Here the messages came with door-to-door service.

In Belgrade's best neighborhood, surrounded by many embassies including that of the United States, we saw the collapsed roof of the Milosevic residence (I thought to myself, "Candy-gram"). Near the television tower, which served no military purpose, my cousin Boba spoke of how the destruction of the city's power plants had thawed the contents of everyone's freezer, forcing residents to serve precious meat dishes while sirens wailed in the night. It turned one aspect of the bombing into a street fair, as neighbors grilled meat for friends. He also recalled, as a boy, how he had cowered in his stairwell as German bombers attacked Belgrade. Now, as a man in his sixties, he got to relive his worst childhood experience. Only this time the bombers were American.

Boba's account of the passenger train bombed in the Morava Valley, killing fourteen, reminded me of a sardonic passage in Fortier Jones's book, which describes the Austrian bombing of Serbia in 1915, among the first such attacks by air:

It is hard to be accurate when sailing high in the air, hard even for those fearless men who with shrapnel bursting around their frail machines calmly drop death upon women and children. I think they are the bravest, perhaps, of all the fighting men, these bomb-droppers in whatever uniform. For, it is not easy to face death at any time, but to face it while in the act of dropping murder on the bowed heads of women, on the defenseless heads of sleeping, playing, or fleeing children, surely it requires nerve to face death thus engaged.

What no one could explain in Belgrade was the intent behind the destruction of the Chinese embassy. When I first read about it in the newspapers, during the war, I assumed a bomb had drifted off course and destroyed the building. I assumed, too, the embassy was in a crowded part of town, not far from the hospital hit when NATO went for a nearby party headquarters. But the Chinese embassy is in New

Belgrade, on a separate plot of land, far from other targets. In addition, it was a new building that looked like it had been built distinctly as an embassy. The rumor in Belgrade was that Milosevic had ties to the Chinese, and thus this attack was yet another singing telegram.

Anatole Germaine: *"so many Balkan lives"*

As our minivan headed toward the highway that runs south, Stasha pointed to a large, now abandoned government center. In this instance, socialist fatigue, not NATO bombs, had closed the doors. Although not more than ten stories, the structure had enormous length, like a government building in Moscow. Here I could imagine Big Brother with his corner office. It could even have been George Orwell's Ministry of Plenty, except that now it looked more like a Trenton housing project, ready for implosion.

"You know," Stasha continued, "Anatole was the architect for this building." The name Anatole brought to mind a small man with a short moustache who visited our house during the years when I was growing up. Once he came in a red van and brought along his dog, Tigger, who slept on our sofa when not chasing the cats. Sadly I had never known Anatole except as one of my parents' distant relatives. As I was growing up, his name was mentioned often and always with affection. The cautionary tale of his life came to represent the dislocations of so many Balkan lives.

He died in Van Nuys, California, in the mid-1980s, and I am sure his neighbors thought of him as a quiet, respectful man who liked to walk his dog. I doubt that any of them knew that his life had begun in Russia or that he had survived the two world wars. From Stasha and my father, I was able connect the dots of his life, a narrative that has always struck me as worthy of Chekhov.

Late in the nineteenth century, Anatole's mother, Evgenia, was a young woman "of good parents" who had a suitor, Constantine Popov, an official in the tsarist government. He wanted to marry her, but at the last moment he was sent on official business to the Pamir Mountains, which run across the spine of Central Asia. Evgenia lost touch with Popov. In the meantime another suitor, by the name of Germaine, appeared and proposed to marry her. She said she would, but under one condition: that if Popov returned from the Pamir Mountains, she would be free to divorce her first husband and marry Popov. Germaine accepted these conditions. They married, and Anatole was the product of that union.

Some time later, Popov returned from the Pamirs, and true to her promise, Evgenia left Germaine and moved in with Popov. It's not clear whether they ever married, but the assumption is that they did. Popov must have been a man of some importance because, in pre-war Russia, he was transferred to the Polish capital, Warsaw. He moved with his wife and step-son. In Warsaw, Anatole contracted tuberculosis. His parents took him to a specialist in St. Petersburg, who recommended that the young boy be placed in a sanatorium above Lausanne. The family traveled to Switzerland and left Anatole there to recover. He was twelve years old.

Anatole was in the sanatorium in August 1914 when war came to Europe. Thus he was caught behind the lines, as Russia was at war with Austria-Hungary. By then Anatole had recovered his health, but he had no way to contact his parents. Assuming they had left Poland—now occupied by a victorious German army—he didn't even know where they were. At some stage the mother of another patient at the sanatorium arrived in Lausanne and said that she could take Anatole to Sweden. From there, she reasoned, he might be able to make his way into Russian-occupied Finland and then to St. Petersburg—the path Anatole chose. The mother, her son, and Anatole traveled by train from Lausanne to England, and then by boat to Stockholm.

Traveling alone, "brave little Anatole"—to use my father's words—crossed into Russia, failed to find his parents in St. Petersburg, and then went south to Odessa. Here he found his mother, but—as only Chekov could explain— she was living with Germaine, not Popov. Sometime later she resumed her relationship with Popov. After the Russian Revolution, which made life difficult for Popov, Anatole took a steamer from Odessa to Istanbul, then under British occupation. He found work attached to the British army. According to my father, he enjoyed swimming off the islands in the Sea of Marmara. He also loved trains and would hang around the Istanbul railway yards. At one point a train engineer offered to take him across the Balkans, which is how he found his way to Kikinda, a railroad town in Voivodina, not far from the Romanian border. There he studied architecture until he moved south to Belgrade, where he married Ruzica, the sister of Stasha's father.

In 1916 Belgrade had a population of 15,000, down from 90,000 at the start of the war. Many residents had been killed during the German-Austrian shelling and subsequent invasion of the city at the beginning of World War I. Others had departed with the retreat across Kosovo and through Albania to the Adriatic Sea. But Belgrade in the 1920s was a growing capital, and Anatole found work as an architect.

According to Stasha, Anatole designed one of the buildings opposite the Hotel Moskva. He was adept at providing any required architectural style: modernist, gothic, Art Deco, etc. You name the design, Anatole could provide it. After designing more than 200 buildings in Belgrade, he was chosen to be the architect for the new government center—the brave old world that we had just passed in the minivan.

For two years Anatole managed the government project, until the bones of five Russian soldiers were discovered at the job site. Someone attending to the bodies asked Anatole for wood from which to build coffins. Although Anatole was Russian with Yugoslav residency, he was also prickly and didn't enjoy outside agitation. He refused the wood, although it isn't clear if it was for patriotic or budgetary reasons. As a result of his refusal, Anatole was arrested, charged with what Orwell called *crimethink*, and sentenced to three years in prison. Stasha summarized the attitude of his accusers: "Who is this Russian guy refusing to bury Russian soldiers?" This was the time just before Tito broke with Stalin, and Russian soldiers were part of the fraternal landscape. After Tito broke with Stalin, who needed a Russian architect at all?

Ruzica—known to us in America as Rose—was distraught that her husband had been put in jail for refusing wood for Russian coffins. She made endless rounds of government offices, trying to secure his freedom. Through her work as a secretary, she knew a high-ranking Tito minister, who managed to have Anatole's sentence shortened to seven months. (*"My husband is an architect, not a politician."*) But when Anatole was released, he and Rose were exiled from Yugoslavia. They only had the choice of going east or west.

They chose to go west, with hopes that my grandfather

could get them a visa for the United States. In 1949, they spent a year in a relocation camp outside Trieste. Stasha's father, who had little money himself in postwar Belgrade, sent them what he could spare for newspapers and cigarettes. At one point my grandfather said as an aside to my father: "You know, I received a registered letter at the post office from Rose. She must want to thank me for something." But it was the news of their expulsion from Yugoslavia. Eventually my grandfather secured for them visas for the United States.

Anatole worked as a draftsman in New York, and later he and Rose moved to Buffalo before settling in California. Rose died of cancer in the 1960s. But Anatole kept working and traveling, visiting our family in New York as late as 1977. When he died in the late 1980s, his ashes were returned to Belgrade for burial next to his step-father, Popov, and Ruzica. His mother, who died in the 1950s, was buried, of all places, in London. My father likes to say: "Anatole was a man of enormous persistence." Concurring, Stasha also admits, with fondness for his uncle: "You know, he had a difficult personality."

Ravanica: *the heavenly kingdom of Kosovo*

ON THE ROAD to Koprivnica, which is about four hours southeast of Belgrade toward the border with Bulgaria, our first stop was at the monastery of Ravanica. Like many such churches in the Christian Orthodox world, the small complex of stone buildings lies tucked in the hills at the head of a valley, offering both a retreat and protection from the Turks. Here, according to legend, are the bones and other relics of Prince Lazar, whose death at the battle of Kosovo in 1389 has inspired so much Serbian poetry and legend.

Then the Turks overwhelmed Lazar
And the Tsar Lazar was destroyed,
And his army was destroyed with him,
Of seven and seventy thousand soldiers.

On the Field of Blackbirds, outside Pristina in Kosovo, it was said that Prince Lazar chose a heavenly rather than an earthly kingdom—that is, spiritual salvation over yet another cavalry charge against the Turks. Defeated, the Serbs slowly abandoned their medieval kingdom in what is now northern Greece, Macedonia, and Kosovo, and drifted north toward the plains around Belgrade. Dispersed over a wide area, the Serbs, according to Pavlowitch, lost "any conception of belonging to a 'nation'...[to] the extent that some did, it was of belonging to a medieval community linked to lineage or territory, not to a later-modern romantic or revolutionary 'nation.'" More pointedly, he begins his book: "This is not a history of Serbia; I would not know how to define Serbia through the ages. There has been no continuous polity or territory with that name. Serbias have come and gone, and they have moved about." Nevertheless, as the Serbs have moved they have remained attached to Kosovo—both the Serbian Orthodox churches that dot its landscape and the mythical lands recited in legend.

On different occasions, Boba and I discussed the current situation in Kosovo. During the week that we were together, I tried to piece together what Serbs think about such hallowed ground. Clearly they think it lost. Boba would say: "Our president cannot even go there, and it's part of Serbia." He was referring to United Nations occupation forces in Kosovo, currently run by the French that are there to keep the peace between Serbs and Albanian separatists. But after the recent fighting, according to Boba, UN forces turned a blind eye to the persecution of Serbs living in Kosovo. After World War II, he said, more than 200,000 Serbs lived there. Now less than 20,000 remain. By comparison, in 1949, the Albanian population was 498,000. Now it's more than two million. He even dug out an article from *Review*, the national airline's in-flight magazine: "Erasing Traces of Serb Presence." The account reads:

> In the recent three-day pogrom (on March 17-19, 2004) alone, as many as 35 Serbian holy sites—monasteries and churches—dating back to the 12th, 14th, 15th, 16th and 19th centuries, and numerous cemeteries and parish homes, several thousand frescoes, icons, church relics and treasuries, went up in flames of hatred and violence.

While I was thinking it odd that an airline magazine should have more graphic coverage of Kosovo than papers like the *New York Times*, Boba went on, somewhat emphatically: "If the United States had an Albanian problem, it would solve it unilaterally. There would be no question." Since the wars in Bosnia and Kosovo, Serbia has had to absorb 800,000 refugees, the most of any country in Europe.

Despite independence, Kosovo's future is as a ward of the international community. Before he retired as the U.S. ambassador to Serbia, I asked William Montgomery what he thought was the most difficult problem in ex-Yugoslavia, and he answered unequivocally: "Kosovo." Even if all the Serbs are driven from the region while the holy sites are given international protection—a possible solution to the conflict— the problem for the Balkans and for Europe remains.

Serbia is not the only country in the region that has an irredentist Albanian population. Other Albanian communities live in Macedonia, Greece, and Montenegro, all of which, following Kosovo's independence, could be emboldened to seek federation with Albania—thus drawing that fractured country into conflict with its neighbors. Pavlowitch writes: "A republic of Kosovo would have opened a Pandora's box." For the Serbs it lives on as a symbol of defeat and ostracism, much as it did after losses there in 1389 and 1915. Jones writes during the retreat: "...never again shall we who traversed the 'Field of Blackbirds' think of war without living again the snow-filled horrors of our march." Writing in 2002, Pavlowitch observes: "Between 1991 and 1995, demagogues were able to mobilize opinion around mystical conceptions of 'Serbia' that stretched over historic sites, holy places and mass graves, while few people actually wanted to go and live in Kosovo." Thus it will remain a heavenly kingdom of defeat.

Zajecar: *the decline and fall of Greater Serbia*

As we were in Ravanica on the Saturday before Easter, a church service was taking place around the sarcophagus of Lazar. The children lit candles, and took pictures, and wandered about, in slightly bored-child fashion. I remember such restlessness well from my own childhood inspection of European cathedrals. Nevertheless, the setting of the monastery, the presence of chanting nuns and monks, the old women in shawls, and the ancient sense of faith in the frescoes did reduce their gentle boredom to something closer to reverence. After a few false starts that included a lost camera and a dead-end road, we ate our picnic on a hillside looking down on the Romanesque arches and domes, and then resumed the minivan march to Romuliana, a Roman ruin near Zajecar.

Not many travelers go to Zajecar, which is about seventy miles north of Nish, and fewer of those inspect Romuliana, which we had to ourselves. Surprised to find a busload of foreigners at 6:00 P.M., the curator kept the city gates open. He delivered a short history about the palace and Galerius—a late Roman emperor who succeeded Diocletian and of whom Gibbon wrote: "The stern temper of Galerius was cast in a very different mould; and while he commanded the esteem of his subjects he seldom condescended to solicit their affections."

"Galerius," continued Gibbon, "was stationed on the banks of the Danube as the safeguard of the Illyrian provinces." He also won fame fighting the Persians in Mesopotamia where he was "invested with purple." As Galerius was born and died near Zajecar, here he made his imperial palace, which he dedicated to his mother, a local villager from Zajecar. The stones to build the palace were dragged from Egypt and Macedonia, and still today it is possible to see mosaics and the marble columns of empire. The boys let off steam from a long day on the road, and the rest of us wandered among the ruins.[1]

Everyone in the entourage was thrilled to check into the Hotel Grinka M in Zajecar. After driving around the dusty town and heading down a dark alley, no one expected much

---

1. April 2004, as the American war in Iraq was raging out of control, was an apropos moment to reflect on Galerius, Mesopotamia, and the roads to imperial ruin. Gibbon writes of his life and times: "The ideal restraints of the Senate and the laws might serve to display virtues, but could never correct the vices of the emperor. The military force was a blind and irresistible instrument of oppression; and the corruption of Roman manners would always supply flatterers eager to applaud, and ministers prepared to serve, the fear or the avarice, the lust or the cruelty, of their masters."

of anything except a hotel catering to the brave old world. Instead, we found that a young couple had renovated a small villa. The rooms were clean and comfortable, the tubs had hot water, and the children could watch such cable classics as *Animal Planet* and a made-for-television movie about the Odyssey.

I was also pleased to stay in Zajecar, as that was where my grandfather went to high school and later returned to teach, before emigrating to America. It is also the hometown of Nikola Pasic, an early twentieth-century Serbian prime minister who represented the new kingdom at the Paris Peace Conference in 1919. When I asked around, no one knew if the old high school was still standing. But I did find a statue of Pasic in the town square. I once asked my father what my grandfather had thought about Pasic. My grandfather had been exiled for articulating a philosophy not that different from that of Pasic's Serbian National Radical Party, which dreamed of integrating Serbia into mainstream European affairs. The king (Prince Alexander's great-grandfather) took exception to my grandfather's democratic sentiments and banished him. But Pasic later became prime minister, blending his progressive sentiments with nationalistic ideas of a Greater Serbia. In answer to my question, I was told that my grandfather felt that Pasic often confused "Greater Serbia with Greater Pasic."

In her excellent history of the Paris Peace Conference, the Canadian historian Margaret MacMillan includes several evocative sketches of Pasic. She writes: "In the turbulent world of Serbian politics Pasic managed to survive, a triumph in itself. Death sentences, exile, plots, assassination attempts, car accidents, he outlasted them all. And he returned the favours to his enemies." In many ways, Pasic was heir to the ideals of the local Timok Rebellion—not unlike America's Whiskey Rebellion—a late nineteenth-century revolt (about the time when my grandfather was born) in which farmers around Zajecar took up arms against the oppression of central government—in this case a monarchy. She continues: "Pasic was a founding member of the Serbian National Radical Party, which stood for the liberation and union of all Serbs, even those in Austria-Hungary. Like so many Serb nationalists, he cared little about Croats or Slovenes; they were Roman Catholic and looked to the West, while the Serbs were Orthodox." MacMillan later describes the split more cryptically: "The Serbs are soldier-peasants; the Croats are passive intellectuals in tendency."

Dinner that night was at long tables, and we were more than thirty. Cousins, and cousins of cousins, all descended upon the restaurant, which served up great mounds of pork, chicken, bread, and coleslaw, more than even our hungry group could finish. I paid for everyone, and the cost was €150, which in Switzerland is a dinner for four, if you are lucky. My wife was distressed that we were leaving behind so much food until Stasha intervened: "Don't worry. I promise you. It all gets eaten."

Milivoy Stanoyevich: *Easter Sunday in Koprivnica*

No DAY ON the trip was more glorious than that Easter Sunday in Koprivnica, which is ten miles north of Zajecar in the Timok Valley. Buds were on the fruit trees, and by mid-morning the temperature under a full sun was approaching seventy degrees. Our minivan pulled up in front of the church, where a delegation of about twenty-five villagers was there to greet us. As we got off the bus, school girls served us bread to dip into salt, and then we passed through an informal receiving line that had congregated outside the church doors. The men, with heavy beards and uneven teeth, freely dispensed hugs and kisses while the women, many encased in shawls, stood shyly to the side.

The reason for the official welcome was that my father and I had donated money to help with a church restoration. They used the money to have a Greek artist, living in Nish, create a mosaic of St. Peter and St. Paul, and we were there to help dedicate the installation over the front door. That morning in the hotel, my wife and I wondered if we would not have to endure a two-hour Easter service, like that we had seen briefly at Ravanica, complete with incense and chanting. But here the service never became any more formal than that of a happy family reunion. We were shown a plaque that listed my grandfather as a contributor to an earlier church renovation. Everyone stood for pictures. The school girls passed around apple juice, and then we were led to the town museum, lodged in the shed of an old barn. Inside the rustic rooms were an old spinning wheel, a peasant bed, kitchen utensils, a photograph of men who fought in the Balkan and First World wars, and a picture of my grandfather wearing a bowler hat. At the time he was in his late thirties and a Columbia University professor. On another wall there was a picture of a prominent local politician—a Pasic man. One of our many eager guides pointed to him and said: "Your grandfather was more popular than he was."

Outside the church a tractor stood attached to a wagon, which was filled with wooden benches. We were to be taken to my grandfather's gravesite, a few miles out of the village. Because the village's lanes are unpaved and were deep in spring mud, it was felt we needed to ride to the cemetery behind the tractor. Everyone piled on the benches by climbing up a small, iron ladder. We traversed the village main street as if on parade and then headed down the muddy path that led to the cemetery. It took a half hour to drive three miles, but we got an excellent tour of the village of several hundred houses and passed the last mile among orchards of flowering plum trees and fields of wild flowers.

I had been down this road before, in 1976, when I buried my grandfather in this cemetery. That summer, after I had graduated from college, I was traveling abroad, and it was decided among the family that I would bury his ashes in Koprivnica. Then it had been a hot summer day, and I buried him with the help of a cousin's uncle (now dead). A few years later, my father had visited the village, and he had laid a headstone over the grave where we now stood. No one in the family, except my father and one cousin had ever been to this remote gravesite, hidden outside the village during the years of Turkish occupation. (At least the dead would be free.) Now we were more than fifteen, poking among headstones tangled with weeds and hanging trees. I read the passage from my book that describes the burial and then we made the return trip in the tractor.

Next to the church, the teacher of the elementary school had assembled many of the village children. For the next hour they sang and danced, and contested Easter games. The benches had been removed from the wagon and lined up on the grass. As visiting dignitaries, we were seated in the front rows. Between some of the dance numbers, the mayor handed out gifts to our family or spoke in remembrance of my grandfather—as if he had left the village in 1988, not 1908. To express thanks, many in our group said a few words, and I made our children sing one of their school songs, which they did (under slight protest) to a gathering that now had several hundred curious villagers standing casually in the churchyard. I could imagine such a scene on the Great Plains, described in a novel by Willa Cather, who wrote often about the dislocations of so many frontier immigrants. (*"I hope he does not see me now. I hope he is among the old people of his blood and country, and that tidings do not reach him from the New World."*)

Lunch was served in the town hall, the size of a school gym, at three long tables, each of which served about a hundred people. All 900 people in the village had been invited, and about a third had accepted. A band played on the stage, and I read a tribute, written by my father to his father, that recounted aspects of the long journey from Koprivnica to the New World:

My father told me that his earliest memory was hearing the sounds of distant artillery, those of the Serbian regular army that King Milan Obrenevitch launched against Bulgaria, and their defeat at [Bregalnica] in 1885. Avid reader and intellectually curious throughout his life, Milivoy early found favor with a professor at Zajecar College where he received a scholarship. Aside from his studies, he took very specific interests in Balkan politics of that period, writing and distributing pamphlets urging a union of all south Slavs, so as to form a democratic republic similar to Switzerland.

As my father pursued his academic life at the University of Belgrade, he continued to advocate his views for reform. Appealing as was the thought of a Greater Serbia, his proposal for a republican form of government drew the ire of King Peter Karageorgevitch and with it the strong suggestion that he seek political asylum. Thus it came about that, in 1908, the year that Austria-Hungary annexed Bosnia and Herzegovina, he sailed for the United States aboard the French liner *Rochambeau*.

After lunch, the party moved across the street to the elementary school, the same school that had launched my grandfather on his way to a master's degree from Berkeley and a Ph.D. from Columbia. Several of us had asked to see the classrooms, and the two principal teachers spoke with sympathy and passion about what it is like to teach in a Serbian school.

The teachers made the point that in a village of 900, only twenty or so residents had jobs that paid a salary. The rest were farmers or got by as they best could. For the moment the village had no running water. Although the water mains were in place, either a billing dispute or a ruptured pipe had broken the service, which meant that for some time everyone was living on well water. This problem, however, did not affect the school, as it had never had running water, a point made clear when my wife asked the teachers what help they most needed and they answered: "A toilet." Despite many hardships, the actual classrooms were bright and cheerfully decorated with student pictures. But the school didn't have heat, computers, or a television on which to show video cassettes. In many ways, it was the same one-room schoolhouse that my grandfather had attended.

In the late afternoon—we had now been celebrating Easter for more than eight hours—those still in the party gathered in the village's only business—a café that doubled as a newsstand and kiosk. The chairs and tables spilled into the main road, but there was so little passing traffic that no one minded sitting in the street. In one corner, a group had formed that was writing a letter to Prince Alexander, asking for help to restore the war memorial and the church. The letter noted that the Communist government had defaced the war monument—missing was an imperial eagle—and they connected the village to the early success of the Karageorgevich clan, in which the men of Koprivnica marched with the first "Black George" on the Turkish garrison at Negotin.

I paid the bill at the café for what seemed like the entire village, and the amount charged was four euros. We went searching for our sons, who had spent the afternoon playing soccer with some local boys and, in the process, had learned a fair amount of schoolyard Serbian. On the way back to the hotel, we visited the crumbling house where my grandfather was born. It remains in the family, although for some time it has only been used on weekends. Located on the edge of the village, the small farm—with its outdoor kitchen—was bathed in springtime warmth. The fruit trees were in bloom. I explained to the children that their great-grandfather as a boy had tended sheep in this yard. One of the boys from the village approached my daughter for her phone number, and then disappeared, shyly.

We slowly returned to the minivan, but the farmyard scene was worthy of Tolstoy. Indeed, my grandfather's Ph.D. dissertation, written in New York City in 1921 but evoking Koprivnica between the lines, carries the title *Tolstoy's Theory of Social Reform*. He describes the devotion at the end of the great author's life: "to work for simple, impressionable, uncorrupted people; to give them pleasure, education and to correct their faults, which arise from ignorance and superstition; to develop their morals; to induce them to love the right."

I wondered what my grandfather would think of Koprivnica today. He certainly would have known the forebears of those we had met in the churchyard, and he would have admired their generosity, knowing they had so little to give. But he would have wanted more than a school without books and running water. In his memoir of growing up, Tolstoy wrote: "Oh happy childhood, never to be recalled. How could one fail to love and cherish one's memories of it? These memories refresh and elevate my soul and are for me the source of all my best pleasures." My grandfather, however, had higher standards for Koprivnica than happy memories. He would have wanted it to share in the political and economic freedoms that he found in the New World. To be sure, the villagers had life, but, to his disappointment and ours, liberty and the pursuit of happiness were proving more elusive.

Last Day in Belgrade: *"as Bosnia goes, so go the Balkans"*

WE HAD A last day in Belgrade as our group of happy travelers broke camp. My sister and her husband returned to Alaska, by way of Milan, Frankfurt, and Salt Lake City. Needing a family break, the older children took themselves shopping, and later reported that Belgrade had what they called "potential." Not that we needed more food, but my wife and I retreated to the hotel dining room and spent what might be called a café afternoon—visiting with friends and relatives who came by to say hello or good-bye. To pay the driver of the minivan took about an hour of figuring and exchanging toasts with plumb brandy.

During the long, pleasant afternoon, in answer to a question whether I felt optimistic about the future of the

Balkans, I described meeting the Bosnian Foreign Minister, Mladen Ivanic, in Geneva before we left on our trip. He had given a speech, and afterwards I spoke to him during the reception. He was born in 1958, and had worked as a journalist and professor in Banja Luka before the war. Surprisingly, no one in his family was killed or wounded during the fighting. From 2001 to 2003, he had served as president of the Republic Srpska, the Serbian enclave in Bosnia that to the outside world seems to exist only to harbor war criminals. But Ivanic told a hopeful story in Bosnia. He said the program to settle the claims of refugees was 95 percent a success. He said no foreign soldiers had been killed in the peacekeeping, and only 12,000 SFOR troops remained in the country. He described Bosnia as a "normal, boring country," where there were many problems, but those of daily life, not survival.

When listing the country's problems, he said the biggest was the economy, in which the gross domestic product had only reached 65 percent of its pre-war level. Unemployment, he said, was either 35 or 24 percent, depending on whose figures you believed. Even many of those with jobs worked on the fringes of foreign aid, which had put more than $5 billion into the country. He hoped for better relations with the European Union, and admitted that the challenge in the Balkans was to find regional, rather than national, solutions. When anyone tried to draw fixed borders, he said, the results were violent—or, as Edith Durham has written, "the borders floated on blood."

He admitted candidly that no one was trying very hard to capture the elusive war criminals, Radko Mladic or Radovan Karadzic. He described the lack of trust between the various countries searching for them: NATO, the United States, Serbia, and Bosnia-Herzegovina. Thus, he shrugged, "it suits everyone not to find them."[2] He worried about the possibility of Islamic terrorists, who fought in the civil wars and who might be loose in the world with Bosnian passports. But aid from the international community could help an impoverished Bosnia to re-issue its passports. Lastly, the threat to peace in the Balkans remains Kosovo, a ward of the international community, neither Serbian nor Albanian—a garrison state with a lot of unhappy garrisons. That said, he remained hopeful that in Bosnia better times were coming. As was learned with the Treaty of Berlin and at Sarajevo, as Bosnia goes, so go the Balkans.

Budapest-Vienna-Zurich-Geneva

To GET HOME, we did not take the night train to Montenegro and fly home from Podgorica, once in my travel daydreams. We missed Cetinje and King Nikola's pool table. Instead we boarded the 8:00 A.M. express to Budapest that passed near the bombed bridges in Novi Sad and also Anatole's adopted town of Kikinda. As we crossed into Hungary, we noticed more European farms and fewer Balkan villages that have to barter something to get running water. Both Budapest and Vienna spoke of imperial splendor. We could even take the waters at the Hotel Gellert in Budapest. In Vienna we walked along the Ringstrasse and through the gardens of the Hofburg, reminded that Austria had been "blind to the advantages of a little kindness and courtesy in dealing with the Balkan peoples."

Leaving Vienna, we hardly fit into the sleeping compartments of our last overnight train, but such were the

---

2. Karadzic was subsequently found and shipped to The Hague.

modern railway locks that my wife finally threw away her door wire. We changed trains in Zurich, and arrived home in Geneva in mid-morning. Slowly the rhythms of our lives resumed. Maybe it had not been a dream vacation for the children. We'd had cloudy, rainy days in Belgrade, and some of the plumbing had lived up (or down to) expectations. We had spent a lot of time on railway berths and in minivans. At more than a few meals, the waiters came by with accordions. But if, in thirty-four years, one of the children returns to Koprivnica, and finds familiar cousins or a better school, it will have been worth the short nights on hard rails. I would not even be surprised if one of them, on the way, didn't make a mad dash in Ljubljana to buy grilled chicken.

Burning Bush

(2004)

*"Whenever a man has cast a longing eye on
[office], a rottenness begins in his conduct."*

—Thomas Jefferson

THE GEORGE W. Bush story was supposed to have a happy
ending, including his re-election as president in 2004.
According to the designs of Karl Rove and Pentagon strate-
gists, after the 2002 mid-term elections, divisions of the army
and marines were to liberate Baghdad from oppression, if not
a little oil from Mosul and Basra. With the flank turned in
the war on terror, U.S. troops could then be withdrawn from
Saudi Arabia—removing the thorn in Osama bin Laden's
beard, that of American forces desecrating the holy lands of
Islam. With a wedge between the Axis of Evil and Israel's
milk and honey, the winds of freedom would blow against
the Syrian regime, evicting that enemy from the Golan
Heights and Lebanon. With Afghanistan under the control
of an American foreign legion—even one that is a mixture
of the 82nd Airborne division and Uzbek warlords—terror's
last redoubt in Iran would find itself besieged by freedom
and, perhaps in time for the footage to roll at the Republican

National Convention, send forth a few mullahs waving white flags. In exchange, a grateful American populace in November 2004 would vote Bush the triumph that he deserved.

The cost of these re-election spots is now approaching $150 billion dollars, and neither Bush nor the nation has much to show for the air time. Osama bin Laden remains the man in motion, still a match, with his handwritten messages, for Pentagon AWACs. The splendid little war in Iraq is now costing the Pentagon $5 billion a month, with no light at the end of any tunnels, even those being searched for weapons of mass destruction. An invisible army of pipe-bombers has tied down America's elite military divisions in such sideshows as Fallujah and Najaf. Instead of gratefully devouring chocolate bars, some Iraqis find themselves in Saddam Hussein's repainted prisons, naked or hooded in hairshirts that might well have been sewn by the Ku Klux Klan. All we know about our terrorist opponents is that they fought the Battle of Lower Manhattan with box cutters and a handful of one-way airline tickets. By contrast, the Bush administration has invested billions in the counterattack, paid for by budget deficits and weary financial markets. Is it thus any wonder that the Bush campaign imagineers thought Ronald Reagan speaking from the grave articulated a clearer election message than did George W. Bush in the bully pulpit?

During this reversal of political fortunes, I read a series of Bush biographies. I started with those by Kevin Phillips, an unfrocked Republican, Molly Ivins, a syndicated columnist who lives in Texas, and David Corn, who covers Washington for *The Nation*. Of other Bush presidency confessionals I only read chapters, for example, in those by Paul O'Neil, the former Treasury secretary, Bob Woodward, of the *Washington Post*, and Joseph Wilson, a State Department official whose wife was outed as a CIA operative after he dismissed claims about Iraqi nuclear intrigue in Africa.

After a while, it became clear that all of these books were telling the same story: the rake's progress of George W. Bush as he makes his way from Andover and Yale to the quagmires of the Marsh Arabs. Along the road he meets temptation and Jesus, businessmen of easy virtue and brave fire fighters. The Knight Errant, searching for both light and terrorists on the road to Damascus, becomes the Knight of the Doleful Countenance, besieged by budget deficits, car bombers, and the memoirs of angry footmen. As Spiro Agnew might have said: if you have read one Bush biography, you have read them all. But while the books tell a familiar tale, they also shine light in some dark corners, no bad thing in an election year.

A REPUBLICAN STRATEGIST during the Nixon years, Phillips remains faithful to the silent majority, the lower and middle classes that he finds abandoned by the Bush presidency's coddling of the rich and famous. He chooses the word 'dynasty' to describe the Bush family's politics, both to evoke the prime-time melodrama as well as to offend George H.W. Bush, who prefers to describe the success of his sons with the word 'legacy'—as if the presidency were a family heirloom. Phillips writes: "That the Bushes have many qualities to commend them as a private family—community involvement, generosity to those who work for them—is not really the point. They are not a private family. They are a public family, and one that is writing a new definition of the presidency. They are bending public policy toward family grudges and interests. What matters is their policy and conduct in that emerging role. The further evidence, since 9/11, of the United States' becoming an embattled imperium, even showing faint specklings of garrison state thinking, only doubles the stakes."

Phillips came to his Bush biography after an earlier best-seller, *Wealth and Democracy*, which makes the argument that "the imbalance of wealth and democracy in the United States is unsustainable [and that] market theology and unelected leadership have been displacing politics and elections." He calls it "plutocracy by some other name," and argues that never before in American history has the nation had such a gap between rich and poor.[1] He prefers the norms of Franklin Roosevelt, whom he quotes: "Such inherited economic power is as inconsistent with the ideals of this generation as inherited political power was inconsistent with the ideals of the generation which established our government." Hence Phillips bristles at both the political and economic inheritances of the Bush clan.

Bush-watching from Texas, Molly Ivins and her co-author Lou Dubose wrote an earlier well-read account of Governor George W. Bush, *Shrub*. In *Bushwacked*, they balance accounts of his life and presidency with after-action reports on ordinary citizens who lack access to the boardrooms of Enron and Halliburton. One chapter tells of failed promises in education (they quote one school administrator: "They're spending less money on education reform than they were

---

1. Phillips uses a number of statistics to develop this thesis. For example, in 1999, he writes, "nearly 90% of all shares were held by the wealthiest 10% of households." In 1998, the top 1 percent had more income than 100 million in the bottom 40 percent. The top 100 CEOs used to earn 39 times the pay of an average worker. Now they earn more than 1000 times. J.P. Morgan, for one, thought the limit should be 20 times.

offering Turkey to accept U.S. troops"), and another tells the story of environmental parsimony. ("The dirty secret is that the Superfund isn't super anymore. What was once a $3.8 billion trust bottomed out at $28 million in 2003—not even enough to cover one of the hundreds of abandoned sites in the country. The money's gone.") Ivins once told a friend of mine that it would be a mistake to underestimate George W. Bush, as, she said, "he is both charming and smart." But her conclusions here are different: "Faith-based domestic policy is scary. Faith-based foreign policy is terrifying—in an apocalyptic way."

David Corn's thesis in *The Lies of George Bush* is that George Bush has advanced his careers in business and politics by "mastering the politics of deception," and that when given the choice of telling the truth or lying, Bush and those around him prevaricate. Corn concludes: "With his misrepresentations and false assertions, Bush has dramatically changed the nation and the world. He has turned the United States into an occupying power. Via his tilted-to-the-wealthy tax cuts, he has profoundly reshaped the U.S. budget for years to come, most likely ensuring a long stretch of deficits that will make it quite difficult for the federal government to fund existing programs or contemplate new ones. He did all this with lies. They were essential to Bush's success."

Corn uses example of Bush's conduct and language to deconstruct the 2000 presidential campaign, his friendship with Enron's chairman, his service in the Texas Air National Guard, the war in Afghanistan, and the invasion of Iraq—all of which relied upon a political style that includes "the frequent deployment of misleading statements, half-true assertions, or flat-out lies." No doubt a student of George Orwell, who wrote that "political language is designed to make lies sound truthful," Corn believes Bush is deceptive even when he does not have to be—as if it were a reflexive impulse, a trait that runs from his National Guard AWOL explanations to the alleged links between Saddam Hussein and Al-Qaeda.

Admirable as are many of the books about Bush and his presidency, the problem with most campaign biographies is that they become dated before the balloons descend from the rafters at the national conventions. None of these books, for example, describes or anticipates America's self-inflicted wounds at Abu Ghraib prison. Nor were they published in time to include President Bush's description of Israel's Prime Minister, Ariel Sharon, as "a man of peace" during the attacks in Gaza. But rather than criticize these books because they lack the timeliness of all-news radio, I chose to imagine that I had discovered them twenty years from now, long after the Presidency of George W. Bush had ended. Seen from that distance, the books of Phillips, Ivins, and Corn can be read as political obituaries, post-mortems on a presidency that failed even before tax cuts eviscerated the federal budget or an American crown prince began tilting at windmills in the Iraqi desert. Herewith are their obsequies:

BORN AT THE end of World War II, George W. Bush was a rank and file baby boomer and thus came of age riding the tricycles of affluence in mid-century America. His father had left Yale to fight in the Pacific and returned a decorated hero. His mother could trace ancestry to, among others, the family of President Franklin Pierce. Bush grew up in Midland, Texas, allowing him to claim heritage to Western civilization, at least that of sage and tumbleweed. But Midland in the 1950s also had aspects of a dude ranch. Phillips writes that many of his parents' friends in the oil business were "transplanted Ivy Leaguers." He notes that "the town's newly paved streets were named after Ivy League colleges."

George W. Bush was also a scion of Eastern establishment board rooms. His paternal great-grandfather, Samuel Bush, "had become wealthy," writes Phillips, "as the president of Buckeye Steel Castings, a railroad-equipment-manufacturing firm, which he headed from 1908 until his retirement in 1927." His grandmother's father, George Herbert Walker, managed G.H. Walker and Company, a St. Louis investment bank that developed business ties with the likes of J.P. Morgan and W. Averell Harriman. It merged into Brown Brothers Harriman, where his grandfather, Prescott Bush, became a partner. Prescott was also the first of three Bushes to attend Andover and Yale, and take the oaths of secrecy from Skull and Bones, a Yale fraternity in which it is possible—to use another of Phillips's reflections—"to contemplate government as a profitable monopoly, and the people as hereditary property."

At Yale, Bush had aspirations to become a stockbroker, as "generally speaking," writes Phililps, Bush "progeny have become almost exclusively financial entrepreneurs." But his bloodline would eventually press him to higher callings. Of Samuel Bush and George Herbert Walker, Phillips writes: "Over the years they led the family to an involvement with the mainstays of the twentieth-century American national security state: finance, oil and energy, the federal government, the so-called military-industrial-complex, and the CIA, the National Security Agency, and the rest of the intelligence community." In addition to investment banking, Prescott Bush was also a U.S. Senator from Connecticut. During the 1950s, he played client golf with, among others, Vice President Richard Nixon, who later appointed his son, George

Herbert Walker Bush, to serve as chairman of the Republican party. Son Bush went from there to become U.S. ambassador to China, director of the Central Intelligence Agency, vice president under Ronald Reagan, and president. But it was also from Prescott Bush that the two presidents Bush inherited aspects of their public Babbittry, as seen, for example, on the flight deck of the carrier *Lincoln*. Phillips describes one of Prescott's campaign events: "Even at age fifty-seven in 1952, introducing presidential candidate Dwight Eisenhower at Yale, he wore a collegian's raccoon coat, acting like a cheer-leader until students started calling "Down, Bush.""

After graduation from Yale, Bush began his years in the wilderness, a wandering that led him from the Texas Air National Guard, to business school at Harvard, to a failed run for Congress, to drink and the oil business. His National Guard fighter group was known as the "Champagne Unit," according to Corn, who also reports that "when Bush entered the Guard, he had to say on his application paper whether he was willing to volunteer for overseas duty. He checked the box that read 'do not volunteer.'" In 1972, Bush laid off the Champagne Unit long enough to live in Alabama, where a family friend was running for the U.S. Senate. By some press accounts, he trashed his sublet apartment in Alabama and never reported to duty for the local Air National Guard, which may explain why his family sent him East to the Har-vard Business School. In three books, the only mention of this education refers to his taste for Wild Turkey, in contrast to that Business School's normal case loads of Scotch.

IF GEORGE W. Bush went east as if sprung from the pages of Hunter Thompson, he returned to Texas in the mid-1970s as if a character in a novel by John O'Hara, who drew inspiration from Yale men with drinking problems. Bush lived in Houston, dabbled in politics, and lost the money he borrowed from relatives and friends. He was voted the sloppiest dresser at his golf club. He lost a run for Congress in 1978. As O'Hara wrote in *Appointment in Samara*: "Ambition is all right, just as long as you don't get too ambitious." Corn quotes from the financier, George Soros, who was an investor in a company that, in turn, invested in George W. Bush's company. Soros remembers: "He was supposed to bring in the [Persian] Gulf connection. But it didn't come to anything. We were buying political influence. That was it. He was not much of a businessman." If he was "not much of a businessman," how did he come to end up with a net worth of more than $10 million when he became President in 2000?

George W. Bush got his start in the oil business in 1979 with $565,000 from an uncle, who headed J. Bush and Company, a New York investment company. When that was gone, Arbusto, Bush's company, came up with $4.7 million from the same pipeline of family and friends. (At the time, his father was Vice President of the United States, so possibly investors viewed an investment in the son as a convertible security.[2]) In 1984, G.W. Bush had merged his company, whose only assets were tax losses, into Spectrum 7 Energy Corporation. After that transaction, Bush owned 16 percent of Spectrum. That wildcat failed to purr, and

---

2. Ivins and Dubose recount the following: "As we reported in *Shrub*, when GeeDubya's company, Arbusto, was in a terminal cash crunch, Uzi [Philip Uzielli] showed up and paid $1 million for 10 percent of a failing company valued at $382,376…In other words, Uzielli paid $1 million for $38,200 in equity….Mr. Uzielli lost his entire $1 million investment but later told reporters he didn't regret it. He described his investment with Bush as a 'losing wicket' but said 'it was great fun.' What a sport."

Bush and his partners were back on the street, looking for an exit strategy, or at least a greater fool. They found both in Harken Energy, "a small Texas firm with high-powered connections that was then gobbling up other small oil companies on the verge of bankruptcy." Bush got $530,000 in stock, a seat on the board, and a no-show job that paid about $100,000.

Harken was a nonprofit corporation, although not by design. While Bush was a member of the board, and also on the audit committee, the company resorted to a series of accounting gimmicks to hide the losses. At one point it booked a $7.9 million gain on the sale of a subsidiary, even though the parent company held a note on virtually the entire amount of the deal. But that slight-of-numbers allowed Harken to show a small loss for the year, not reservoirs of red ink. It also enabled George W. Bush to sell $848,560 in Harken shares to an investor who has never been identified. Corn writes: "The Harken deal was all very Enron-ish. An insider selling stock before the price tumbled." Phillips concludes: "Harken was not Enron, but it was certainly Enron in the making. What Bush took out of Harken was also twenty times as much as Bill and Hillary lost in a crummy Arkansas real estate deal that cost American taxpayers seventy million dollars to investigate." Ivins and Dubose are more direct: "George W. Bush should declare himself a conscientious objector in his own war on corporate crime."

By 1990, Ivins and Dubose continue, "Bush walked away from the Texas 'awl bidness', with almost a million in cash— after a career during which he lost more than $3 million of other people's money." But he needed the money so he could repay a loan of $600,000 that he had taken to invest in the Texas Rangers baseball team. In 1989, a group of Texas businessmen had agreed to buy the team, and they invited Bush into the syndicate. He paid $600,000 for 2 percent of the team. The offer came the same year his father was elected President of the United States, which has a way of juicing the ball and shortening the fences.

Like the oil businesses, baseball is another oligopoly that is well-suited to a family with the political connections that are second nature to the Bushes. Exempt from antitrust regulations, the owners of professional baseball teams are, nevertheless, free to blackmail their fans should the local municipality not come across with assorted tax breaks or a new stadium, to keep the team from leaving town. Bush and his co-owners so threatened Arlington, Texas, which paid the following in ransom to the Rangers' owners: a new $190 million stadium that was financed by a local bond issue ($135 million) and a ticket surcharge. After only $60 million was repaid, the ownership of the $190 million stadium, and nearly all the revenue, transferred to the team owners. Suddenly a second-division team, acquired for less than $100 million, was worth $250 million when it was sold in 1998 (by then George W. Bush was governor of Texas, and the buyer had made money investing state funds). As if to acknowledge the leverage of Bush's political influence, his grateful co-owners voted him stock options that turned his $600,000 investment into almost $15 million.

BEFORE BUSH WAS elected governor of Texas in 1994, he gave up drinking and came to Jesus. Phillips writes: "The biblical role in which he so easily and comfortably fell was that of the prodigal son (Luke 15:11–24)—a wayward sinner, in this instance reclaimed from near-alcoholism or worse and brought to God and salvation with the preacher [Billy] Graham in 1985, just a year or so before his fortieth birthday." He might have wished to avoid an appointment in Samara. But his choice of churches, the Southern Baptist Convention (65 percent of whom agreed that the Bible was the literal word of God), also coincided with an emerging bloc of the Republican Party. The prodigal son believed his father had lost the presidency in 1992 because he had failed to unbuckle the Bible belt. Now a fundamentalist, Bush threw his lot in with what Phillips calls "a new militancy" that "was church-driven. Instead of Episcopalians, Methodists, and Presbyterians, the congressional Republican Party was now dominated by the fast-growing South Baptists, many of whom belonged to the denomination's newly ascendant conservative faction." From now on, Jesus would be his copilot, even if he had never tasted champagne.

George Bush served as governor of Texas from 1994 to 2000. When he ran for president in 2000, he presented himself as a "compassionate conservative," someone who—while balancing the budget, cutting taxes and standing tall with the police—had reached out to school children and embraced social justice. Nevertheless, Ivins and Dubose offer this cautionary tale: "As president, Bush had his first big legislative victory in a tax cut that turned a $127 billion surplus into a $288 billion deficit. Been there. As governor, Bush inherited a $6 billion surplus, pushed through two major tax breaks for property owners, and promised they would 'grow the economy' so much the state would never even miss the money. Two years after he left we're looking at a $10 billion budget deficit, and rising."

Few campaigning for Bush in 2000 were under any illusions that he should be president because of his record in Texas. Despite his claims of having been "the education governor," more than 50 percent of students in the large Texas cities never graduated from high school. Instead, as Phillips observes, "George W. Bush had become a rare rallying point for notions of restoration, legitimacy, and personal responsibility." He would remove the stains from the Oval Office. Pollsters would not guide his campaign. Decency, not campaign contributors, would move into the White House. Nevertheless, as Corn writes, Bush's 2000 campaign became one of "nasty ads, pandering, expedience-driven position-shifting, cover-up, and assorted spinning." (For example: "His switch from 'pro-choice' to 'pro-life' had escaped public notice.") Still, he had what in marketing is known as "brand recognition." Since 1976, either a Bush or Dole had been a candidate for national office in every election. Theodore Roosevelt said of Mark Hanna that he had "advertised McKinley as if he were patent medicine." In this campaign, the Bush trademark was promoted for its restorative powers.

Selling snake oil came naturally to Karl Rove, whom Phillips quotes: "The great majority of mankind is satisfied with appearances, as though they are realities." Appearance alone, however, did not elect George W. Bush president. That was left to the Supreme Court, which voted 5-4 against allowing Florida to conduct a state-wide recount of cast ballots. The next day, Al Gore, who had won the popular vote, conceded. But before the Florida case went to the Supreme Court, the Bush campaign spent, according to Corn, $13.8 million in the Florida recount wars: "Roughly one hundred lawyers were sent to Florida and Texas, and frequent use was made (with recompense) of Enron and Halliburton corporate aircraft."[3] Even before that fight in Florida, Ivins and Dubose remarked that "Governor George W. Bush was a creation of Enron."

THE DAY AFTER George W. Bush was inaugurated president, he invited Kenneth Lay, chairman and chief executive officer of Enron, the energy corporation, to the White House for lunch. After Enron collapsed later that year, costing investors and employees losses of $68 billion, Bush made his friendship with Lay appear casual, someone he had met only in 1994, when he first ran for governor of Texas. He even described Lay as more of a friend and supporter of his opponent, Governor Ann Richards. But in describing the links between both presidents Bush and Lay, Corn quotes the Enron chairman himself on the origin of his relationship with the current president: "In 1989, Lay spearheaded a drive to convince the first President Bush to locate his presidential library in Houston. That's when I probably spent a little more quality time with George W.'" Ivins and Dubose elaborate: "When he ran for Governor in 1994, Enron gave Bush $146,500; he got $47,500 in direct contributions from Ken and Linda Lay. Lay gave Ann Richards $12,500." In the 2000 election, besides giving candidate Bush access to the corporate plane, Enron donated $700,000 to his campaign—even in Texas, something more than lunch money.

---

3. The Republicans had James Baker III, perhaps the rival of Mark Hanna in marketing presidencies, as its point-man. By contrast, the Democrats, who spent only $3.2 million, had a soft-spoken lawyer, Warren Christopher, there for the commonweal. He would never have quoted Hanna who once said that "all questions of government in a democracy are questions of money."

Enron was the largest corporate donor to federal candidates between 1993 and 2001, giving $5.3 million to assorted campaigns, including those of Lay's now-estranged friend, George W. Bush. In return for this civic pride, Enron was allowed to convert the staid business of natural gas transmissions into one of the rings of the Chicago Board of Options, in which Enron both ran the trading pit and made the largest bets on future energy prices. It was work that began under the first President Bush, who used Enron's help in passing the Energy Act of 1992. Phillips describes that bill: "This act, which mandated the deregulation of electricity at the wholesale level, also obliged utilities to carry privately marketed electricity (like Enron's) on their wires and permitted states to deregulate retail electricity. Transmission lines, in short, became common carriers. It was one of several breakthroughs that made possible Enron's exponential growth during the 1990s." During these years it did not hurt that Enron benefited from $7.2 billion in publicly funded financing for projects in twenty-nine countries or that the first Bush administration exempted Enron from oversight by the Commodity Futures Trading Commission, even though it was trading energy futures as if they were pork bellies. Enron stood at the center of a new Gilded Age. Phillips quotes Mark Twain on the first: "I think I can say with pride that we have legislatures that bring higher prices than any in the world."

Enron turned out to be on the wrong side of many markets, not unlike one of George W. Bush's oil ventures. Like some executives at Harken, Enron's insiders decided against sharing the bad news with investors and quietly sold stock into the bubble of artificial earnings. Corn reports that Lay

sold $50 million in Enron shares "while advising Enron
employees to buy on the dips of Enron's share price." But the
looting was wholesale, as Ivins and Dubose describe: "On
October 17, 2001, Enron locked workers out of the 401(k)
plans while a new investment firm took over management
of retirement accounts. Executives and directors were not
locked out. They saw the company collapsing and dumped
$1.1 billion in shares. By the time workers could get to their
401(k) accounts, the Enron stock they had for retirement
was worthless. One coincidence sure to be mentioned in the
shareholders' suits is the fact that the employee 401(k) losses
were $1.2 billion—just $100 million shy of what Enron's
insiders walked away with." None of the authors mentions
the fate of Karl Rove's portfolio, as at one time he owned
$108,000 in Enron shares.

ROVE, HOWEVER, HAD bigger problems than figuring out
how to go short against the box. His candidate faced the
risk of becoming known as the honorary president of Enron.
Senior members of the Bush administration included former
executives of Enron. His father was one of its more prominent frontmen. Hence for the 2002 mid-term elections, and
beyond, Rove cast Bush in the role of a wartime president,
someone there to lead the nation in a time of crisis. True,
the United States lost a group of office buildings and suffered 3,000 casualties in the attacks of September 11. But
was the analogy of these losses Pearl Harbor or the sinking
of the Hudson River steamer *General Slocum*, which cost the
lives of 1,000 New Yorkers in 1904? Bush never paused to
reflect. Instead he sent troops to the Philippines, Afghanistan, Yemen, Iraq, and the former Soviet republic of Geor-

gia to search the caves of terrorism. Still the war on terror remained a blur, as the front lines stretched from the Sudan and rundown German apartments to Moroccan Internet cafés. As Corn writes: "Terrorism is a methodology—used for centuries by various forces. After he left the white House, Bush speechwriter David Frum bemoaned this device: "All this talk of fighting 'terrorism' made as much sense as a war against 'sneak-attackism' would have made after Pearl Harbor. Terror was a tactic, not an enemy.""

To give a face to battle, the Bush administration chose Saddam Hussein, the Iraqi president who had done America's bidding in the 1981 to 1989 trench war against Iran. For that effort he was given chemicals of mass destruction and a blind eye until he raised taking Kuwait as a spoil of war. Had he only liberated a few oil reserves in northern Kuwait, Hussein might have succeeded. But his troops emptied Kuwait City of color televisions and stretch limousines, and menaced the Saudi monarchy, thus prompting an Allied coalition to remove Hussein's forces from Kuwait. Iraq then became a good safe menace during the 1990s, a place to denounce at the United Nations or useful to train pilots over the no-fly zone. Compared to the United States, which was spending $399 billion annually on its military, Iraq was spending $1.4 billion. Hussein practiced barbarism against the Kurds, but was no more ruthless than NATO-member Turkey, which had the same violent agenda against Kurdish irredentism.

How DID IT come that George W. Bush decided to gamble his presidency, as if it were one of Enron's out-of-the-money futures contracts, on bringing democracy to the Sunni triangle? Phillips offers this observation: "None of the Bushes has ever been a serious intellectual in defense or foreign policy matters. For them, physical activity—especially sports such as golf or speedboating—has been more appealing than long evenings devoted to abstract thought. The effect has been to leave George W. Bush, like previous Texan wartime president Lyndon Johnson, at the mercy of second-rate defense intellectuals, this time ones who had changed the gray pinstripes of neoconservative think tanks for Pentagon togas of neoimperialism."

He continues:

> After the election of 2000, son George II followed the Iraq warpath of George I, even attacking similarly near the midpoint of his term. Arguably more parentally motivated in his foreign wars than England's restored Charles II, George W. Bush was demonstrably more Bourbon in vengeful recollection than France's Louis XVIII. This is based on his reappointment of officials charged, indicted, or tarred in his father's best-known scandal (Iran-contra): Elliot Abrams, John Poindexter, John Negroponte, et al. The younger Bush also promoted the 1989–92 Bush warhawks most eager for a follow-up with Iraq—Paul Wolfowitz and Douglas Feith—and likewise selected his father's Gulf War defense secretary, Richard Cheney, as vice president....Yet one could plausibly argue that the pull on George W. Bush toward war with Saddam Hussein was as much a family legacy as were his admissions to Andover, Yale, and Skull and Bones.

The same messianic streak that doomed Woodrow Wilson at Versailles proved George W. Bush's undoing in Iraq. There was Wilsonian piety in the doctrine of preemptive war, enunciated at West Point in June 2002. On other occasions he proclaimed: "We are committed to rid the world of evil."[4] Phillips describes how Bush after September 11 "came to feel that the Almighty was speaking to him and had chosen him for a great role."

For Cheney, who held on to his Halliburton stock options when he became vice president, Iraq was less a war of liberation and more a profit center. A lot of the war to seize Baghdad was out-sourced, following plans pushed by Cheney when he was secretary of defense that privatized phalanxes of the American military. He then moved over to run Halliburton, which, as Phillips writes, "is first and foremost among the two dozen or so U.S. firms that fit the new category of 'private military companies' (PMCs)—primarily service providers of high-tech warfare, including communications and intelligence, logistical support, and battlefield training and planning. Since 1994, the Defense Department has entered into just over 3,000 contracts with PMCs, valued at more than $300 billion; 2,700 were held by just two companies: Kellogg, Brown and Root, the Halliburton subsidiary, and the Virginia-based management and technology consulting firm Booz, Allen, and Hamilton."

The problem with out-sourcing the war in Iraq was that, as Soros remarked, Bush wasn't "much of a businessman." For example, some of the interrogators at the Baghdad prison, Abu Ghraib, were hired guns, and thus their prosecution fell outside either military or American justice. A few Iraqis with pipe bombs shut in Iraq's oil reserves, the third largest in the world, so oil went to $40 a barrel. Nor were the books in

---

4. When Ivins and Dubose heard this, they wrote: "That could take a while. This is frankly ridiculous and has already led to glaringly inconsistent policies. Quite a shift from John Quincy Adams' 'We go not abroad in search of monsters to destroy.'"

the war on terror balanced any better than the balance sheet at Harken Energy or Enron. The cost of the war effort was $5 billion a month, after Congress voted a down payment of $135 billion. The budgets for the Defense Department, the Central Intelligence Agency, and Homeland Security, not to mention the Star Wars missile shield, exceeded $470 billion annually, although for that investment Osama bin Laden remained as footloose as Kenneth Lay.

Such expenditure came at a time when, because of the Bush tax cuts, the forecast of the 2004 budget deficit was estimated at $521 billion, down from the $127 billion surplus he inherited in 2001. But as one Harken investor said: 'His name was George Bush. That was worth the money they paid him.'

Those Magnificent Medici

(2005)

ALTHOUGH I LIVE in Europe and first went to Florence in 1970, I cannot say I know the city well. Of that first visit, as part of a family Grand Tour, I have no memory of Brunelleschi's dome or Michelangelo's David, although we undoubtedly saw both. Then a high-school sophomore, brooding on the baseball practices I was missing, I recall fleeing the tedium of the Pitti Palace and walking the Boboli Gardens in a light rain, happy to have escaped a soporific world of madonnas and children. After moving to Switzerland in the 1990s, I would occasionally brush Florence. In 1992, my wife and I were there for a day with young children, but limited our appreciation of the great masters to ice cream and inquiries, in bad Italian, on where it would be possible to purchase a wading pool. A few years later, working in banking, I had a sumptuous lunch in a Florentine counting house—a Tuscan reverie of white wine, salad, veal, dessert, and coffee—but all I saw of Florence were glimpses of Giotto's campanile from the car that took our business delegation to and from the Pisa airport.

Even from afar, I continued to have a love-hate relationship with the city. Over the years I collected books about its political and literary history, absorbed Niccolò Machiavelli's *The Prince*, and, when the children got older, made dinnertable noises about how they should study art history for a semester in Florence. But I never returned to the city, even though from where we live it is an easy flight or an overnight train ride. When I thought of Florence in the summer, I thought of the hordes laying siege to the Duomo, the lines outside the Uffizi Palace, and my teenage museum feet in the Pitti Palace. Hence when I dreamed of romantic weekends or family vacations, Florence held as little appeal as a Renaissance theme park where I could imagine long lines outside such attractions as Dante's Dungeon or Michelangelo's Marble Mountain.

One reason, among many, that I am indebted to Tim Parks, and his history of the Medici bank—*Medici Money: Banking, Metaphysics, and Art in Fifteenth-Century Florence*—is that it has allowed me to give Florence another chance. I was not cast adrift in a sea of religious art, but I could connect the dots of a story that interested me, Florentine banking, and see it in the context of a family, the Medici, whose greed for power, money, and splendor makes them as much figures of modern business as variations on Machiavelli's princes. With Parks under my arm, I even ventured back to the city, braving the crowds before Ghiberti's doors and crossing the Ponte Vecchio, described in one of my guidebooks as a "squalid mixture of souk, airport lounge, and dormitory." I also tracked down the Medici palaces, inspected their crypts, found their bank (or the sidewalk on which it did business), and followed the footsteps of their rivals and assassins. I even rented a bicycle to find the hillside village to which Machiavelli was exiled and where he wrote *The Prince*.

In this sense, *Medici Money* became the guidebook I never had for Florence—something to make the Renaissance marble come alive. Another Florentine, Dante Alighieri, whose house I passed often while crossing the city, wrote of other inhabitants in other circles: "Let us not speak of them but look, and pass on." That's easy to do in Florence, where everyone brushes past a work by Leonardo da Vinci to find lunch or something cold to drink. Hence my gratitude to Parks and his short, accessible, well-written narrative of a bank's rise and fall. Without it I might have abandoned all my hopes for Florence; with it, I could sit with a coffee in the early sunshine of the Piazza della Signoria, knowing that the sparks of Savonarola's Bonfire of the Vanities, which burned in this square, were lit with Medici conspicuous consumption.

Parks, an Englishman born in Manchester, is best known for his accounts of Italian expatriate living, *Italian Neighbors* and *An Italian Education*. They are in the vein of the travelogues that sprang from Peter Mayle's *A Year in Provence*. Although he describes Italian living outside Verona, his accounts have many of the same eccentric neighbors and wacky tradesmen who roll up to Mayle's provincial farmhouse. By training, Parks is a professor of literature, but based on his perceptions of the Medici's financial house, he could well add the credential of historian to his dust jackets and curriculum vitae. In the introduction, he writes:

> The Medici bank came before the sacking of Rome (1527), before the sieges of Naples (1527–28) and Florence (1529–30), before the cruel and suffocating inflexibility of the Counter-Reformation, before Italy lost any

practical independence for more than three hundred years. Hence, despite the many wars and occasional torture, the murders and corruption, the interminable vote-rigging and tax evasion that will have to be chronicled in this book, we might nevertheless think of fifteenth-century Florence, the ninety-seven years of the Medici bank, as a quiet parenthesis in the troubled transition from medieval to modern words. A time in which usury and art could flourish.

The book's subtitle makes reference also to metaphysics and art in fifteenth-century Florence. While those subjects are subplots to the bank's history, I suspect Parks's publisher wanted to link his book to the broader themes of the Renaissance, fearful it would otherwise be dismissed a primer on bad banking. Alas, there is more here about finance than the dividends that supported the likes of da Vinci and Michelangelo. But what elevates this book from those studied in business schools (I remember one called *A Brief History of Panics in the United States)* is that Parks can write gracefully about bankers and traders as if they were figures in Renaissance paintings, as, indeed, many of them were.

FLORENCE IN THE fifteenth century is a republican city-state that straddles the banks of the River Arno behind fortified walls and hilltop ramparts. The Renaissance historian Jacob Burckhardt calls it "the first modern state in the world... at once keenly critical and artistically creative." The arched entrance to the Palazzo Vecchio, the crusader fortress that doubles as the city hall, still has a series of maps and murals showing the progress of Florence from a small walled encampment to a city on a hill, something as inspiring as Periclean

Athens or Cicero's Rome. As local residents such as Dante and Giotto are pulling Europe from the Dark Ages into the Renaissance, the city takes its political inspiration more from Roman republicanism than baronial Europe. Government consists of various rotating councils in which local nobility has a turn but rarely dominates. Instead of a standing army for protection, Florence defends itself with diplomatic guile and, when necessary, mercenaries, coalitions of the willing whose courage can be purchased in the coin of many realms.

At the same time the aspiring republic is unsure whether to find inspiration in man or God. Parks writes: "Florence had two visions of itself: It was the true inheritor of ancient Rome, eternal renown, wise republicanism; and it was also the city of God. Why else would the government insist that prostitutes dress as described in the book of Isaiah?" He also describes other incongruities: "Foreign visitors to Italy in the fifteenth century frequently remarked on two peculiarities: Everybody had illegitimate children and everybody was extremely concerned with etiquette."

IN ADDITION TO manners, gold and silk are among the items traded in the city's markets, and in the *loggia* (covered sidewalks) near the stalls are the tables of the moneychangers. Parks describes them: "Bank, Italian *banco* (later *banca*): a bench, table, or board, something to write on, to count over, to divide two engaged in a transaction. That was all the furniture you needed. For some people a bank was just a *tavola*, a table. The Medici have their table in via Porta Rossa, they would say. Some things passed above board, and some below."

The emergence of the Medici family as a powerful banking and political family begins around the tables of Giovanni di Bicci de' Medici (1360–1429), who in 1393 started his bank in Rome, and later opened branches in Florence, Venice, and Naples. Rather than barter primitive toasters for deposits of ducats, Giovanni, according to one historian, "accumulated a vast fortune, mainly by collecting papal revenue from distant points, by clever exchange operations, and by advancing ready cash to popes for immediate expenditure." At his death, his fortune is estimated at a modern value of about a hundred million dollars, and his business passes to his son Cosimo (1389–1464), who has dreams of following the travels of Marco Polo to the East before he enters the family bank. He shares with J.P. Morgan the distinction of having inherited a thriving family banking business, but still getting credit for creating a dynasty.

By the mid-fifteenth century, Florence is one of the money centers of European finance. But it faced the monetary and spiritual problem that to charge interest was sin. Parks writes: "Indeed, as they approached their deathbeds, it seemed that usury was not just *a*, but *the* sin on the minds of wealthy men. Their illegitimate children, the sex they had enjoyed with child slaves from North Africa or the Slavic countries, their greed, gluttony, and general intemperance worried them far less." He elaborates: "Usury makes money 'copulate', said the theologians, quoting Aristotle. Which is unnatural." A practical man when it came to the arbitrage of time deposits and salvation, Cosimo the Elder, as he came to be known, expands the bank across Europe through what might be called offset trades, dealing that is absolved of the sin of usury. As a result, the Medici bank thrives.

All the hallmarks of modern banking can be found on the green velvet covering Cosimo's tables. He has deposits from the collection of papal dues, not just in Italy, but also as far north as Bruges. He also has clients, trading silk and other fabrics into northern Europe, who need to collect on the letters of credit upon which they have dispatched their goods to northern markets. Cosimo obliges both debtors and creditors with what today are known as bankers' acceptances, negotiable instruments that pay interest and principal after a fixed period of time. Parks describes his inventive genius: "Across the banker's green table you could make the move from one world to another, from silver to gold, modesty to riches. At the price of a small commission."

The Medici avoided having this paper condemned as usury by convincing their clients to give the bank discretion over their bank accounts. Parks describes a system still very much alive in Switzerland and elsewhere: "So discretionary deposits involve discretion in two senses. The name of the deposit holder is kept secret, hence the arrangement is *discreet*. The holder's return on the money he deposits is at the *discretion* of the banker, and thus is a *gift* and not a contracted interest rate at all, even if it can usually be expected to work out in the region of 8 to 12 percent per annum." For the purpose of eternal salvation, this arrangement is not considered usurious. The modern equivalent would involve a papal encyclical blessing the gains of insider trading. Parks notes that the "money had the advantage that it could be deposited secretly and, in the event of trouble, withdrawn in a foreign city"—something familiar to any Citibank client today.

As Cosimo's business flourishes, he opens branches in Bruges (1439), Pisa (1442), London (1446), Avignon (1446) and lastly Milan (1452). He is paying about 8 percent on his deposits and earning anywhere from 12-30 percent on his loans. But he is also wise in the arts of investment banking, becoming a broker-dealer in state bonds needed to finance both war and peace. Parks describes this new line of business: "In the early fifteenth century, the Florentine branch of the Medici bank became a major dealer in debt bonds, which by 1426 were trading only at 20 to 35 percent of face value. Clearly the idea of the government's ever paying interest was considered a very long shot." But the Medici are not ordinary bondholders, because without money from the likes of the Medici to fund mercenaries, the city will be lost. Another historian estimates that "the annual interest on war loans to Florence in the years 1429 to 1932 was never less than 15 percent and the take was far more likely to go up to 60 and even 100 percent." Still, the Medici have most of their eggs in the papal basket, as Parks concludes: "Throughout Giovanni de Bicci's life, and Cosimo's, more than 50 percent of the Medici bank's profits came from Rome."

Banking today continues to profit on wheels tilted toward government money. Witness the trade in government bonds, in federally guaranteed mortgages, and how investment banks, like Goldman Sachs, funnel money to Washington to sustain the national debt. By contrast, Cosimo had a more practical side. "Don't trade in wine," he would tell his branch managers, "it's not worth it." But, according to Parks, "he regularly consulted astrologers. Money and magic go together." Parks writes:

> Time is on the Medici side. Cosimo is getting richer. The branches in Rome, Venice, and Geneva in particular are producing healthy profits, the first through collecting Church tributes, the other two through exchange deals along Europe's busiest trading routes. To the sick, cash-starved city of Florence, Medici money seems to possess curative powers.

Cosimo is also a patron of the arts, funding the transformation of Florence into a city of Renaissance splendor. He is christened "Pater Patriae," the father of his country. It reflects his strong leadership and support for the government. But it may also reflect sentiments he held, but which only his grandson, Lorenzo the Magnificent, expressed: "It is hard for the rich to live in Florence, unless they rule the state." Parks quotes from Stendhal that it was "only through the drug of aesthetic passion and pleasure that the Medici were able to subdue the Florentines' 'passionate love for liberty and implacable hatred of nobility.' They accepted the Medici, that is, because the family filled the city with beautiful things."

Cosimo builds his family's palace not far from the Duomo and the old church of San Lorenzo, geographically on the right and left hand of God. On a courtyard pedestal, he displays Donatello's David so that the androgynous bronze warrior would be visible from the street. Upstairs he lines the walls with important works of art, and even builds a chapel, much the way wealthy homeowners today install a home cinema or Jacuzzi—for spiritual purification. The scenes on the chapel walls, in theory, depict the Procession of the Magi, although on closer inspection the murals illustrate the progression of the Medici. At the head of the parade are Cosimo and his brother, leading not just angels and various family members, but also important officers and clients of the Medici bank. Heaven is depicted as a Medici summer villa, and the Holy Father is hard to distinguish from some of the remittance men. Clearly showing God as an advisor to the Medici board is a way of protecting Cosimo from the sin of usury, and the Medici chapel can be read as an early attempt at regulatory disclosure. Now bankers must show reverence for Messrs. Sarbanes and Oxley; then it was more important to be compliant with the Father, Son, and Holy Ghost.

RECOUNTED BY PARKS and others, the story of the Medici bank is a story familiar to many family businesses. Giovanni and Cosimo build up the bank and establish the family fortune while Cosimo's son, Piero (1418–1469, who lived only six years after Cosimo), and his grandson, Lorenzo (1449–1492), run it into the ground. It is not quite of a story of 'shirtsleeves-to-shirtsleeves in three generations,' and the Medici line in the sixteenth century is restored to grand ducal powers. But by the end of the fifteenth century, the bank is bankrupt, the Medicis are expelled from Florence, and Savonarola is running the city-state from their Palazzo Vecchio.

Lorenzo, so-called the Magnificent, inherits the bank and family fortune in 1469. Unlike Cosimo, Lorenzo never understood the business. Cosimo knew figures and he knew his clients, of whom he said wryly: "A couple of lengths of red cloth, and you have your nobleman." On another occasion, recounts Parks, an archbishop asks him to support a drive to stop the clergy from gambling. To which the banker replies: "Maybe first we should stop 'em using loaded dice." He knew a debit from a credit, matched his assets and liabilities, and knew how to liquidate collateral. But for Lorenzo, business and banking are the honey pot from which he can indulge in his aesthetic passions. It is a bottomless family trust, for which both he and Florence are the beneficiaries

After his father's death, Lorenzo is head of the bank, and by extension, its subsidiary, the Florentine government. But he reserves his passion for poetry and public works. By one account he composed "41 sonnets, wrote several acclaimed plays, was an accomplished architect, played the lyre and the organ to accompany his own compositions, was the most admired patron of the Arts in Europe and became famous for his philanthropy." Parks elaborates: "Lorenzo would eventually be able to think of Florence as becoming—through his government, his marriage-arranging, his manipulation of available patronage to painters, poets, sculptors, and architects—his own personal work of art."

If portraits of Cosimo make him look like Cortez conquering Mexico, Lorenzo is depicted with a scruffy beard, perhaps only happy when chanting verse with his poetic friends. But he presides over Florence as if a Roman emperor. "And," writes Lauro Martines, the author of *April Blood*, a history of a plot against the Medici, "as he worked to make Florentine public authority the possession of the Medici, his constant claim was that the good of Florence and the good of the Medici family were one and the same. He even came to believe it." But Parks quotes one historian that "Lorenzo's greatest failing was suspicion", and concludes, "the best way to destroy Lorenzo would be to lend him money and watch him waste it."

In effect, that scheme is what cost the Medici the family bank. The decline begins when the Medici move away from counter-trade business, with its steady but sure profits, and increase the loans they extend to governments, notably those of the Papal States. (Citibank's former chairman Walter Wriston liked to quip that "countries don't go bankrupt," but that did not mean they repaid their loans, including those to Citibank.) Parks writes: "From the 1460s onward, the Medici bank was lending out more to the Curia than it was taking in with the commission on papal tributes." It opens branches, notably that in Ancona, for political rather than financial reasons. To secure its monopoly in the alum trade—a mineral used to dye garments—it agrees with the papacy what is known as a red clause letter of credit, which means the Medici are forced to pay the pope before any of the minerals are shipped. In 1474, the pope closes his accounts with the Medici, following an audit of the Florentines' books; two years later, he ends their alum monopoly while neglecting to pay the papacy's outstanding obligations ("the pope is as stubborn as a corpse" is how the branch manager in Rome describes his slow-pay client). Thus the bank is squeezed between nonperforming loans and a run on deposits.

Between the late 1470s and early 1480s, the Medici bank fails—as would have many American banks, including the large ones, had not the U.S. federal government in the 1980s and 1990s tolerated bad loans on their balance sheet, and had not the Federal Reserve not indirectly fueled the recapitalization of the banking system by drastically cutting interest rates. But Florence in the 1480s had no such thing as deposit insurance or a central banker as malleable as Alan Greenspan. In the end, even Lorenzo is taking money from client accounts.

Of the bank's failure, Parks writes: "One would have thought that the crises of the previous years would have demonstrated once and for all the folly of tying up a bank's capital in loans to a monarch who not only was barely solvent but liable at any moment to be overwhelmed by civil war." But the men running the Medici bank are adornments at a rich court, not practical bankers. "Yet one can't help feeling that at a very deep level the whole Florentine attitude to banking had changed. The old humility, the old enthusiasm for the nitty-gritty of moneymaking, was gone. The families traditionally involved in banking were now used to their wealth and looking for other forms of excitement." Lorenzo, and many others at the table, Parks concludes, were "only *playing* at banking in order to be close to kings and queens."

Among the collateral damaged in the failure of the Medici bank is the run on confidence in the Florentine government. For too long Lorenzo has confused the state treasury with his private accounts—an overdraft he could rollover so long as the bank had liquidity. Martines writes: "His beautifully-orchestrated 'reforms' had been a matter of timing, numbers, disinformation, intimidation, bribery, and electoral machination. This was Renaissance statecraft as art: the paradigm of what it was to rule by 'civil' and 'constitutional' means in Medicean Florence." In response, in 1478, members of the powerful Pazzi family plot to assassinate Lorenzo and his brother, Giuliano, and the attack finally takes place near the altar under Brunelleschi's cupola. Giuliano is killed, but Lorenzo escapes to his palace, from which he orders the elimination, Mafia-style, of the Pazzi clan. Their family is killed and deported, and their palace sacked. Among those who witness Pazzi family members hanging from the parapets of the Palazzo Vecchio is the nine-year-old Machiavelli. For a brief period, the purge maintains the Medici's grip on Florence. But Martines observes: "The plot, however, was also a hinge for the history of Florence, with a lively republic on one side of the turn, stretching back to the thirteenth century, and on the other, after 1478, an incipient principality or 'tyranny'."

NOT ONLY DID Parks's history rekindle my interest in Florentine history, I also found his cautionary tales on modern financial management similar to my own conclusions on why some banks do well and others founder. As it happens, I came to Parks's account of the Medici after spending twenty-one years working in banks around the world. As a trainee in New York, I worked in the credit and commodity departments, assessing the net worth of potential borrowers. Later, in the international division, I visited companies in Australia and Asia, always keeping in mind a quote that appeared in the *Economist*: "When it comes to getting into trouble, commercial bankers are hard to beat." In the last thirteen years of this career, I even worked in Geneva for a Swiss private banking family that had Medicean pretensions: they flew the world on a private plane, lined their villa with Impressionist art, and thought nothing of abusing their employees with midnight phone calls.

Along this pilgrim's progress I came to conclusions expressed in Bertolt Brecht's *Threepenny Opera*: "What is robbing a bank compared with founding a bank?" Or, in the case of the modern corporation, managing a bank. I reported to a series of executives who were paid millions—in salary, bonuses, and stock options—whether or not the banks actually made money for the shareholders. In one bank for which I had worked, the chairman earned over the past eight years an average compensation of $13.6 million, according to *Forbes* magazine, while in that time the price of the bank's stock actually went down. A few bankers I encountered were serious—in the mold of Cosimo the Elder—about protecting the interests of the banks' clients or shareholders. But the vast majority of my colleagues were robed figures at court—there to do a prince's bidding in exchange for a two-car garage in the suburbs. And I often felt like one of them.

In the end, I spent twenty-one years in the vineyards of compound interest. In that time, I found myself inside banks that prospered and others that flirted with collapse. I realize now that not much has changed in banking since the Medici set up their tables near Florence's New Market. The green velvet may now be a computer screen, and the benches are upholstered sofas in corner offices with views of the Thames or Hudson rivers. But the goal of modern bankers, in one sense, is still to sanctify money—to say unction over large corporate salaries or chant blessings on corporate behavior, like that at Enron, which had many of the largest and most prestigious banks as its lenders or advisors.

What I liked about banking was the challenge to make an enterprise thrive, to employ more staff, and to watch the clients prosper. I saw those favorable winds on several occasions, and thus I can share vicariously with Cosimo the thrill that comes from a bank that is expanding into new markets. What I did not like about the banking world is that, after serving princes for twenty-one years, I found myself having to sue in several jurisdictions just to collect the salary and pension that I was contractually owed. The experience made me think I was dealing with the son of *il Magnifico*, of whom Parks writes: "He had inherited Lorenzo's suspicious nature but not his charm." Cosimo would have honored his commitments; Lorenzo would have reneged, perhaps using language I once heard from a superior at Christmas: "If I pay you a bonus, it will have to come out of mine."

Reading Parks about Medici money, I see little difference between today's banks and fifteenth-century Florentine palaces. Most of the banks I know today are dominated by dynastic families or corporate princes, to whom the companies supply cars, drivers, club memberships, and pay envelopes stuffed with stock options, restricted shares, and insurance annuities. (Martines observes that "office of the higher sort in Florence was all about being honored, feared and flattered.")

A corporate hierarch traveling abroad demands, as a matter of course, limousine pickups at every airport, the right restaurant, theater in the evenings, and golf on the weekends, to the point that the job becomes a series of pontifical blessings more than actual business discussions. I was never criticized for my professional work, but I can recall being disparaged because I served Swiss, not French wine, at a board dinner and another time because I had dared to collect the bank's chairman at the airport in a Mercedes taxi, not a stretch limousine. Clearly I had forgotten the letter written by Cardinal Giovanni de' Medici, the son of Lorenzo the Magnificent, who became Pope Leo X. Upon his election he wrote to his brother, the Duke of Nemours: "God has given us the papacy...now let us enjoy it."

Imperial Vapors:
A Journey from Beirut
(2006)

SHORTLY BEFORE THE summer 2006 war between Israel and the Party of God (Hezbollah), I spent a week traveling around Lebanon and, by chance, visited many of the places later bombed. I spent most of my time in and around Beirut, including the southern suburbs. I also traveled in the Bekaa Valley and into south Lebanon, both of which are heavily populated with Shiites. A month ago Lebanon was at peace, although once I traveled outside the capital, it became routine to pass through various military checkpoints, which cropped up with the frequency of phantom tollbooths. In most cases those soldiers manning the checkpoints were members of the Lebanese army, the national armed force that emerged after civil war ended in 1990. In my travels I was told repeatedly that were push to come to civil unrest, the Lebanese army would be no match for Hezbollah, the only Lebanese faction that refused to disarm after the end of the civil wars and, later, the Syrian withdrawal.

My trip began either late on a Sunday or early on a Monday, depending on whether 3:00 A.M. is morning or night. The predawn arrival felt like a hangover. After leaving Vienna, I had eaten the midnight supper, skimmed the pages of my book (*Pity the Nation* by the *Independent* correspondent Robert Fisk) and dosed in my seat—sleep that came fitfully as the man next to me was juggling two toddlers in his lap. In fact, what struck me about the night flight was that it had an air of a day-care center. There were children literally everywhere, and one of my row-mates spent his time spilling Coca-Cola and trying to crawl under the seat in front of us to surprise his mother, who, instead of dosing or reading, was occupied with two other children.

The flight from Austria to Lebanon tracked across Serbia, Bulgaria, and Turkey—the Middle East cauldron of the nineteenth century—and landed at the seaside airport to the south. Even at 3:00 A.M. Beirut was brightly lit, as if perhaps host to a country fair. Remembering photographs of the civil war, I recognized the hotels along the Corniche, saw shadows of the mountains in the background, and craned my neck as we touched down, to pinpoint the location of the Marine Corps barracks that a suicide bomber had destroyed in 1983. Indeed, even at night, as the blue lights of the rebuilt runway bracketed the plane, I saw the Beirut airport as a montage of terrorism's greatest hits: the hijacking of TWA flight 847, the taking of so many hostages on its access roads, and the death of 241 marines, victims of unimaginable road rage. But a new airport has replaced that which the marines were guarding, and inside, as I lined up to purchase a visa and wait for my bag, it felt more like I had landed in Dallas than in one of the capitals of random violence.

Above all, it was ignorance that led me to Lebanon, and the knowledge that needed improving was my own. In my Near Eastern travels, I have spent a lot of time in Israel, including the West Bank and the Gaza Strip. My wife and I once drove a dilapidated rental car around Jordan; and on a fool's errand for my work, I passed the better part of a week in Kuwait, where most of my time was spent in a seaside palace eating meals at about 2:00 A.M. On other travels I have inspected Greek ruins in Turkey, attended meetings in Azerbaijan, and haggled for carpets in Armenia. But I had never been to Lebanon, except vicariously in headlines. I might not have gone this time, had I not had a rambling conversation about the Middle East in which it became clear to me that I was clueless about the faith of the Druze (they are considered Muslims, at least on paper) and wobbly in understanding the origins of either Islamic Jihad or Hezbollah. Of course, that never stopped me from having off-the-shelf opinions about the future of the Middle East. But at the same time I knew that only a trip to Beirut would allow me to visualize passages in civil war histories or assemble a line-up of the various holy warriors.

In planning the trip, I had no idea what to expect in Beirut. I knew that the country had been largely peaceful since the early 1990s. At the same time, in recent years, several prominent journalists, not to mention the prime minister, had been assassinated with car bombs. Nor did I think it appropriate to ask the travel agency arranging my hotel if they are still kidnapping foreigners. I knew Hezbollah to be on the State Department's list of terrorist organizations, and I think of organizations like Abu Nidal and Islamic Jihad as virulent strains of anti-American fever. Various official Web sites caution Americans from visiting Palestinian camps in Beirut and the southern border shared with Israel. None of them declared the country out-of-bounds. But I wondered if the airport road was still in the hands of rival militias, and I recalled passages from *An Evil Cradling*, a hostage narrative by Brian Keenan, which I read, transfixed, in 1994 on a flight from Zurich to Boston. He writes:

> I was barely away from the gate and the fence which enclosed the garden when an old Mercedes, hand-painted dark green with a cream roof, pulled up alongside me. The driver's door opened, preventing me from passing on the narrow street. Out jumped four men, the driver with a hand pistol and three other young men in their mid-twenties, each with a Kalashnikov in his hand and hand gun in his belt.

Every account I have ever heard of a hostage taking in Beirut always read about like this one. Even though the last American hostage, Associated Press correspondent Terry Anderson, was released in 1991, I did something I rarely do in my travels, and that was to have a pre-paid taxi await me at the airport. I was following logic that said no one gripping a voucher had ever been taken captive.

IN THE RECONSTRUCTION of Beirut, which was conceived in 1982 but which only began in the early 1990s, the government connected the airport to central Beirut with the Middle East equivalent of the Cross-Bronx Expressway. During the hostage era, the airport road ran along the slums of the southern suburbs, which, after the Israeli invasion of 1982, filled up with Shiites who had been forced from the borderlands. Thus in the mid-1980s (not that all kidnappers were Shiites) taking hostages was often no more difficult than setting up the seine of a primitive roadblock and then hoping to catch a Western big shot on his way upstream to the airport. Now the airport road is a divided highway, lined on both sides with high walls, and driving into Beirut has the slight feel of the opening chapters of Tom Wolfe's *The Bonfire of the Vanities*, when investment banker Sherman McCoy vanishes into the Bronx: "In the darkness, amid this red swarm, he couldn't get his bearings. His sense of direction was slipping away....His entire stock of landmarks was gone, left behind. At the end of the bridge the expressway split into a Y."

My own ride into the city was less dramatic. But there is also a Y at the end of the airport freeway, with the largely Christian East Beirut to the right and West Beirut, which is largely Muslim, to the left. The highway runs just west of the Green Line, a name imported from Cyprus that also split along its Christian-Muslim seams. During the worst of the civil wars, the Green Line demarcated a line of urban trench warfare. Now most of the gutted buildings have been torn down, but some riddled with bullet and artillery holes are still standing, and their ruined façades stand at odds with nearby new high-rise towers, which project the Green Line as a castaway from Miami Beach.

Much the way I had deliberated over how I would get from the airport into the city, I also puzzled over where and what kind of hotel I should choose. In the civil wars many heavy blows—from artillery, ships, airplanes, and kidnappers—were delivered against West Beirut, which straddles the Corniche and has many of the seaside hotels that epitomized Beirut's cosmopolitanism in the 1960s and early 1970s, before the fighting started in 1976. I liked the idea of a room with a view, and the prices of even luxury hotels in Beirut are reasonable. But the seafront palaces struck me as slightly removed from the central business district, which envelops both sides of the Green Line near the waterfront. At the same time I did not want to check into a modern business hotel, a Sheraton or a Renaissance Plaza, and find that my room in Beirut looked exactly like one in Detroit or the Frankfurt airport. So I scrolled back and forth on an Internet booking Web site until I found the Berkeley Hotel in West Beirut, several blocks south of the American University. A few of the people I was to meet were professors, so it made sense to stay in the neighborhood. At 4:50 A.M., then, I presented my voucher to the taxi driver and signed the registration forms at the Berkeley, and struggled with my bag into a room that Willy Loman would have known as a commercial single.

Beirut is the kind of city where you have no need for an alarm clock; jackhammers do that work more efficiently. At about 9:00 A.M., I was vibrated out of bed to discover that my shower had no more force than a rain forest mist and that the chief features of the hotel breakfast buffet were watermelon and hard-boiled eggs. The morning room at the Berkeley was off the bar, and the other travelers I saw grappling with eggshells struck me as tourists and businessmen from various Gulf States. The hotel lobby lacked air conditioning with conviction, so even at early hours it had the stillness and choked air of the American South before everything that moves was encased in frosty air. I ate breakfast with my maps—one of the city and another for the country—and then climbed into the front seat of a suburban utility vehicle owned by a friend, in which I was given a cursory tour of the city in bright sunshine.

What became immediately clear is that the Green Line is now paved with petrodollars. West Beirut still has the feel of an Arabic Greenwich Village, in which the side streets are jammed with small grocery stores, CD outlets, and shops selling an assortment of modestly priced clothes. But the Bourj or the central park of Beirut now looks more like Dubai than any outtake from a war zone. There are high-rise apartment buildings, glass-fronted office towers, and, often on the same street, a reconstructed church and mosque. At first the new buildings have the super-sized feel of tasteful suburban malls—as if a Barnes & Noble designed with steroids. Many of the buildings also seem disproportionate to the scale of a Mediterranean seaport. But the longer I stayed in Beirut, the more I began to appreciate the elegant grandiosity of the design, which mixes the elements of Ottoman, French, and Mediterranean styles, in ways to suggest that while the old Beirut was lovely and lost in the wars, the new one will be better.

Nevertheless, the masque of the red death, to use Edgar Allen Poe's expression, is also on display in downtown Beirut. As my driver weaved the car through increasingly frantic city traffic, he motioned with his head or pointed fleetingly to sidewalks where this hostage was taken captive or that journalist killed. Throughout the tour we remained within what might be called a gunshot of the Murr Tower, a half completed high-rise that in the urban fighting served both Christian and Muslim snipers. Tall and narrow, like some upended coffin with empty windows, the Murr evokes the darkness of Poe's prose, which in *The Bonfire of the Vanities* Tom Wolfe summarizes:

> A mysterious plague, the Red Death, is ravaging the land. Prince Prospero—Prince *Prospero*—even the name is perfect—Prince Prospero assembles all the best people in his castle and lays in two years' provision of food and drink, and shuts the gates against the outside world, against the virulence of all lesser souls, and commences a masked ball that is to last until the plague has burnt itself out beyond the walls.

And where the Red Death is most at home in Prospero's Beirut is the spot where former Prime Minister Rafik Hariri was assassinated by a car bomb.

A Lebanese businessman with strong ties to the Saudi royal family, Hariri was killed in February 2005 as he drove his car (surrounded by a large and well-armed security detail) on a seaside boulevard between the St. George Hotel and a branch of Hong Kong and Shanghai Bank (HSBC), the British bank. Before entering the fratricidal world of Lebanese politics, Hariri had run a large construction company and counted the Saudis among his most faithful clients. A Sunni Muslim, but initially with good relations both in the Christian and Syrian communities, he was assassinated precisely on the center stage of reconstructed Beirut, a dream that he had conceived in 1982 and then carried out, as prime minister, first from 1992 to 1998 and then from 2000 to 2004. Several times my driver crept near the bloody angle, which now was covered with a large white tent, as you might see at a state fair. Presumably UN investigators were inside, collecting evidence to determine whether the Syrian government had commissioned the hit. Several blocks away, Hariri and some who were killed with him lay in state under other temporary white tents. More than one Beirut resident told me his more permanent resting place depended on whether his friends or enemies were ascendant in Lebanon's political future.

JUST BEFORE LUNCH I called at the law offices of Dr. Chibli Mallat, a prominent jurist whom I had met in Geneva, when he was on a visit to the United Nations. We share a common friend, Edward Mortimer, a senior aide to the UN Director General, Kofi Annan. Before leaving for Beirut I had arranged to meet Mallat on my first day for lunch. His cabinet, to use the French word for a law office, was refreshingly old world. The doors and paneling were made of heavy dark-stained wood, and the floors, at least in memory, were a mixture of tile and faded marble. I have no recollection of air conditioning, but the thick walls of the older building provided cool air. When I walked into the office, I sensed that Mallat was revising either a legal brief or a chapter from a forthcoming book. He took a break from his manuscript, and we talked as a secretary set in front of us a small tray with Turkish coffee. I might well have been calling in Lebanon around 1908, when Lebanon became a leading center of Ottoman dissent.

A man in his mid-forties, Mallat has about him the air of a Young Turk, someone who believes that only a more democratic Lebanon and Middle East can end the cycles of domestic and international violence that have turned the region into a medieval cauldron. Toward that end he is a candidate for the Lebanese presidency, but as we spoke he expressed frustration that no date for an election had been scheduled. Worse, the issue of the current president's term of office—extended, probably illegally, by parliamentary fiat—has become the flint that sparked much of the recent violence that has engulfed Lebanon, including, in part, the recent war with Israel.

As Mallat explained, under the National Pact that has governed the nascent state of Lebanon since independence in 1943, a power-sharing arrangement gives the presidency and the key security positions to Maronite Christians while the prime minister is Sunni, and the speaker of the parliament is a Shiite. In September 2004, under pressure from Syria, parliament extended President Emile Lahoud's term in office. It did so after senior officials in Syria had physically threatened Lebanese Prime Minister Rafik Hariri, who resigned from his office rather than acquiesce to the presidential extension.

Probably as a result of his opposition to Syrian interference in Lebanon, Hariri was assassinated in February 2005. A UN report concluded that his opposition to Lahoud's extended term in office had set in motion the plot to kill him. Rather than reinforce Syria's stranglehold on Lebanese politics and economics, the Hariri assassination subsequently provoked more than a million Lebanese demonstrators to go into the streets of downtown Beirut, and those rallies, plus a UN resolution, became the catalyst that forced Syria to withdraw its occupation forces from Lebanon. Nevertheless, they left behind President Lahoud as "their man," and also counted on Hezbollah to do the bidding for Damascus in hot and cold wars with Israel.

Mallat is not the heir to a warlord family, the usual path to the Lebanese presidency. His grandfather, of the same name, was well known and admired throughout the Arab world as "the poet of the cedars." His father, Wajhdi Mallat, is a respected lawyer and served as the president of the Lebanese Constitutional Council. Mallat defies many stereotypes associated with Middle Eastern politicians, most of whom, to quote the Beatles, find happiness in a warm gun. He speaks fluent English, French, and Arabic. Over the years he has taught international law, in the United Kingdom, at the University of London, and in the United States at Yale and Princeton universities. His many books are available in Arabic and in English. On paper, however, he looks less like a Lebanese academic who has achieved success in the West and more like someone who should have a chance to bridge some of the violent chasms of Middle Eastern politics.

While in London, in the 1990s, he published, with Cambridge University Press, *The Renewal of Islamic Law: Muhammad Baqer as-Sadr, Najaf, and the Shi'i International*, an early study in English of *shari'a* and the revolution brought about in Iran when Ayatollah Ruhollah Khomeini proselytized about the legal canons of an Islamic state. For almost two decades Mallat supported and encouraged both the Iraqi opposition to Saddam Hussein and enfranchisement of the Shiite majority in southern Iraq. On another front, believing that the law is mightier than the sword, he brought criminal charges in Belgium against the subsequent Israeli Prime Minister, Ariel Sharon, for his complicity in the 1983 massacres that killed several thousand Palestinians—many civilians—in the refugee camps of Sabra and Chatilla. Maronite Christians, in Lebanon anyway, are rarely experts in Islamic law. Nor do they often, if ever, represent Palestinians in legal cases involving a senior Israeli politician. But it's hard to run for president in a country where elections are in a state of suspended animation.

During our conversation, we spent a lot of time talking about Syria's influence in Lebanon. When we spoke, Syria had withdrawn from Lebanon, but the long arms of its security apparatus were apparent in the Hariri killing and in the subsequent assassination of Samir Kassir, a journalist, politician, and friend of Mallat's, who had spoken openly about the malevolence of Syria's Lebanese occupation. My notes taken during the meeting, however, are sketchy. It was only later, when I read the transcript of an interview Mallat had given the BBC, that I recaptured the same points that he had made when we spoke. For example, on the term-of-office extension given to President Lahoud, he said: "It's the first time in the history of our country, nay in the history of any country that you have president of a foreign country [Syria] putting pressure and threats on your sitting prime minister in order to force a constitutional amendment. It's quite an extraordinary set of circumstances all of which are not only bizarre but had tragic consequences including the killing of our prime minister." He went on to make the point that Syria could only oppose its weakened position in Lebanon through violence. "They have to blow up parliament, blow up the candidates, that's the only choice. They cannot stop it." Asked if he feared for his life, he said: "Well not only *my* life, I think a lot of candidates will be in that position."

Mallat raised the wild card element that Hezbollah posed in Lebanese politics. Despite the country's image as the domain of factional opposition, it surprised me to learn that Lebanon has few political parties. In fact, according to Mallat, Hezbollah has the largest block of representatives in parliament, with 14 out of 128 seats. Lebanon's fault lines are drawn along religious rather than party lines. Mallat spoke with foreboding tones when he described Hezbollah as both a state within a state, and as the only national body that had refused to disarm after the Lebanese civil wars. Paradoxically, Hezbollah had not been an active participant in the domestic violence that swept Lebanon from 1976 to 1990. But rather than give up their weapons, as the other private armies had done at the end of the fighting, Hezbollah had become a freelance militia that saw a future in manning the ramparts of south Lebanon against Israel. Nor did Mallat think that the Lebanese Army was in a position to disarm Hezbollah, which numbered, he guessed, about 15,000 guerrillas.

Prior to the Hezbollah-Israeli war, in which the entire state of Lebanon suffered most of the collateral damage, Mallat believed that it might have been possible to integrate into Lebanese politics the positive elements of Hezbollah—those which ran schools and clinic, and distributed bread and drinking water—and give the militia fewer reasons to stand at arms. He told the BBC: "Hezbollah has two faces. There is a revolutionary dimension of Hezbollah, and there is a national Lebanese dimension. What I want to offer Hezbollah is for this Lebanese dimension to prevail over on the other one because it is much more fruitful for them and for us." He elaborated: "Well, I have something better to offer them than carrying arms that cannot be used against Israel at this stage because the fight against Israel through the blue line is totally illegal under international law. I am offering Hezbollah two things that are much more interesting for them than what Lahoud or any other contender can offer them. I am offering them, first, a higher ground for the fight against Israel because I do think that we have a lot of problems with Israel, but that these problems must be solved in a nonviolent way and that we can win the fight against Israel, in that manner, far better than with weapons that we can't use. And the second thing that I want to offer Hezbollah is to remove the terrorist label that they have internationally by going to the U.S. government in particular and saying, 'Look we are into a new stage and these people are our people and you cannot call them terrorists.'" But Hezbollah chose to make common cause with Syria and Iran, themselves implausible allies, than with the ideas that Mallat had on offer in his campaign.

Mallat spent some of the years during the previous civil wars outside Lebanon. He studied at the University of California at Berkeley and the School of Oriental and African Studies at the University of London. As he wrote in his book, *The Middle East into the 21ˢᵗ Century*: "The Middle East has been cruel to my generation. Most of my high-school friends in Beirut are scattered throughout the world, where they have well succeeded, but they are also lost to the country and the region." Admirably, his own optimism never wavered: "As the war was raging in my native Lebanon, I had, like so many other compatriots, spent long moments networking and discussing ways out of the impasse."

No doubt the violence of Israel's response to Hezbollah's cross-border raids stunned him and made him fear for his family. But within a few days of the attacks, he had petitioned the UN Security Council for a new resolution, "insisting that Lebanon take full charge of its territory." He wrote further: "Until a lasting ceasefire is at hand, the Israeli government should resist three temptations: the reoccupation of any part of Lebanon, the equation of Hizbullah with the Qa'eda and a policy of assassination which is by nature irreversible, and the punishment of the whole of Lebanon for an action that a small faction has brought upon a largely reluctant population and government. For my part, I have never taken comfort in the killing of Israelis." To the *New York Times* he wrote: "A robust international force can help the Lebanese government assert its exclusive sovereignty over its territory against any possible Syrian, Iranian or Lebanese encroachment." I later asked him in an e-mail what might be the cornerstones of Middle East peace, and he wrote back: "freedom of movement, centrality of individual rights, federal arrangements. It needs a lot of political work and education, but the trend goes now in the opposite direction." Then he concluded more ominously: "On the medium run, however, as things continue not to work, people will be looking for new avenues."

WITHOUT, SEEMINGLY, TIRING of my naïveté, Mallat took me to lunch, first parking his car in the garage of St. Joseph's College of Law, where he is a professor of law. The American University of Beirut may be better known, among Americans anyway, than St. Joseph's University, which dates to 1875.

(The first Jesuits came to the area of Mount Lebanon in the 1640s, and the Maronite Christians claim an early affinity with the Church of Rome, dating to the fifth century AD.) But in all likelihood, St. Joseph's has graduated more prominent alumni, in large part because its law school was the only one in Lebanon from 1913 until the early 1960s.

The assassinated journalist Samir Kassir had taught at St. Joseph's. A columnist for the *Daily Star* newspaper, Michael Young, described him as "the media figure who contributed the most to denouncing the hegemony over Lebanon of the Syrian and Lebanese intelligence services," and called his killing "a warning to the opposition." Ironically, according to Young, Kassir had supported Syria, but "his enthusiasm was not for the despotism of the Assad regime or the contemptible kleptocracy it has presided over; it was for the Syrian people and the opposition; for those countless men and women thrown into the dungeons of the Ba'ath Party during the past decades...." Young goes on: "He had ideas and openness in a system that rewarded mediocrity and intolerance," adding ominously "the army doesn't forgive its critics." Later in my stay I would come back to the law school and attend a memorial conference in Kassir's honor, where many of the speakers echoed some of Young's observations: "He was someone, I steadily learned, who had the patience to listen. That came with the territory of teaching at St. Joseph's University."

Strolling around the law school, and discussing the life and death of Samir Kassir (according to Young, "Samir was a leading figure in the Democratic Left movement, one of the parties that had demanded a Syrian pullout from Lebanon"), Mallat and I settled for lunch at a restaurant that from the terrace overlooked some of the new buildings in downtown Beirut. No doubt I had expected to eat Lebanese food, as my wife and I did often when we lived in New York. But this restaurant, while elegant, had more the offerings of an international hotel coffee shop, and we ate pizza and then sushi rather than *humus* or *baba ganoush*. I suppose if you can eat kebab on Atlantic Avenue in Brooklyn, it follows that you can eat Japanese food in Beirut.

I REGRET, IN hindsight, that I knew so little about Lebanon when I had my meeting and lunch with Mallat. Here I was with someone who had thought and written extensively about Lebanon and its future. But I was reduced to simplistic questions: Who are the Druze? What caused the fighting in the Lebanese civil wars? Where were the American hostages held? Why did the fighting finally end? At one point, I took out a large map from my briefcase, and Mallat patiently filled in some of the gaps in my knowledge, tracing with his finger the contours of Christian Lebanon (roughly a large circle around Beirut) versus the Muslim areas (Shiites are mostly in the south while Sunnis tend to be closer to Beirut and north in Tripoli). But one reason I travel is to fix images to my reading. That afternoon at the coastal town of Byblos, I paid eight dollars for a deck chair and an umbrella, and then—in the mid-afternoon heat—spent several enjoyable hours reading *A House of Many Mansions: The History of Lebanon Reconsidered* by Kamal Salibi, which tells a story not unlike the one that Mallat told over lunch.

Born in 1929, Salibi is listed on the book jacket as a professor at the American University of Beirut (AUB). When I asked someone on campus if I could meet him, they said he had retired, perhaps to Jordan. His book, which includes a chapter entitled "The War Over Lebanese History," makes the point that, "To create a country is one thing; to create a nationality is another." Over and over, he argues that Lebanon, while admirable in many ways and at times peaceful and prosperous, began nationhood as a political and geographical abstraction. He writes: "The real problems of the country, however, were to come blatantly into the open as soon as the French mandate came to an end [1943], leaving an independent Lebanon at the mercy of external and internal forces acting in the name of Arab nationalism with which the Lebanese state, in the long run, was unable to come to reasonable terms." His writing is graceful and his arguments are subtle, as when he states: "Since 1920, it has been repeatedly argued that Lebanon, until that time, had been part of Syria. Politically, the argument is meaningless, because there was no nation-state before 1920 called Syria from which the State of Greater Lebanon was artificially separated."

Brushing Lebanon with broad strokes, the lands between Tyre and Tripoli have been, in the last several thousand years, Phoenician, Greek, Roman, Byzantine, Arab, Crusader, Ottoman, French, and Lebanese. Salibi makes it clear that the coastal settlements were worlds apart from those of the hinterland, even if in modern times it is possible to drive from Beirut to the ridges of Mount Lebanon in less than an hour. To complicate matters further, regions of Lebanon link up with some of the larger, if divergent geographic distinctions of the Middle East. As Salibi writes: "The Greeks, and the Romans after them, distinguished between an *Arabia deserta*, or desert Arabia; an *Arabia eudaemon*, or *Arabia felix*, meaning fertile Arabia, which referred in a special way to the south-eastern parts of the peninsula, in the region of the Yemen; and an *Arabia petraea*, or rocky Arabia, which was taken to comprise the Syrian highlands east and south-east of the Dead Sea along with the west Arabian ridges of Hijaz."

Not only does each of these different Arabias slice into modern Lebanon; the country has also been home to numerous religious sects during the years of its many occupations. From my reading I have counted ten Christian sects in Lebanon: Maronite, Syrian Orthodox, Syrian Catholic, Greek Orthodox, Greek Catholic, Armenian Orthodox, Armenian Catholic, Chaldean, Assyrian (Nestorian), and Roman Catholic; I am sure I have missed a few. On the Muslim side, the country has more than a million Sunnis and Shiites, leaving aside the schisms within both of these branches of Islam. Then there are the Druze, Muslims who for the most part live in mountaintop villages around the Chouf, one of the ranges that look down on the Mediterranean Sea and Beirut.

In most cases, each of these religious groups—when they thought at all of their nationality (and I think few did until the twentieth century)—found affinity with a host of rival nations. Salibi writes: "In these areas the Christian leaders represented feuding political clans and so were no different from the Druze, Shiite or Sunnite bosses of the various rural and tribal regions. In the coastal cities, including Beirut itself, the Arabism of the Sunnite Muslims, with external support from Damascus and other Arab capitals, was determinedly pitted against the Lebanism of the Christians, and had echoes among the Sunnites, Druzes and Shiites of the hinterland."

Part of the problem in Lebanon has always been the conflicting national antecedents of the various sects, tribes, families, and groups that were vying for power. For example, the Maronites claim ancestry from the Crusaders, which places Lebanon in the role of a Western redoubt in an otherwise hostile world of infidels. By contrast, as Salibi writes, "Druze and Shiites were willing to subscribe to the theory that justified the existence of Lebanon as a historical refuge for the minorities of Syria. This theory, however, did not work politically with Sunnite Muslims, even though they normally admitted that there was a degree of historical truth in it, as already observed. On the other hand, the Sunnites insisted that Arab rule in Syria under Islam had always been outstandingly tolerant and fair in its treatment of minorities, and there had never been cause for anyone to flee to Mount Lebanon." Just to make national matters even more complicated, certain Christian communities were descended from the Phoenicians.

Needless to say, once most of these ancient sects woke up to the modernist idea of nationalism, governing the lands between the Lebanon and the Anti-Lebanon (two parallel mountain ranges separated by the Bekaa Valley) became a balancing act beyond the talents of most local administrators. In the mid-nineteenth century, after Muslims slaughtered some of the Christians, the Ottomans established the area as a privileged *sanjak* (administrative region) of the empire. The local governor was an Ottoman Christian, called a Mutesarrif. Bizarrely, although no doubt for local consumption, not to mention papal blessings, the powers that guaranteed this form of Lebanon were Britain, France, Austria, Russia, Prussia, and Sardinia. The mutesarrifate lasted until the British routed the Ottomans from Palestine and Syria in 1917.

In the postwar settlement, the British had hoped to reward their loyal wartime ally, Sharif Feisal, with suzerainty over Syria, then a geographic abstraction. T.E. Lawrence had made that promise when the two were out in the desert, blowing up trains. But then the British got nervous about losing the oil fields of Mesopotamia. Instead of buying into the small type of the Sykes-Picot Agreement (made public in

November 1917), it decided to hang on to latter-day Iraq, and after the war France was awarded a mandate over what are now Syria and Lebanon. From this artificial divide emerged, in 1926, something called the State of Greater Lebanon. In 1943 it became an independent republic, although the Christian heartland was saddled with surrounding Arabic *vilayets* in south Lebanon and around Tripoli. In her history of the 1919 Paris Peace Conference, Margaret MacMillan writes:

> To bring Syria under control, the French shrank it. They rewarded their Christian allies by swelling the borders of Mount Lebanon with the Bekaa Valley, the Mediterranean ports of Tyre, Sidon, Beirut and Tripoli, and the land in the south, north of Palestine. Thousands of Muslims now joined a state dominated by Christians. The result was a Syria, which even after the French finally left still remembered what it had lost, and a Lebanon dancing uneasily around unresolved religious and ethnic tensions. In the 1970s Lebanon blew up; to no one's surprise but the outside world's, the Syrian government took the opportunity to send in its troops, which have stayed ever since.

In a larger sense, as Salibi explains, the problem with the lines drawn in the sand of the Paris Peace Conference is that "the colonizers had divided the Arab national territory into diverse countries against the national wishes of the people." None of the borders drawn around the imperial mandates corresponded either to local geography or national aspirations. (Syria, which included Palestine and Trans Jordan, "was not a national territory on its own, but part of a greater Arab homeland.") To make matters worse, he writes, "Syrians, Palestinians, and Transjordanians chose to think of themselves as Arabs, although Lebanese were always Lebanese first, and then Arabs or Christians second." The result meant that the State of Greater Lebanon, like so many other countries in the Middle East, existed only in the imagination of colonial mapmakers.

DURING MY DAYS in Beirut, I tended to have appointments in the mornings, and then in the afternoons I would hire a taxi from the stand near my hotel and explore the countryside. Sometimes I met people for drinks in the late afternoon. I rarely had formal dinners. On some afternoon excursions I would leave after lunch and get back to the Berkeley around 9:00 P.M. As a country, Lebanon is smaller than you think. From Beirut to the Syrian border is about ninety minutes by car, depending on traffic and military checkpoints. From the Israeli border in the south to Tripoli in the north, on average the drive would never take more than three hours. Ironically, the slowest travel in Lebanon is around the hills above Beirut. Like the Italian spine, Mount Lebanon and the Chouf range are lined with gorges, many of which have villages at improbable angles or on steep hillsides. North of the Beirut-Damascus highway, many villages are Christian. To the south, they tend to be Druze. Where these demographics overlapped between 1976 and 1990 accounted for some of the deadliest fighting in the civil wars. Those encounters were dress rehearsals for Bosnia and now Chechnya, wars fought along the fault line between Islam and Christianity.

To visit the Roman ruins at Baalbek, I had originally conceded to take an organized tour. It was cheaper than hiring a car, and one left at a convenient time. In fact, the tour bus either forgot me or was canceled, due to lack of interest. I waited for an hour in the hotel lobby, had an unpleasant phone conversation with the tour operators, and then headed east over Mount Lebanon in an old yellow Mercedes taxi that billowed diesel exhaust in the steep curves that lead above Beirut.

Much of the Lebanese civil war was fought over and along the Damascus highway that connects Beirut to Syria. Even fifteen years after the fighting, it is still possible to see gutted apartment buildings in nearby valleys and towns. When the Israelis invaded in 1982, they attacked north through the Bekaa Valley and then moved west on the main highway, cutting off Beirut from Syria. We stopped for gas in Aley, one of the higher towns in Lebanon, and I remembered visiting Kuwait in 1994 and being shown a home video of a Kuwaiti-owned house that was burned and destroyed in the Lebanese civil wars. Many Arabs came to Aley in the summers to escape the heat of the Persian Gulf and enjoy the views of the Mediterranean. Various Christian militias, notably the Phalangists, had put some of their holiday homes to the torch.

Along this stretch of highway—something between an autoroute and a Brooklyn boulevard—I passed through my first Lebanese checkpoint. As we were far from any border, I had not expected the wooden gatehouse, the barbed wire, or the soldiers sitting on machine gun nests of piled-up sandbags. Much of the civil war was fought from these makeshift barricades, which became as numerous as the many militias that sought to assert control over some small section of a road or through one of the mountain passes. In our case, the taxi elicited no interest from soldiers on duty. But I could see them rummaging through Syrian trucks off to the side, and a few minivans, clogged with itinerant workers, were getting searched. Here the guards were members of the Lebanese Army, but the British correspondent of the *Times* (London) and later the *Independent*, Robert Fisk, describes a similar drive to the Bekaa in 1982: "After a visit to Baalbek in the autumn of 1982, I drove home through checkpoints manned by Iranians, Palestinians from the PFLP [Popular Front for the Liberation of Palestine], regular Syrian troops, plain-clothes Syrian *mukhabarrat* agents, Syrian Special Forces units, Israelis, Phalangists, Lebanese soldiers, French para-troopers and U.S. Marines. There were, in all, at least 33 foreign armies and local militias in Lebanon when the MNF [Multinational Force] arrived."

When the highway crested, I could finally look down on the broad, fertile Bekaa Valley. I associate the name with news dispatches in which Israeli warplanes are routinely striking "suspected guerrilla positions." Because of the sun and the heat and the feeling that I was approaching the San Fernando Valley, I was also reminded of passages from John Steinbeck, who in *East of Eden* writes "of great virtues and great sins." Clearly the Bekaa harvests both in vast quantities.

Between Chtaura (the word means cross) and the Chris-tian city of Zahlé, the driver stopped at the château of Ksara wines. At first I suspected one of those tourist moments when you end up in a brother-in-law's gift shop. But Ksara is in the "Levantine Napa," and I was happy first to hear how Jesuits had first cultivated the vineyards and then to sit in an elegant restaurant, tasting excellent wines. Many of the oak casks are stored in underground caves that are thought to date to the Roman era (Baalbek, itself, is dedicated to Bacchus), and the business has grown to produce more than two million bottles a year despite the occasional bombing or Israeli tank lodged among the vineyards. I loved the chardonnay and carried home a bottle of Cabernet-Sauvignon, but as we resumed the drive to Baalbek it became clear that the Bekaa cultivates other crops, including radical Islam.

Although the fact has been known for more than twenty-five years, I had not associated the Bekaa Valley with either Iran's Revolutionary Guards or Syrian occupation of Lebanon until my taxi drove down a long stretch of a divided highway between Zahlé and Baalbek. To our right were the dry, windswept mountains of the Anti-Lebanon, the range of hills that separates Lebanon from Syria. In the distance to the left were the peaks of Mount Lebanon, including those that have winter ski resorts and others that are covered with what is left of the country's cedars. But straight ahead, waving from streetlights as we drove toward Baalbek, were numerous billowing billboards that promoted the images of Shi'a's leading clerics. I recognized some but not all of the imams. In a few posters, Ayatollah Ruhollah Khomeini was shown welcoming the faithful with both a genial smile and an AK-47. On other banners he was joined with a portrait of Imam Musa Sadr, the Shiite cleric who disappeared in Libya in 1979, perhaps done in by jealous Sunni rivals. Here and there, my driver pointed to pictures of Hasan Nasrallah, the spiritual head of Hezbollah who came across on the billboards as an odd cross between a mayoral candidate and a local car dealer. (Would you buy a used religion from this man?) During the half-hour ride, my eyes darted from these flags of convenience to cars coming from the opposite direction, which, to save time, often used the shoulder on our side of the highway to make the short journey between villages. The practice gave new meaning to the word *freeway*.

I was not surprised to learn later, during the course of

my reading, that Baalbek is both a stronghold for Hezbollah and a forward position of Iran's Revolutionary Guards. It is known that Hasan Nasrallah has both a home and an office here. In one of the more comical events during the recent border wars, Israel dispatched an airborne strike force to Baalbek to capture Nasrallah, and, in fact, brought back to Israel an entire household of suspects from a house listed in the directory under the name of the Hezbollah leader. Alas, while interrogating the prisoners, the Israelis learned that Hasan Nasrallah is a common name in Baalbek and that those they had kidnapped had nothing to do with the town's more notorious resident of the same name. Israel's blunder at sending keystone cops to Baalbek, however, in no way diminishes the town's more sinister occupations.

Many American hostages, taken by extremists in the 1980s, were often held captive in or near the town. A correspondent for CBS television, Lawrence Pintak, in his memoirs of the civil wars, describes the experience of CNN reporter Jerry Levin, seized on the streets of Beirut: "From the movement of the truck and the length of the trip, Levin knew he was being taken to the Bekaa. He later confirmed that when he surreptitiously scratched out a tiny hole in the pane that covered the window of his room and saw the Baalbek ruins and Mt. Lebanon to the west." Next door to where he was held, together with other Americans, were the headquarters of the Iranian Revolutionary Guards, who bartered captives like Levin and Father Lawrence Martin Jenco, to the Reagan administration in exchange for surface-to-air missiles and aviation spare parts. In that sense, Baalbek was one of terrorism's commodity exchanges, not unlike a stockyard.

The presence in the 1980s of several thousand Iranian Revolutionary Guards—including, perhaps, the country's current president, Mahoud Ahmadinejad, himself one of the Ayatollah's anti-Christian soldiers—prompted war gamers for the Reagan administration to propose preemptive strikes against the forerunners of Hezbollah. For example, in the 1980s neoconservative professor Daniel Pipes called for air strikes against Baalbek, prefacing his remarks by writing: "Fundamentalist Muslims direct terror primarily against those Americans associated with major institutions.... They formed alliances with Lebanese organizations such as Islamic Amal and eventually established an Islamic government in Baalbeck along Iranian lines. More Iranians were sent to Baalbeck; by the end of 1982 they numbered about 1,500." At the time that TWA flight 847 was hijacked from Athens to Beirut, he argued: "Punishment of the terrorists who are most implicated and most vulnerable—those in the Baalbeck region—presents the best opportunity to protect Americans and their interests in the Middle East." In the 1980s Hezbollah was an emotion, akin to sympathy for the Ayatollah, rather than a political party or a reinforced brigade. But even twenty years later, driving into a dusty town ripped open with road work, it was hard to see how America could hope to win the region's hundred year's war by taking out the swarming touts who man the souvenir shops outside the Roman ruins.

RIGHTLY OR WRONGLY, I associate the imperial columns at Baalbek with the emperor Hadrian (AD 117–138, succeeding Trajan who adopted him on his deathbed), who thought Rome needed to reinforce its splendor where the road forked between Damascus and Palmyra, not to mention the north-south roads between Antioch and Jerusalem. My taxi dropped me near the front entrance, which was hard to find in the scrum of hawkers flogging "original" Roman coins. I bought

water and sunglasses from one of the more aggressive market-
ers, who impressed me as someone who spent his evenings
brainstorming over a new spring line of hostages. But once I
was inside Baalbek, on the broad marble steps of the Propy-
laea—as timeless as those of the Acropolis in Athens—the
world around me went silent, save for the distance cries of the
muezzin summoning the faithful to prayers. It was hot and
the scorching sun was overhead. Either because of the midday
heat or the cacophony around Baalbek, I found it disconcert-
ing to be standing in a Roman temple but to be reminded of
Ayatollah Khomeini.

To anyone brought up in the classical tradition of the
sparseness of the Roman Forum or the elegant proportions
of the Parthenon, Baalbek appears to have been pumped up.
Nowhere in Asia Minor have I seen larger pedestals or columns. While there is grandeur to the ruins that are on a
scale of those of the Mayans, Baalbek feels neither Greek
nor Roman in its execution, but rather the work of some successor master race that inherited the license to the imperial
trademarks. In fact, the temples and the surrounding struc-
tures neatly summarize Hadrian's greatness and insecurities
as emperor.

Hadrian was one of the so-called adopted emperors, in
that he succeeded to purple thanks neither to slow poison nor
to his legions. His sensibility was that of an aesthete, like a
Byronic grand tourist. Above all he believed in the wonder
of Periclean Athens. Elisabeth Speller, the author of *Following Hadrian*, describes him as "a man of almost modern
sensibility: intelligent, aesthetic, insecure in himself, given
to that particular form of nostalgia that the Portuguese call
saudade—the longing for a past happiness one never really

possessed." He had, in fact, commanded Roman legions and he wisely knew the limits of empire, which in the north of Britain he defined with the defensive fortification that bears his name. But his pleasures came from his imperial wanderings, described by Speller as a "traveling court." She continues:

> He traveled his empire, assiduously as he believed, recreating a lost Hellenistic earthly paradise, where his buildings stood not only as a reminder to his subjects after he had gone but as a memorial to his beloved Greece, to exceed his predecessors and as a legacy to the posterity which would judge him. He used art to bind his empire with his own past and unknown future.

Hadrian was among the first politicians to press the flesh with his constituents, although few of them got close to the head of a procession of five thousand. Still his presence was felt. Speller describes the emotions of one follower in his wagon train: "If I have learned one thing on this journey it is that we are an empire held together by entertainment." At Baalbek he left behind an imperial line in the sand, but one that mutes the heavy treads of legionnaires with soft Greek marble and the soothing rows of columns that implied order in chaotic worlds. Speller concludes on Hadrian's era: "The dream of a Roman empire united by Hellenic nostalgia had reached its zenith." What might Hadrian think of the Persian mercenaries now stationed at his temples? In Marguerite Yourcenar's *Memoirs of Hadrian*, the fictional emperor is quoted: "I could see possibilities of Hellenizing the barbarians and Atticizing Rome, thus imposing upon the world by degrees the only culture which has once for all separated itself from the monstrous, the shapeless, and the inert, the only one to have invented a definition of method, a system of politics, and a theory of beauty."

DRIVING BACK TO Beirut, the taxi driver indulged my curiosity to see the Syrian border and meandered along a series of backcountry roads to the ruins of Aanjar. I had not obtained a visa for Syria, even though Damascus is less than an hour from Baalbek and many Lebanese, at least before the recent war, went there for lunch. On this trip I had just wanted to visit Lebanon, although I came to realize that Syria is the wild card in Lebanese politics, and the presidential administration of Bashir al-Assad, the son of the former president Hafez al-Assad, is fond of dealing from the bottom of the deck.

At Aanjar, we stopped for fresh orange juice and a walk through the ruins, which were a summer market town of Caliph Walid I. Not much is left of the Umayyad outpost, which flourished only for about forty-five years, until 705 AD. It reminded me of sections of Pompeii in that all that remains are the footprints of shops and houses and a few arched columns of the caliph's summer mosque, laid out like the cross of a Roman temple. Like Baalbek up the road, Aanjar was sited astride the caravan lanes that ran north toward Byzantium and east to Damascus. As I walked around, I sensed that its citizens had qualities both of Phoenician traders and Ottoman shopkeepers. Arabic speaking, the Umayyads developed a commercial empire from Spain to Central Asia. But not long after the construction of the summer quarters at Aanjar—there to catch the cool breezes that drop from Mount Lebanon into the Bekaa—Abbasids, who founded a successor

Arab dynasty, sacked the city, opening yet another rift in the Muslim world.

Lebanon is a distant heir to this broken family. Sunni Muslims settled around the ancient port of Sidon while Shi-ites moved to Tripoli in the north and Tyre in the south, one reason Lebanon is described as one country with many nations. Indeed, Aanjar itself has changed hands repeatedly in the shifting sands of Middle East politics. In 1939, for example, about 6,000 Armenians came here from the legendary town of Musa Dagh, which, during the 1915 Turkish genocide of the Armenians, held out for forty days against the Ottoman army. The Austrian novelist Franz Werfel later wrote an account of the Armenian last stand, *The Forty Days of Musa Dagh.* The book begins with the fateful question, "How did I get here?"—words that are still spoken by the Armenian residents of Aanjar. British sailors and warships rescued survivors of the 1915 siege, and after World War I some were resettled in the ruins of Musa Dagh, which was then part of the French mandate over Syria. In 1939, so eager were the French to enlist Turkey on the side of the Allies against Hitler, the colonial officials gave Musa Dagh back to Turkey (although that failed to enlist the Turks to the Allied cause). Yet again the survivors of Musa Dagh fled, this time to Aanjar, where about 3,000 in the town claim Armenian ancestry. Is it any wonder that Armenian mothers sing "The Song of Coming and Going?" as a lullaby to their babies? One verse goes like this:

> *The world is an inn on the road, oh, singer,*
> *The people, its guest, they come and they go.*
> *Mother Earth embraces her well-taught child,*
> *While ignorant nationals may perish, and go.*

I BEGAN TO understand the depth of Lebanon's anger over Syria's occupation when I met Michael Young for a drink. He writes a regular column for the Beirut *Daily Star*, an English language newspaper. We had not met before, but we had exchanged e-mails, after I read an Op-Ed piece that he had published in 2004 in the *International Herald Tribune*. In that column, which had turned dog-eared in my "Lebanon Trip File," he had written: "For decades, Syria has been the unavoidable force in Lebanese politics." When I suggested getting together, he had recommended the Gemayze Café, which I found in a taxi. The café turned out to be on the top floor of a recently finished mall, something easy to imagine in Malibu, but probably incongruous for anyone who, like Young, survived the Lebanese civil wars. I arrived early and decided to price replacement sunglasses, as those I had purchased outside Baalbek, from the revolutionary salesmen, had not survived the ride back to the hotel. But the pair I tried on cost $200, which suggested that one of the strengths of radical Islam is its pricing models.

Because Michael Young writes grammatically perfect sentences—of a kind I rarely encounter even among native English speakers—I was surprised to find that he is Lebanese, not an expatriate Englishman or American. He explained that his position at the *Daily Star* was part-time and mostly involved writing the column from his apartment. Then in the afternoons, he was free to pursue other projects, including his passion for reading. Almost immediately I sensed someone with a worn library card, and we spent much of the late afternoon discussing recent Lebanese affairs in the context of the many books published about the country. More often than not, his views came back to the malevolent shadow that Syria has cast over Lebanese politics.

Young graduated from AUB, and thus knew first hand many of the authors whose books I had dragged to the Berkeley Hotel and was trying to read at night, after my days on the road. He liked, as I had, *A House of Many Mansions* by Kamal Salibi. At AUB he had taken courses from Judith Harik, who wrote a history entitled *Hezbollah: The Changing Face of Terrorism*. She was someone I had hoped to meet on this trip. When I brought up Robert Fisk's monumental work, *Pity the Nation*, a journalistic account of the civil wars, he said, somewhat cryptically, that he had not read it. Nor, he added, did he plan to add it to his list of things to read. (Fisk is not someone who generates lukewarm appraisals. Mallat had said that Fisk's book, published in 1990 as the wars were ending, was "comprehensive." But another acquaintance, who covers the Middle East for a major magazine, said: "It should come with one of those surgeon general health warnings." Yet another friend told me: "He writes like a dream. But I have to tell you I don't believe any of it.") After our drink, Young walked me over to a large bookstore in the mall and pulled from the shelves three or four books, in French and English, that he encouraged me to read. He also recommended a used bookshop across the city where I later loaded up on some hard-to-find titles. I left the country with the feeling that if even I were to read ten or a hundred books about Lebanon, it would never be enough.

Having grown up in Beirut, Young broke down the many phases of the civil wars, noting that the violence had not been a continuous battle but rather the occasional outbursts of a deadly volcano. He described the first phase, 1975 to 1976, as violence between Christians and Muslims in and around Beirut. Next came the Israeli incursion into southern Lebanon in 1978, followed by the fighting for Zahlé, the Christian city on the edge of the Muslim Bekaa Valley that I had visited earlier in the day. Next came the fighting in the mountains, often between Phalangists (a Christian militia) and the Druze (a group best described as secular Muslims). After the Israeli invasion in 1982 to 1983, there were the battles of the foreign occupation, when American, French, Italian, and other troops took up the white man's burden around Beirut. Pax Syriana followed the withdrawal of western forces, as Syria occupied Lebanon with several divisions and installed its proxies throughout the political system. For most Beirut residents, the heaviest fighting of the civil war came just before the war ended, when between 1988 and 1989, the Green Line once again became a Great War trench. Through it all Young had gone to school, gotten his degree, and begun his career.

Neither of us had any notion that in a few weeks Israel would be at war with Lebanon. Nevertheless, Young spoke at length about Hezbollah's refusal to disarm at the end of civil war. As he wrote a few days later: "Hezbollah denies this, but benefits from having carved out a virtually autonomous territory for itself in the border areas of southern Lebanon and in Beirut's southern suburbs.... Hezbollah effectively operates in a parallel environment to the state, which is not unusual in a sectarian society, but alarming when accompanied by a paramilitary and intelligence structure over which the state has no control." He did not think that the Lebanese army had the strength to dislodge Hezbollah from its caves in southern Lebanon. In effect, he was describing a state within a state. "Hezbollah," he said, "is caught between conflicting loyalties—to Lebanon and the consensus between its religious communities, and to Iran and Syria." More prophetically, he wrote that same week: "Since Syria's withdrawal from Lebanon, the Iranian side of Hezbollah is said to have gained ascendancy over the Syrian one."

We were discussing the many Syrian interventions in recent Lebanese affairs, beginning with the occupations of the late 1970s and continuing with its role in the assassination of Prime Minister Hariri. It was toward the end of our meeting. On my maps, I had Young outline Shebaa Farms, that part of the Golan Heights claimed by both Lebanon and Israel. For strategic purposes, he said, Syria avoided direct military confrontation with Israel over the Golan, preferring to dispatch the likes of Hezbollah to do its territorial bidding. But the constant skirmishing over the disputed land allowed Syria to maintain its posture as a front-line state and to save face with its Arab brethren. Equally improbable was the strange alliance that Syria shared with Iran in support of Hezbollah, a movement among Shiites, few of whom live in Syria. Although the ruling Assad family is Alawite, a minority Shiite sect, the country is largely Sunni and the one-party Ba'athist government tolerates religious freedom, although not Islamic fundamentalism.

Previously Damascus had found common ground with Tehran over a shared loathing of Saddam Hussein's Iraq. More recently each had rallied to the cause of Hezbollah, although for different reasons. Iran was in southern Lebanon to export the Shiite revolution, and to fight the holy war against Israel, if not its American patron. By contrast, once Syria withdrew from Lebanon, the self-sufficient Hezbollah, standing armed outside the Lebanese system, gave Damascus a proxy in Beirut's political affairs. It was a wedge that could be inserted, at will, into Lebanon's fragile democracy. As Young made clear, when that didn't work to unhinge the

Lebanese, Syria always had recourse to its standby solution: political assassination.

To UNDERSTAND THE events around the killing of the former Lebanese prime minister, I arranged to meet Nick Blanford, a correspondent for the *Times* (London) and *Time* magazine, who has written an account of the assassination. We met in a café where many patrons smoked water pipes and played backgammon while the rest were watching reruns of games in the National Basketball Association. A man in his mid-thirties with short blond hair and an engaging manner, Blanford had come to Lebanon as a stringer for several newspapers. He had married a Lebanese woman, with whom he has two children, and settled into the life of a foreign correspondent, which I sensed involved numerous trips to southern Lebanon. When we met, he was trying to convince his editors in New York that Hezbollah was worthy of a major story and the next day was planning a trip along the border with Israel, to take a measure of the Party of God's political intentions.

On the morning that Rafik Hariri was killed with what was most likely a car bomb, Blanford had been working at home. It was just after lunch when he heard a tremendous blast coming from the direction of the waterfront. Not knowing who or what it involved, but seeing the billowing smoke over what in Beirut is called the marina district, he got to the assassination site in less than fifteen minutes and found the remains of what looked like an airplane crash. Between the St. George Hotel and the branch of HSBC were the twisted metal remains of Hariri's motorcade and a huge crater, as if a meteor had struck the former prime minister. Blanford told me that the road looked like it had been heaved upward, as in an earthquake, and then he saw all kinds of state security agents arrive at the crime scene, although it was clear that no one organization had control of the chaotic situation.

When Hariri was killed, he was heading to his large home in West Beirut, together with numerous aides and bodyguards, although he was driving his own Mercedes. Watching him leaving his downtown office were numerous plotters, who had staked out the three possible routes for Hariri to get home. Using a network of stolen or anonymous portable phones, the plotters communicated with the driver of a white Mitsubishi van, who then stationed himself near the St. George Hotel, based on the spotters' information that Hariri was taking the seafront boulevard. The United Nations Security Council commissioned a report on the assassination; it has since come to be known as the Mehlis Report, named after the lead investigator. The UN concluded that the Mitsubishi van had been stolen in Sagaamihara, Japan in October 2004 and then driven into Lebanon by a colonel of the Syrian Tenth Army Division. Experts differ on the amount of explosives it contained. (The figures I have seen vary between 300 and 1200 kilograms of military-grade TNT.) It isn't clear if the assassin in the car was a suicide bomber or if he triggered the bomb with a remote-controlled device. As we spoke, Blanford raised another possibility, also explored in the UN report: that the assassins had tunneled under the road in front of the hotel and thus detonated explosives both above and below ground. Evidence for that possibility is the huge crater, testimony from the hotel manager, and the fact that the hotel's underground foundations were nearly destroyed. But then Blanford recounted how, in the hours after the assassination, much of the key evidence at the crime scene was destroyed.

By nightfall after the assassination, the crater had filled with water. But that isn't what compromised the investigation. As the UN reports: "A bulldozer was introduced into the crime scene on the day of the explosion, February 14, 2005, in the evening for no justifiable reason." It continues: "The decision to fill the crater at the crime scene, to remove the motorcade vehicles and to re-open the street on the day after the blast, is confusing, assuming that there was a collective will to preform a professional crime scene investigation in order to track down the perpetrators and bring them to justice." Later on, UN investigators erected what looked like a wedding tent over the assassination site and did the best they could to reconstruct what kind of explosives were used and who might have set them off. But in the early hours of the investigation, the filling in of the crater, and the dragging away of the motorcade's tangled wrecks, made it that much harder to pin the killing on either senior officials within Lebanon's own government or their overlords in Damascus. The damning conclusion of the UN is: "There is probable cause to believe that the decision to assassinate former Prime Minister, Rafik Hariri, could not have been taken without the approval of top-ranked Syrian security official [sic] and could not have been further organized without the collusion of their counterparts in the Lebanese security services."

In the almost two years since the assassination, numerous conspiracy theories have been advanced to explain the circumstances of Hariri's killing. He was a billionaire businessman, with strong ties to the Saudi royal family, and had run a government in the most volatile region of the world. Some theories suggested he was killed to cover up a massive bank fraud, and others, inevitably, pointed to the likes of the Central Intelligence Agency and Israel's Mossad. But the scenario that has refused to fade away is that Hariri was killed because he opposed the extension by fiat of President Lahoud's term in office and thus found himself leading the opposition to Syria's control. According to both Blanford and the UN report, in September 2004 the Lebanese parliament had passed a law to extend the president's term in office. Hariri opposed such legislation and, as a result, was summoned to Damascus where he met with senior officials, including the President, Bashir al-Assad, who is quoted in the UN report as making all sorts of wild threats during the meetings. He told Hariri: "Lahoud is me. I want to renew his mandate." He threatened to "break Lebanon over your head" if Hariri did not agree, as prime minister, to implement the extension. He also said: "If you think that President Chirac and you are going to run Lebanon, you are mistaken." In October 2004, Hariri resigned from office rather than do Assad's bidding, and during the winter of 2004 to 2005 Syria could feel itself losing its grip on its Lebanese franchise.

In life as in death, Hariri was hugely popular in Lebanon. A Sunni from Sidon, the city south of Beirut, he had ties to the Saudis, to world leaders, to the Christian and Shiite communities. He was rich and hard working. He was synonymous with the reconstruction of Beirut, including the construction of an enormous mosque on the main square. He also restored numerous Christian churches. He seemed above the street politics of the civil wars. Nevertheless, it was inevitable that he would clash with Syrian interests that had much to gain from a Lebanese occupation. As Blanford explained to me, Syria needed Lebanon as a buffer with Israel, especially after the United States invaded Iraq. From the ports around Beirut, Syria had access to world markets, both for legal and illegal goods. By one account I read later, Syria produced $1 billion in hashish in Bekaa Valley. Control over Lebanon also evoked the conquests of a Greater Syria, which was denied when British and French voided the Sykes-Picot Agreement and parsed the Middle East into the Balkans of the twentieth century. As Salibi writes: "The colonizers had divided the Arab national territory into diverse countries against the national wishes of the people."

Late on that summer afternoon, as the sun was setting behind the gutted remains of the Murr Tower but also the shimmering apartment towers of restored Beirut, I walked with Blanford across the remnants of the Green Line and into downtown. He wanted to check on his car rental for the next day. Mostly we made small talk about children and vacations, but he did say that Syria and its leadership faced a looming crisis if, for example, its president were put on trial for the assassination of Rafik Hariri. Blanford thought Cyprus rather than The Hague would be the logical venue for such a war-crimes trial, and he said that many Lebanese would take satisfaction in bringing the Hariri killers to justice. One witness for the UN report "claimed that a senior Lebanese security official went several times to Syria to plan the crime, meeting once at the Meridian Hotel in Damascus and several times at the Presidential Palace and the office of a senior Syrian security official." But a trial of Syrian officials raises the question, for example, of American interests in Damascus.

At the beginning of the Iraqi invasion, it looked as though the United States had the intention of rolling up the Syrian flank, once American forces were "greeted as liberators" in Baghdad. The Bush administration made threatening noises against the Ba'athist regime of Bashir al-Assad. As one observer wrote: "Washington seems to be pursuing a policy of regime change on the cheap in Syria." But then came the Iraqi quagmire, in which the United States needs Syrian cooperation to end the violence. As Professor Joshua Landis wrote in the *New York Times*: "Washington must choose between destabilizing Syria and stabilizing Iraq." He continues: "Worse, if Mr. Assad's government collapsed, chances are the ethnic turmoil that would result would bring to power militant Sunnis who would actively aid the jihadists in Iraq." After the Israeli attack on Hezbollah in southern Lebanon, the *New York Times* ran a story about how Secretary of State Rice is "seeking to peel Syria away from its alliance of convenience with Iran." That statement is at odds with then Secretary of Defense Donald Rumsfeld's allegations that Syria has supported Islamic resistance in Iraq and Lebanon. Only the Middle East, it seems, could have the Hobson's choice between justice for a horrific crime in Lebanon and increased violence for the unhappy lands between Beirut and Tehran.

FOR MY DAY job, I spent many mornings in Beirut calling on the local banks. Lebanon has eighty-five banking institutions, not to mention countless financial intermediaries—all of which are heirs to the Phoenician counting houses. In recent years, with the boom in deposits from the Persian Gulf states, many Lebanese banks built new headquarters along the Green Line. I had meetings in many of these towers and spent as much time gazing at the Mediterranean and the surrounding buildings as I did listening to the presentations. I still found the monetary history of Lebanon as compelling as any of the stories from its recent political past, and this was before Israeli bombers scored a direct hit on the local economy, taking out bridges, dockyards, the new airport, and the country's refining capacity. It may not have smoked Hezbollah from its caves in southern Lebanon, but the run it will generate at the banks ensures that the options held by radical Islam will stay in the money.

Although it is rarely discussed in the political conversations about Lebanon, the gravest threat to the country's future is the potential for default on the national debt. Ironically, at the time of the fratricidal civil wars, Lebanon was largely debt free. On its books were only about a half billion in government bonds. In the second quarter of 2006, as I was making my appointed rounds, external and state borrowings had reached $40 billion. Annual interest costs on such indebtedness was running at $2–3 billion, some 80 percent of the government's annual budget. Overall, the debt amounted to 185 percent of Lebanon's prewar gross domestic production. (The recent fighting will have cost Lebanon at least $3–4 billion in tourist revenue.) But no one thought the loan sharks had teeth, because, put broadly, Lebanon was a flourishing emerging market.

Looked at in purely economic terms, Prime Minister Rafik Hariri was the great middleman in repaving the Green Line with Saudi and Gulf states' petrodollars. By rough estimates the Lebanese civil wars (1975–90) destroyed about $25 billion in local infrastructure. When the street fighting ended in the early 1990s, the new prime minister hoped that domestic tranquility could be restored through the redevelopment of downtown Beirut. He incorporated a private real estate development company, Solidere, kept ten percent for himself, and turned the Beirut waterfront into a glittering skyline of apartment buildings and bank towers. The easy money for these projects came from the Gulf, where not all the investors wanted to stay long on radical Islam.

Especially after September 11, when the U.S. Treasury saw in every Arab bank transfer the potential of terrorist front money, wealthy Arabs decided that Lebanese banks were more in their interest than compliance officers in London or New York. Some of this flight money went into real estate projects. (A lot of Beirut office towers can be understood as the high-rise equivalent of Swiss bank accounts.) But a lot of the oil money also was put on call at Lebanese banks, in which the deposit base reached $65 billion. Emerging from the shadows of civil war and an earlier Israeli occupation, Lebanon's financial markets flourished. Beirut became a city that never slept.

The ministers with sleepless nights, however, were those at the government treasury offices and the Lebanese central bank, which had to keep pace with the edifice dreams of the prime minister, one of the few real-estate tycoons who now could print his own currency. Private equity, to be sure, covered some of Lebanon's war reconstruction. But the government pumped the real-estate bubble with budget deficits and a burgeoning national debt. To the outside world, Beirut was a renaissance city; to those who could read a balance sheet, it had fewer assets than a failed savings and loan association.

What kept the wolf from the door of the central bank was a financial slight of hand: the government leaned on the privately owned banks to invest their abundant deposits in state bonds. As a result, many banks now have more than their book equity invested in government debt. That paper may, at face value, pay 8 to 9 percent annually in interest. (It must now be assumed that Israeli bombers have added a few rollover points.) To complicate matters for the Lebanese government, the central bank issued many of its bonds in U.S. dollars. Hence, debasing the local currency is not an option to reduce the debt burden. Lebanon's economy has been "dollarized," and bondholders are expecting to be repaid with greenbacks. Meanwhile, since the war ended, the same Gulf states depositors with the most to lose in the liquidation of the Lebanese economy have become lenders of last resort and pumped enormous liquidity in the country's financial markets—hoping that they are not throwing good money after bad.

Tragically, the investor with the most to gain from Lebanon's potential insolvency is Syria, which may well have had an invisible hand in the death of Rafik Hariri. He had wanted Syria out of Lebanon, because, among other reasons, he believed it lorded over the Mediterranean economy as if it were a protection racket. One source I read in my travels said that Syria had extracted $20 billion from its Lebanese occupation, including about $5 billion in various illicit trades— hashish from the Bekaa, guns from Iran, etc. If it looked askance or even encouraged Hezbollah to pick a fight with Israel, Syria has only profited since the summer 2006 border war. Israeli bombers took out the economic interests of an anti-Syrian coalition government in Lebanon, and the rise of Hezbollah, coupled with the looming American withdrawal in Iraq, makes the Syrian government look like one of the few winners in the game of Middle Eastern roulette. Even if Lebanon does not go to the wall, Syria may find itself the ascendant power in Beirut while its hated enemy, Saddam Hussein, is out in Iraq, and its ally, Iran, is increasingly influential in the Shiite quarters of Iraq and southern Lebanon. In banking terms, this is known as cashing naked options, and the country on the wrong side of most Middle Eastern markets is the United States.

OF THE MANY books that I read during and after my visit to Lebanon, none made a bigger impression than *Seeds of Hate:*

How America's Flawed Middle East Policy Ignited the Jihad.
The author is Lawrence Pintak, and the book was originally
published as a journalistic account of the Lebanese civil wars,
which he covered for CBS television. Pintak's account is not
unlike that of Robert Fisk, in that he blends journal entries
of the fighting with reflections on the background causes of
the many local conflicts. He has since written other books and
articles about the inability of the United States to comprehend
or deal intelligently with Middle Eastern affairs. This 1980s
history, I sense, was reissued in 2003 with a new title and new
chapters, to capture the market curious to know how things
could have gone so wrong in the region. In many ways, Pintak's book is out-of-date, in that it mostly describes the events
of the Lebanese civil wars, especially as they related to the
United States: the 1983 attack on the U.S. marines in Beirut,
the taking of American hostages during the 1980s, etc. But
Pintak writes well and vividly about American blunders in
the Middle East, which, quoting another scholar, he refers
to as "the fireworks of a frustrated power."

Pintak is among those who believe that Lebanon was
doomed from the start. He writes that "the day the state of
Lebanon was born was the day its destruction began.... The
Lebanese civil war was probably inevitable. It is doubtful
that the Christian minority could have held on to power
indefinitely without a fight." He believes that "it was an economic struggle of rich against poor, a political struggle of
conservatives against liberals, an ideological clash that pitted
Lebanese nationalists against Arab nationalists, and a feudal
struggle of dynastic warlord against dynastic warlord.... And
all the players had guns." James Baker, then chief of staff for
President Ronald Reagan, spoke for the administration in

the early 1980s when he said "we don't have a dog in that fight." But what changed the United Ststaes from the mythological "honest broker" into just another dynastic power with guns were the events set in motion after the 1982 Israeli invasion of Lebanon.

Prior to launching its 1982 incursion, Israel had tried to play its hand in Lebanon with proxies. Pintak writes: "During the Christian confrontation with Syria in the spring and summer of 1981, Israeli advisors were with the Phalangists in the mountains above Zahlé, the main Christian town in the predominantly Muslim Bekaa Valley." After crossing the border in 1982, Israel had originally hoped to create a twenty-five mile buffer zone in southern Lebanon. But the Israeli Minister of Defense, Ariel Sharon, instructed his commanders both to encircle Beirut—by cutting off the highway to Damascus—and to push Israeli troops into West Beirut. In September 1982, while occupying Beirut, Israel either condoned or looked the other way when Phalange gunmen went on a killing spree in Sabra and Chatilla, a rampage that left several thousand dead, wounded, or missing. Pintak argues that these events pushed the United States across a local Rubicon because the U.S. negotiator in the region, Philip Habib, had guaranteed the safety of civilians in the camps after the Palestinian Liberation Organization had withdrawn its fighters from Lebanon earlier that same month—as part of the truce that followed the Israeli invasion. Pintak believes that Sabra and Chatilla are "where the seeds of the American disaster in Lebanon were planted —a disaster that would spawn a global terrorist nightmare that few could even begin to imagine at that time."

The sacking of the refugee camps prompted the Reagan administration to land U.S. marines as part of an interna-

tional peacekeeping force. They splashed ashore for waiting cameramen in September 1982 and took up positions
around the airport runways, much as they had in 1958,
when President Eisenhower sent in the marines to forestall
an earlier confrontation between Christians and Muslims.
Marines landing in the languid surf made better copy than
the mangled remains that were being unearthed in the
camps. But in fact, the mission revealed the marines in
the role of not-ready-for-prime-time players. They were
assigned the low ground around the airport, thus in the
sites of every militiaman dug into the surrounding hills.
Their guards stood watch, effectively unarmed. Gilbert
and Sullivan might have cut their orders. Fisk writes:
"For some unfathomable reason, the marines at the airport were ordered to salute every Pan Am jet taking off."
Patrols, armed largely with chocolate bars, were sent into
the nearby southern suburbs and to the area around the
American university. As time passed, it became clear to
the marines on the ground that they had been assigned the
mission of sitting ducks. One marine told Pintak: "We're
serving no purpose just sitting here."

The rules of disengagement changed in 1983 when Robert C. McFarlane, Reagan's national security advisor (later
of Iran-Contra fame), tilted the American forces in favor of
the Christian militias. When he was inspecting the troops
on the televised front, Druze forces in the Chouf, mountains
that literally overlook the Beirut airport, were threatening to
defeat Phalange forces around the hillside resort of Souk al-
Gharb. American battleships shelled what they hoped were
Druze positions. Suddenly the Americans were players, not
brokers, in the Lebanese civil wars. Pintak writes: "What the
Reagan administration didn't seem to be able to grasp was

that by propping up Amin Gemayel's regime, it *was* taking sides." He notes a further irony in the confrontation: "The Phalangist militiamen would not have been in the Druze-claimed areas of the mountains in the first place if Israel had not brought them in under its wing." In response, the Druze shelled the marine positions around the airport. The marine battalion commander issued brave sound bites: "Our mission is to support the Lebanese government and the Lebanese Armed Forces," but, as Pintak notes, neither existed. He writes: "There were at least four readily definable conflicts, not counting a score of localized quarrels, going on inside Lebanon in late 1983 as the marines scrambled to figure out whom they were fighting and why."

Using the currency of innocence, the Reagan administration paid for its lost illusions in the Middle East with the lives of 241 marines. In October 1983, a suicide bomber rammed through the main gates of the Battalion Landing Team headquarters at the airport. The guard on duty was shouldering an unloaded weapon and remarked later that the driver was smiling, presumably because he was on the road to paradise. As violent as the Lebanese civil wars had been for the previous seven years, the fighting had not yet included suicide bombers. Pintak expresses his astonishment that there were the likes of kamikaze, even in the cauldron of Beirut. Nor did the marines have an inkling of what could hit them. Pintak writes: "As Shi'ite resentment toward the Marines had risen in pace with American involvement in the fighting, that lack of intelligence expertise [about Shiite anger] had become crucial and, finally, fatal."

Until today, it has not been established exactly who attacked the marines as well as the French paratroops stationed nearby. Assuming it to be the work of a cell within the general terrorist rubric known as Islamic Jihad, Pintak establishes the link that targeted the Americans as architects of the brutal Israeli occupation of southern Lebanon. He writes: "The Shi'ites hatred of Israel was building to a fever pitch and they would never forget who provided their enemy with money, weapons and political support." When Israel had first crossed the southern border, Shiites had truly greeted them as liberators from the harsh Palestinian occupation. But those hopes were short-lived. When Shiites fled from the south into Beirut's southern suburbs, they suddenly found that only thin strands of barbed wire separated them from the marine encampment, a target perhaps more inviting—or at least more accessible—than an Israeli stronghold. After the attack, the Reagan administration announced that the remaining American troops would be "deployed" to offshore carriers. It was another word for retreat, but Pintak writes: "Where U.S. military and diplomatic expertise had failed, American PR know-how was called in to save the day."

During my time in Lebanon, I tried hard to find the location of the destroyed marine barracks. One of my taxi drivers took me to the beach where they had landed. Another driver said the newly constructed airport had covered its location and shared little enthusiasm for my interest. On one trip out of the city, when passing the airport, I tried to stand on tiptoe to peer into the airport, to at least imagine the setting. I had thought that perhaps a marker might commemorate the spot where 241 marines had died. But in a civil conflict that claimed several hundred thousand lives over fifteen years, the loss of an American company was, as Lincoln might have said, "of little note" nor "long remembered."

I did, however, drive up into the Chouf to Souq al-Gharb, where the fighting had prompted, according to Pintak, the

Americans to take sides in the civil wars. The Druze reminded me of Bosnians. They dress in black shirts and tight leggings, and most wore white skullcaps. My driver said: "Well, it says Muslim on their passports. But there are no mosques and no fasting." Their battles may have engaged Muslims against Christians, but I sensed little connection between the mountaintop Druze and either the Sunnis or the Shiites along the coast. Their villages are collections of stone houses along steep hillsides, as you might encounter in Sicily or Albania. I have my doubts that shells from the battleship *New Jersey* actually hit "Druze strongholds." More likely they tore holes into family houses.

Wanting to learn more about the origins of Hezbollah, I brought with me to Lebanon yet another book, this one entitled: *Hezbollah: The Changing Face of Terrorism*. The author is Judith Harik, who on the back jacket was identified as a professor of political science at the American University of Beirut. In fact, I had tried to write her an e-mail before coming to Lebanon, but had no response. Some people that I met in Beirut knew her, but they said she was probably up in the mountains, renovating an old house. Finally, I stopped by the dean's office at AUB, and they gave me a cell phone number, on which I left several messages. Just about ready to give up, I got a phone message from her husband, which confirmed that they were outside Beirut. He said they were happy to meet me, but it would have to be in the mountains. I arranged to drive up the next day, to arrive late in the morning.

Judith and her husband, Antun Harik, live in Bteghrine, about an hour's drive from my hotel in West Beirut. On the way I passed Bikfaya, hometown to the Gemayel clan, where

Pierre Gemayel founded the Phalange party in the 1930s. Critics saw it as a spiritual heir to the fascism of the period. Followers hoped it was a guarantor of the Christian homeland, much of which is centered in the deep valleys around Bikfaya, which reminded me of the Italian spine south of Rome.

The taxi driver found Bteghrine, but I needed to duck into several small stores before someone could point me toward the house. Directions in Lebanese villages tend to involve phrases like "go past second gas station" or "turn left at the bread shop." I had been told to look for an old stone house under renovation, and I had to circle the block until I found a way into the garden. There I found Judith pulling weeds, and Antun supervising workmen. The house, built with local stone, had belonged to Antun's ancestors. For more than twenty years—probably on a lot of weekends—the Hariks had been renovating with the idea of moving here as they got toward retirement ages. Eastern Switzerland, around St. Moritz, has similar square stone houses, as do certain villages in Corsica. What makes this house distinctive are its thick, ancient walls—as if the Romans had sunk the foundation— and an elegant rectangular cupola, the Lebanese equivalent of what on Nantucket is called a widow's walk.

I toured the house, they made me coffee, and then I sat in the garden with Judith, who spoke about her research into Hezbollah. She had come to the American University in the early 1980s, during a bad moment in the civil wars, to teach Latin American politics. Her expertise was the politics of Peru. The fighting in and around Beirut scared away students interested in South America, although clearly her familiarity with such groups as the Shining Path gave her insight into the origins of such movements as Islamic Jihad and Hezbollah. She surprised me by saying that during all the years of the civil wars the university had remained open and that she had often commuted across the deadly Green Line. She said that Antun had listened carefully to local radio and thus knew which sectors were quiet and which were at war, and directed her commute accordingly. She described the eight checkpoints that she would have to pass between AUB and her house in the mountains. The worse moments of the wars, she said, were when the battleship *New Jersey* was called to quarters. In her book she writes that "it was anchored less than a quarter of a mile from home [in Beirut], and the first blast of its giant guns shattered all windows facing the sea and blew my front door right off its hinges." In the garden she said it was as if someone "had launched a freight train." Fisk calls the *New Jersey* "a true representative of U.S. policy in Lebanon: unthinking, unwieldy, hopelessly out of date."

Before the 1982 Israeli invasion, no one had ever heard of an organization called Hezbollah, which means Party of God. But around the time the *New Jersey* arrived on station, she and her husband, who worked for the United Nations, began hearing about militia members in the southern suburbs wearing black head scarves. They had vowed, as she writes in her book, "to conduct jihad against the 'usurpers of Muslim lands'—the Israelis." But, she pointed out, as these guerrillas were not in the violent mix of the Lebanese civil wars, it took a long time for anyone to link them to one organization, if, indeed, Hezbollah is a hierarchical organization.

Until Hezbollah's recent battles with Israel, not even experts like Judith Harik could be certain whether the Party of God was a religious movement, a social organization, a political party, a terrorist network, or a private army. At different times it has had the characteristics of all five. In his book Fisk writes: "The Hezbollah was founded on faith, not patriotism. The living image of that faith was Khomeini." The catalysts were both the Iranian revolution, exported to Lebanon through gateways such as Baalbek, and the Israeli occupation of a buffer zone below the Litani River. Hassan Nasrullah, the party's chief, credits Israel for the genesis of Hezbollah, saying in 1997: "Had the enemy not taken this step [invading], I do not know whether something called Hizbullah would have been born. I doubt it." Pintak writes about how Hezbollah inherited the mantle that Israel squandered when it treated Shiites so harshly after the 1982 invasion. Its military mission from its earliest days was to fight the Israeli occupation of Lebanon and to liberate what it called occupied Palestine.

In my conversation with the Hariks, and later in my reading, I explored whether Hezbollah was more a social than a terrorist organization. Viewed from the Israeli side of the Lebanese border, Hezbollah is simply an army of Iranian and Syrian mercenaries, there to kill Israeli soldiers and to terrorize the population in the north of the country. Seen from Beirut, Hezbollah has social qualities as elusive as its guerrillas posted to the caves outside Tyre. Pintak writes: "It delivers powdered milk." Indeed Judith Harik spoke at length about the schools and health clinics that Hezbollah operates in Beirut's southern slums, where neither police nor sanitation men dare to tread. It had also contested numerous elections and now had the largest single block of members in the Lebanese parliament. Nor did Judith Harik believe that Hezbollah in the last fifteen years had targeted Western interests (other than Israel) with acts of terrorism. Nevertheless, in 1985, there may have been a link between Hezbollah and anti-American terror through the shadowy presence of

Imad Mugniyeh, who may have been among the hijackers of TWA flight 847.

Harik made the point that the iconography of Hezbollah—whether it is a resistance (to the Israeli occupation of Lebanon) or a terrorist organization—is often a function of great power politics. In 1996, hoping for a comprehensive settlement in the Middle East, the Clinton administration acknowledged Hezbollah more as a resistance group. In 1998, an Israeli government report concluded: "Only when the Israeli Defense Force escalates its activities, do they [Hezbollah] launch rockets toward towns and villages beyond the border into Israel." The U.S. endorsement of a Pax Syriana to end the civil war in Lebanon allowed Damascus to sustain the presence of Hezbollah in the south of the country. (Harik writes: "Ironically, leaving Syria in charge of Lebanon established exactly the conditions Assad needed to guarantee the sustainability of Hezbollah's jihad in South Lebanon.") After September 11, when American policy shifted to fighting an unconditional global war against something labeled "terror," Hezbollah was easy to add to the list of terrorist organizations; it had unlicensed guns and rockets, not to mention black head scarves. Pintak, however, makes the point that "for Israeli Prime Minister Ariel Sharon, there was huge currency in getting Washington to buy into the notion that Israel and the U.S. faced the same terrorist onslaught....[He] was the expansionist general whose actions had dragged U.S. into Lebanon...laying the seeds that spawned this new, vicious, face of Islamic terror...to satisfy his own ambitions." Yet again the United States became hostage to the fortunes of the Israeli army in southern Lebanon.

The problem for U.S. interests in the Middle East is that Hezbollah can now add a public relations firm to its organizational chart. On the basis of having survived the Israeli assault, it can lay claim to broader Arab sympathies in the so-called struggle for Palestine. Previously, radical Islamic militants had charged Hezbollah with a bizarre covert mission. As a Saudi journalist wrote: "The impression among Al-Qaida activists is that Hezbollah is guarding Israel's northern border instead of protecting Lebanon's southern frontier." This matched the sentiments of Abu Musab al-Zarqawi, the leader of Al-Qaida in Iraq until he was killed. He charged: "The party (Hizbullah) has raised false banners regarding the liberation of Palestine while in fact it stands guard against Sunnis who want to cross the border into Israel." But Hezbollah fought its recent war with Israel as if filming thirty-second Pan Arab election spots or perhaps trailers for propaganda films entitled: "Why We Fight Israel." It also emerged from the fighting with its television station, al-Manar, still on the air, and a reputation for having fought a respected army to a draw. I sense that Harik was among the first to recognize Hezbollah's love of the spotlight, writing: "Militantly religious, disciplined and skilled in modern communications techniques, Hezbollah leaders, coached by Syria and backed by important resources Iranian leaders make available, have learned how to put their version of activist Islam across to the Arab and Muslim peoples in ways not likely to be forgotten."

DURING MY STAY in Lebanon, I found no more tranquil setting than the Hariks' garden. Trees shade the terrace, which overlooks a gorge of pine trees and houses wedged into the mountainous slopes. A cat prowled at my feet and, in between talking about Hezbollah and the civil war, we all sang the praises of restoring old houses. Toward the end of my stay, Antun joined the conversation. I had taken out my map to ask Judith if it was safe to travel into the south of the country. Had I asked the question several weeks later, I would have been inquiring whether it was feasible to visit a war zone. But at the time of my question, the border between Lebanon and Israel had been quiet, save for skirmishing that went on around the contested Shebaa Farms.[1] Both Judith and Antun encouraged me to see as much of the south as I could. I was nervous that it was off-limits, dangerous, a variation on the chaos that reigned when it was called Fatahland. But they said I would be fine, especially if I just followed the coastal road down to Tyre.

I then asked if it was safe for an American to visit the Palestinian refugee camps of Sabra and Chatilla. From my drive in from the airport, I had a rough idea of where they were—adjacent to the soccer stadium. But a State Department Web site I consulted had advised Americans not to visit the camps. My question prompted Antun to retell the story of the massacre. At first he spoke in broad generalities about what had happened and when, but as his account grew longer I began to realize that he had been perhaps the first outsider to have uncovered this tragedy.

By many accounts of the massacre, on the night of September 15-16, 1982, illuminated Israeli shells floated over the southern suburbs, including Sabra and Chatilla, which are two contiguous camps in one section of the city. (In New York City terms, I would estimate their size to be twenty

---

1. Fisk describes it as "a small section of disputed territory wedged between the borders of Lebanon, Israel and Syria, called Sheba'a Farms by the Arabs and Mount Dov by the Israelis. Israel, which occupied the area in 1967, considered it part of the Golan Heights, and thus did not withdraw from there when it left South Lebanon. Beirut and Damascus both insisted the territory was part of Lebanon. Hizbullah kidnapped three Israeli soldiers there in October 2000 and periodic clashes erupted between the two sides in subsequent years."

square blocks.) At that moment, no one in Beirut knew that Phalange militiamen—perhaps in response to the car bomb assassination elsewhere in Beirut of their leader, President Bashir Gemayel— had gone on what Antun called a "revenge rampage." An official of the UN, Antun sensed something wrong there on the afternoon of the next day. Israeli soldiers were patrolling the main roads around the camps. Nevertheless, to enter the camps, Antun had to commandeer construction equipment from some nearby job sites. At 5:00 A.M. on Friday, September 17, at the head of this makeshift convoy, he entered Sabra through its southern gates. His description of that descent into one of Dante's infernos matches that of Robert Fisk, who entered the camps on Saturday the eighteenth: "It was the flies that told us. There were millions of them, their hum almost as eloquent as the smell." Antun spoke of finding numerous dead women and children, and even now recoiled at recalling how pregnant women, in particular, had been disemboweled in the slaughter. Great numbers of Palestinians had been shot against a wall just inside the camp gates. Using the construction equipment, Antun led the burial parties, telling me: "We buried 1,450. I know. We numbered them." But he spoke of several thousand other residents who on that day went missing and were never seen again. Some, he was sure, had been flown to prisons in Israel. Others had inexplicably vanished.

On my way back into Beirut from the mountains, I had the driver take me to Sabra and Chatilla. Antun had given him precise directions as to where I should be taken, and we parked near the vacant lot where so many had been executed. Fisk writes: "The bodies that were found in Chatilla were buried in a plot of land just to the right of the entrance to the camp in a ceremony of great grief and nauseating stench."

Now the small parcel of land is overgrown with weeds, and the billboard to mark this as the Square for the Martyrs is in a state of disrepair. Leaving the Square, I took a walk through the camps. Mostly the camp buildings are two stories of concrete blocks, and everywhere are clothes hanging to dry. Along the main streets the feeling is of a third-world market. I saw great stacks of fruits and vegetables, and it is possible to buy tools, clothing, and hubcaps. There is a feeling of resignation about the back alleys; Sabra and Chatilla are the Arab world's September 11.

The camps date to 1948 and the Palestinian exodus from Israel, although Antun said that some Lebanese, especially poor Shiites, lived there alongside the mostly Palestinian population. I asked him about the role of Israel in the massacre. His answer had two elements. In a strategic sense, he believed that the Israeli army had targeted the camps with the goal of, once and for all, "rounding up the terrorists." He did not think that Israeli soldiers had participated in the actual killings, but he pointed out that most Palestinian guerrillas had shipped out of Lebanon, from Tripoli, earlier that week. Left in the camps were women and children. His views echoed the words of Fisk, who writes: "If the Israelis had not taken part in the killings, they had certainly sent the [Phalange] militia into the camp." I asked if he believed Ariel Sharon had been personally involved, and he answered: "He was there Friday morning. At the Kuwaiti embassy, across the street. He was looking down on the camps. I saw him."

I SPENT MY last afternoon in Beirut at the American University of Beirut. It was several blocks from my hotel, and the campus is an oasis in an otherwise park-less city. In addition to graceful Arabic architecture and palm-shaded walkways, the university looks down on the Mediterranean, as if it were a deluxe resort. No matter how hot and steamy Beirut can get, AUB always seems to have a gentle breeze rustling through its lush gardens, and I paused many times in my Lebanon schedule at the picnic tables that the administration has scattered around the campus.

On this particular afternoon, I was early for my meeting with Professor Samir Khalaf, so I passed the time reading in the shade and wandering through some of the university exhibitions. Missionary academics founded AUB in 1866. Its original name was Syrian Protestant College, and among the first professors and students were zealous graduates of Yale, Amherst, and Princeton. Sometime later, the Dodge family, of Phelps-Dodge prosperity, donated significant money to the college, which in 1920 changed its named to the American University of Beirut. An article in the *Chronicle of Higher Education* that I picked up in a waiting room states: "Among its graduates have been nineteen of the delegates who signed the 1945 United Nations Charter in San Francisco; two prime ministers of Lebanon and two of Jordan; George Habash, one of the founders of the radical Popular Front for the Liberation of Palestine...." For a long time the United States Agency for International Development (USAID) contributed up to 40 percent of tuition costs, and thousands of mostly Lebanese and Arab students took advantage of these grants to obtain undergraduate and graduate degrees, on a level that is offered at similar universities in the United States. At present USAID contributes only 2 percent of the university's costs, which amounted to $158 million in 2006. AUB has 7,342 students, and 544 full-time faculty members. Tuition for the year is $12,000. Less than 20 percent of the students are from abroad, many of them Americans studying abroad in their junior year. While a private university, AUB must be the most significant American institution in the Middle East, but by my estimates, the United States spends more on an average day in the war in Iraq than AUB costs to run for a year.

Walking the grounds of the campus, I came across the memorial and grave of Malcolm Kerr, the university president who was assassinated on campus in 1984. Judith Harik had told me that, overall, AUB had suffered few losses in the fifteen years of civil wars, but the killing of Kerr was the most grievous. Hooded gunmen shot him outside his office. They fled and were never captured. Pintak writes in *Seeds of Hate*: "The anonymous voice Islamic Jihad again claimed credit. It didn't matter that Kerr was a friend of the Arabs. He was 'victim of the American presence in Lebanon,' the caller said." He is buried under the head of a Corinthian column, and the inscription on his headstone says eloquently: "He lived life abundantly." In fact, although American, he was born to parents who were both teaching at AUB in the 1930s. In a memoir of her husband, his wife, Ann Zwicker Kerr, writes: "His earliest memories of Lebanon were formed in the pre–World War II days of the French Mandate before the establishment of the state of Israel and the full flowering of pan-Arab nationalism." He studied international relations at Princeton and got his PhD from Johns Hopkins in Baltimore. His best known book was, *The Arab Cold War: Gamal Abd al-Nasir and His Rivals, 1958-1970.* "His concern," writes his wife "was to dispel the notion of Arab politics as a projection of decisions made in Washington." He taught political science at UCLA and, when he had the chance, spent time at numerous colleges around the Middle East. He clearly had a love of sports, once comparing the June 1967 Arab-

Israeli War to football. "The June War," he wrote, "was like a disastrous game against Notre Dame which Princeton impulsively added to its schedule, leaving several players crippled for life and the others so embittered that they took to fighting viciously among themselves instead of scrimmaging happily as before." He was the father of the professional basketball player, Steve Kerr, and served as president of AUB for seventeen months. "The irony, of course," his wife wrote of his death, "was that they had killed a man who understood and loved the Middle East as much as any foreigner could."

I sensed the presence of two other AUB presidents as I strolled around the campus. Kerr's successor was David Dodge, a descendant from the same line that has endowed the university so handsomely. Not long after Kerr was killed, Dodge was taken hostage, held captive in the Bekaa Valley, and then put in a crate and flown to Iran. The only reason he knew he was in Iran is that he heard people speaking Farsi and glimpsed a Tehran license plate when his blindfold slipped. He was later moved to Zabedani, in western Syria, and from there he was released, apparently due to the intervention of Rifaat al-Assad, brother to the then president of Syria. By chance, Dodge later retired to Princeton, New Jersey, and moved into the house next to my parents. I met him in their living room, and we talked about how the Dodge family had endowed the university and how he survived captivity. "I didn't get sick," he reflected, "and I took it one day at a time, although I never knew if it was my last." He had only three books in the year, one of which was *Ragtime*, but he could speak Arabic with his captors, and my guess is that he felt more Lebanese than they did.

I did not meet the current president, John Waterbury, but I did walk around an exhibition of his photographs, which were on display in a gallery in one of the main buildings. The photographs are largely impressions of people and places around Lebanon, and I would describe Waterbury as an empathetic photographer, someone who spends his off-hours driving narrow Lebanese mountain roads, seeing the landscape as if his eyes were part of a camera lens. On the day that Rafik Hariri was killed, he went down to the Corniche along the waterfront and took a picture of smoke billowing over the skyline of downtown Beirut. That picture is entitled: "No Comment."

I finally met Professor Khalaf in his office on the ground floor of Nicely Hall, of which he said: "I like the building. Not everyone does." I could see their point. Nicely Hall is built in a modernistic but slightly faux Arabic style. It could be a Moroccan restaurant in a suburban mall. Whoever designed it clearly was trying to maintain the integrity of the AUB campus while staying within a budget. Costs explain a lot of second-rate buildings. But it was a pleasure for me to sit in Khalaf's office where one long wall is covered with books. We had friends in common, he had studied and taught at Princeton, and we both like talking about what makes a great city. He is a man, I would guess, in his early sixties, with a full head of gray hair. I admired his vitality, his humor, and the absence of cant in his speech. Touched by the memorial, I asked him about Ann Zwicker Kerr's memoir of her husband and AUB, *Come with Me from Lebanon*. Khalaf had known Kerr well and liked him and his wife. But of the book, he said: "Well, it's a bit sentimental." My favorite professors were always those who never minced words.

Because I noticed that Khalaf had on his shelves the complete works of Edward Said, our conversation turned to the Columbia University professor and author of numerous books, whom both Khalaf and I had known. I am sure Khalaf had known him better than I. They had numerous meals together in the United States and in Lebanon. My dealings with Edward Said were in the 1970s, when I was a student at Columbia and attended his lectures, and in the 1980s, when I edited some of his magazine articles and published an interview with him. I confessed to Khalaf that I had found his celebrated work, *Orientalism*, heavy going and that when I had edited his stories, I often found the prose tortuous. But I told Khalaf that, nonetheless, I wanted to read Said's memoirs, *Out of Place*, because during our dealings together, he had often spoken about growing up in Jerusalem, moving to Cairo and then Lebanon, and then finally attending a prep school in northern Massachusetts.[2]

Officially Professor Khalaf is a member of the department of sociology at AUB, but such a classification restricts the depth and breadth of his learning, and his ability to teach. I would prefer to describe him as a social historian, some-one able to divine truth about civilization from a novel, a cityscape, or a column of figures. When I met him, I had just purchased a copy of his latest book, *Heart of Beirut: Reclaiming the Bourj*, which is perhaps the most optimistic statement about Lebanon's future. The Bourj (the city center, from which comes the word *bourgeois*) in Beirut is the area around

---

2. During an interview Said told me: "I became aware of the fact that I was different partly through personal accident. My family is a Christian family, and the Christians are a minority in the Middle East. And, within the Christians of the Middle East, we belonged to a minority. We are Protestants.... All of the countries in which I grew up—Palestine, Egypt, Lebanon—I cannot return for one reason or another.... My roots are at best metaphysical, or in the past, and that has drawn me to subjects like exile itself and writers like Conrad and to movements and to ideas about travel—across boundaries, across disciplines, across cultures. But at bottom, I have a sense of isolation and separation and probably estrangement."

the parliament and the large downtown buildings. It is the site of ancient civilizations—Roman ruins are here—plus parts of the Green Line, numerous churches and mosques, restaurants and cafes, many banks and apartment buildings, and, most recently, the makeshift tomb of Rafik Hariri, not to mention the place where he was killed. According to Khalaf, the Bourj is "a compelling setting for political mobilization." Indeed, to protest the killing of Hariri and the Syrian occupation, more than a million Lebanese flowed into the area, which on that day became an Arabic village green.

Khalaf is an effective multi-tasker, and on the evening we met he had to appear, briefly, at a book signing, and then get home to have dinner with his son, who was back home from university in the United States. But he said I was welcome to walk home with him. As he lived in the Bourj, as if in the pages of his book, I was thrilled. Without overstating the case, I felt like I had the chance to stroll through Edinburgh with James Boswell. We swooped into the book signing and then headed to the city center, about a twenty-minute walk. Along the way Khalaf dragged me into churches, down small alleys, and up obscure staircases, all to make the point that Beirut is among the most dynamic and modern cities in the world—either despite or because of its destruction in the civil wars. He writes in *Heart of Beirut*:

> Beirut today is akin to a living laboratory where one is in a sustained state of being captivated by the perpetual thrills of new discoveries unfolding, as it were, before one's very eyes.... Indeed, in the popular imagination a plurality of images is invoked: a future Hong Kong or Monaco, a Mediterranean town or Levantine seaport, a leisure resort, a playground or tourist site.

As we walked, he spoke at length about the idealism and high quality craftsmanship of Solidere ("foreign architects and local contractors"), the company Hariri founded to manage and plan the reconstruction of Beirut. With many of the renovated buildings, it had guarded the dimensions and designs of prewar Beirut. It also built the nearby modern towers and office complexes, although using stone and glass in such a way that the modern does not drown out the old.

Today Beirut is a city of more than one million—Khalaf said it captures "the dream of Lebanon." Despite the Ottoman arches and Roman ruins, it is not an old city. One hundred fifty years ago its population was six thousand. Only between 1932 and 1980 did it grow ten times. But such exponential growth may have sealed Lebanon's fate. Khalaf explained that when people moved to the city, they moved with their "village loyalties intact." He calls it the "ruralization" of Beirut: that is "the tenacity and survival of large residues of non-urban ties and loyalties." By Khalaf's estimates, during the wars there were 280 factions in battle. He elaborates in his book: "The 'Lebanism' of the Christians was pitted against the 'Arabism' of the Sunni Muslims with reverberations among the Shi'ites and Druze of the hinterland." In short, the pot never melted until it blew up.

One reason Solidere was founded to buy up large tracts and many central Beirut buildings is because during the civil wars, Shiites from the south and the southern suburbs, fleeing the fighting, had moved into downtown Beirut as squatters. Thus as it flipped properties, Solidere also sought to keep downtown Beirut from becoming a Shiite neighborhood. Despite such a political agenda, according to Khalaf, the reconstituted Bourj has more churches and mosques and religions than anywhere else on earth. (In answer to my question of astonishment, he said: "Yes, more than Jerusalem.") We even visited a Maronite church that was rebuilt with arches that manages to evoke those of the Romans as well as the Ottomans.

Not yet to open when we were on our walk was the dominating al-Amin Mosque, a personal project of Hariri's, overlooking Martyr's Square. It was hard to reconcile secular Lebanon—that of Phoenician traders and bankers—with the manifestation of so many different religious symbols in downtown Beirut, especially a supersized mosque. But Khalaf does not see the religious revival in the Bourj as evidence of new sectionalism among Lebanon's many ethnic and religious groups. Instead, he spoke to me about how Lebanon's survival depended on the "need to seek shelter in cloistered communities." In short, in the new Bourj, everyone would feel at home and welcome. No one would be the angry, excluded outsider, bringing the vendettas of the villages into the city.

When I said good-bye to Khalaf, we were near Martyr's Square. In rapid-fire English he was explaining how Baron Haussmann's Parisian influences had reached to the wide Beirut boulevards that spiral around the Bourj. He then pointed out to me the delightful irony that a bank would have excavated Roman baths in its courtyard. ("Both have a way of relaxing morals," he chuckled.) He was proud of sitting on the architectural commission that was deciding how to fill in the last empty spaces of the Bourj, the great no man's land of the Green Line that remains the last divide between Christian East and Muslim West Beirut. We discussed the possibilities: should it become a paved paradise with high rises and Starbucks or should it remain the equivalent of Lebanon's Washington mall, available to the people for popular demonstrations? Should the Green Line become a wall memorial to those killed, or carted away like the Iron Curtain? Looking into Lebanon's future, Khalaf said his greatest fears are for what he calls "retribalization" and "collective amnesia." He loves what Beirut has become since the wars ended, but he worries that in the city's passion to forget its past, it may yet dig up foundations that supported the violence for almost twenty years. He brought up the changes in Europe, whether it was healthy or not that the continent has largely forgotten its pre-1945 history. In a more local sense, he asked what should be done with the remains of Rafik Hariri, still lying in state under a makeshift tent on Martyr's Square. Should a memorial in his honor be built on the site or should his remains be quietly moved to a family plot in his native Sidon? By letting him rest where he is, which would be safer, the future or the past?

BEFORE LEAVING LEBANON, I decided to follow the Hariks' advice and take a drive through the south. It meant leaving my hotel at 7:00 A.M., and the taxi driver I had come to know and trust had another client that morning. But he sent me off with a relief driver, and we stopped before 8:00 A.M. at the waterfront section in Sidon. For the most part, everything, except for a few cafés and market stalls, was closed. I wrote postcards and sipped Turkish coffee overlooking the remains of the crusader fortress that connects to the city walls by what looks to have been a drawbridge. Along the seafront the young sons of fishermen were repairing their nets. Then I explored the souk where the heavy metal shutters were just beginning to rattle open. There was a sinister quality to some of the areas I visited, although no one approached me to say that I didn't belong. Maybe because of the still fetid air on a hot summer morning, I found Sidon suffocating.

In hearing descriptions about the south, I had heard that while Sidon was largely a city of Sunnis, further south, including Tyre, was Shiite, and largely in the control of Hezbollah. The Hariks had said it was safe to drive along the road that runs parallel to the Israeli border all the way to Syria. But my taxi driver said I would need a pass from some official in Tyre and that it would take hours to obtain. I passed the remains of the day in and around the city of Tyre, the objective of so many Israeli bombing runs during their various Lebanese incursions.

I wondered how I might be received at the checkpoint alongside the Litani River. But the guard simply waved us through. Although the Litani has come to symbolize the internal border between the worlds of the Lebanese government and Hezbollah's state-within-a-state, in summer the river is little more than a stream. To the right of the coastal highway, as you head south, are great fields of banana palms and then the sea. To the east are rolling hills, softer than the mountains of the Chouf, and numerous Shiite villages, including Qana, where, in the war to follow my visit, Israeli warplanes accidentally destroyed a building full of cowering women and children.

I had expected Tyre to be another strident Shiite city, a coastal Baalbek, if you will. Near where the city begins, I saw the obligatory banners of Ayatollah Khomeini and Hassan Nasrallah. But after taking in those welcoming banners (Do spiritual leaders really carry so many machine guns?), I explored the part of the city that extends into the Mediterranean Sea.

During the July 2006 Hezbollah battles, Tyre became a point of no return for many refugees who fled inland villages but then became stranded in the city because no ferries or boats were allowed to pick them up. Aircraft repeatedly strafed the city. An Israeli bomb killed a number of Canadian aid workers holed up in a guesthouse. But the Tyre I saw at high summer had few qualities of either a rebel stronghold or a hotbed of radical Islam. I have no doubt that residents of both persuasions live in the city. At the same time Tyre struck me as a forgotten city, hard up against a closed border, the sea, and villages that share few of its historical origins. In Lebanon, the divide has always been between the coast and the mountains, or between *Phoenicia Maritima* and *Phoenicia Lebanum*. As best as I could judge, the sleepy port district of Tyre looks west to the worlds of Carthage and Athens. Less than ten miles to the east, but in what could be distant worlds, the inspirations are Mecca and Najaf.

After wandering through the city, I found a shady spot among the Roman ruins and curled up with my book, in this instance, Fisk's *Pity the Nation*. I had been working my way through it for weeks, and only finished the last of his 727 pages when I got home to Switzerland. To readers who have come this far in the story, it must seem odd that I spent so much of my time in Lebanon reading. In fact, at most of the principal historical sites—Byblos, Baalbek, and the Ottoman palace of Beit Ed Dine—I spent as much time with my nose in a book as I did climbing around the ruins. I found I had no choice but to let books be my guides. The few professional guides that I met—such as my Armenian friend in Aanjar— spoke the pigeon-English of guiding, a grating patter about this dynasty or that caliph done in by an earthquake or a sandstorm. Tyre was no exception. But there is no better place in Lebanon to reflect on the layers of the country's history than on the sacred way of the Roman port.

Many Roman columns astride this triumphal path leading to the shore remain standing, which gives the city the sense that gladiators might any day disembark from their long boats and escort Hadrian ashore with his "traveling court." From where I was hiding from the noonday sun, I could look along the columns into the blue waters of the Mediterranean or tilt my head slightly south and see the low, dry hills that roll toward the UN compounds at Naqoura and then the fortified border with Israel. On other trips, I have stood on the Israeli side of this divide, and looked from the Golan Heights into both Syria and Lebanon. From either side of this political divide, the guiding fixed point is the gently sloping peak of Mt. Hermon, in many ways the Mount Ararat of the Middle East in that it represents, for many, the unobtainable dreams of divided nations.

The Hariks had spoken at length about this range when we sat on their terrace in Bteghrine. Repeatedly they made reference to *Water Wars* by John Bullock, in which there is a chapter on Mount Hermon and the River Jordan as the source not just of the region's water table, but of many ensuing conflicts and battles. In short, the abundant rain that falls every year on this mountain drains into an underground Nile, so to speak, that flows south under the Jordan River and does not end until well into the African rift. Beginning with its occupation of the Golan Heights, and the southern slopes of this range, Israel has diverted a lot of this water to make its deserts bloom. The Hariks described the rival claims to Shebaa Farms in the Golan essentially as a battle for water rights—a remake of the movie *Chinatown* in lands where both crusaders and Bedouin have died of thirst.

Mt. Hermon looms over southern Lebanon, much the way Hezbollah dominates it politically and militarily. But it is not visible from the shade of the Roman ruins. There I pressed on with my Fisk reading, which, while a detailed account of the civil wars from the late 1970s to 1990, can be read as an explanation of why the numerous Israeli invasions of the south Lebanon have failed. Critics who despise Fisk—there are many—see him as an apologist for terrorism, as someone who is stridently anti-Israeli, as a reporter who would much rather interview Osama bin Laden than cower with a family in Haifa under attack from Hezbollah's rockets. At the same time Fisk has been a reporter in Beirut for the *Times* and the *Independent* since the 1970s, and much of what he does in his journalism is describe what he has seen or been told on his many trips to Lebanese battle fronts.

In his book Fisk covers the Syrian occupation, ethnic cleansing in the Chouf, the Phalange, the Druzes, the massacres at Sabra and Chatilla, the 1982 Israeli invasion, the attacks against the French and Marine Corps barracks, the hostage taking, and several incarnations of the so-called security zone in southern Lebanon. On any number of occasions he put his life on the line to cover a particular story. My problem in assessing his accuracy is that I respect those who warned me to read him with caution. At the same time, as a writer I admire his precise use of language, his apparent obsession with checking facts in person, his longevity in Lebanon. Plus I agree with his linguistic attacks on the word *terrorism*, an expression, he writes, that "had become not just an obsession but an amorphous military objective with neither end nor meaning."

As the Israeli army was to overrun the south of Lebanon several weeks after I lingered in Tyre, I found it instructive to read Fisk on the results of the many earlier Israeli attacks into Lebanon—all with the stated goal of "securing" a hostile border and routing out terrorists from the caves of the Jabal Aamel. When Israel launched its forces into southern Lebanon in 1982, Prime Minister Begin spoke of the goal to "root out the evil weed of the PLO." At one point in 1982 Israel had 100,000 troops in Lebanon. One report estimated the casualties from this invasion as 14,000 killed and 20,000 wounded. Air raids on the port city of Sidon may have killed a thousand civilians, some of whom Fisk himself counts in that city's morgue. When Israel pulled back from Beirut and established its security zone south of the Litani River, it armed a local militia, the South Lebanon Army, much the way it had earlier armed the Phalangists, as guns for hire. But as Fisk writes, the idea of a buffer zone, even one that had 6,000 peacekeeping forces, did not work: "In one form or another, this 'security belt'—often one of the most *insecure* and dangerous areas of the country—was to become a permanent feature of southern Lebanon."

Fisk describes the 1982 to 1983 Operation Peace for Galilee: "The Israelis came like the Syrians, with expressions of innocence and with promises that they had arrived only to restore the sovereignty of Lebanon." Israel withdrew from southern Lebanon in 2000, only to return, in force, in 2006. Between 1982 and 2000, it spent some $20 billion on the occupation and suffered thousands of casualties. It succeeded in driving the PLO from Lebanon. In its place it contributed to the breakdown of Lebanese society by arming proxies in the civil wars. (Fisk describes earlier mercenaries: "The Phalangists here were dressed from boot to helmet in Israeli clothes.") Its harsh rule in the south proved the perfect incubator for the rise of Hezbollah and the influence of it Iranian patrons. Obviously, the United States, which footed some of the $20 billion invasion costs, had hoped that a pacified southern Lebanon would lead to a comprehensive Middle East peace. Instead, it had to accept the criminal Syrian occupation of Lebanon, and saw its honest-broker status reduced from that of a disinterested party to just another armed militia fighting for a piece of Lebanon. Twenty years later, the "war on terrorism" looks a lot like the Lebanese civil wars, with the *mise en guerre* having moved to places like Iraq and the World Trade Center.

Fisk's conclusion about Lebanon is dark: "Its tragedy—its history—was one of constantly invading armies, negotiating, cajoling, intimidating, storming their way into Beirut." Certainly not even the Roman Empire had managed to hang on to Tyre, not to mention Baalbek, now Hezbollah's primary tourist attraction. Looking around the seafront ruins for the last time, I thought of all the empires that had hoped that by controlling this spit of land (once an island) they might remain dominant in the Middle East. After the Phoenicians, the pretenders to the throne here had included Persians, Greeks, Romans, Byzantines, Arabs, Crusaders, Ottomans, French, British, Lebanese, Syrians, and, in short stretches, the Israelis. Others now courting influence here include the United States and Iran, although few citizens of either republic are present, letting mercenaries in nearby caves and in Israel do their bidding. Even Pericles, Shakespeare's "prince of Tyre," associated the city with all that was virtuous in his life. As his friend Helicanus proclaimed:

> *We have no reason to desire it,*
> *Commended to our master, not to us.*
> *Yet, ere you shall depart, this we desire:*
> *As friends to Antioch we may feast in Tyre.*

Leaving the city to drive to Beirut, I had no sense that in a few weeks Tyre would be under attack by land, sea, and air. Perhaps because it is on the fault line of so many empires, and has broken so many of them, it did not come as a surprise when I heard that it was yet again on the front lines of the region's great game. Shakespeare sensed well the dangers of these lands, noting, wryly: "With golden fruit, but dangerous to be touched."

Remembering the
Twentieth Century Limited
(2005)

As a child of the 1960s, traveling the United States by train with my father, I often stopped in Chicago. He would do business, and, in the company of an off-duty secretary, I would see the city-of-the-lake, which to this day fills me with small-town wonder. Then under the influence of Superman, I was sure Chicago had the coordinates of Metropolis. To a boy of ten, business was synonymous with the skyline of the Loop, elegance was the department-store windows at Marshall Field's, luxury meant checking into the gilded Parker House hotel, and the gothic type and tower of the *Chicago Tribune* met all the requirements for Clark Kent's *Daily Planet*.

More recently—instead of arriving on the red carpet that was laid out for the passengers of the *Twentieth Century Limited*—I flew to Chicago, from my home in Switzerland, on airliners that looked like empty movie theaters. To be sure, it was a business trip like many others, punctuated with such mantras as "transparent," "synergy," and "viable options." But for me, the best trips are those which align business with pleasure. So I did my best to mix into "the calls" what Robert Louis Stevenson called "travel for travel's sake."

Because of security checkpoints, O'Hare was a vision of Bedlam, although these inmates had better access to Starbucks. Crowding onto a hotel courtesy bus, I recalled in contrast those trips of childhood when the echo of footsteps on marble greeted sleepy overnight passengers in the parthenon of Union Station.

Nostalgia may not be what it once was, but, nonetheless, I checked into the Parker House, strolled along North Michigan Avenue, crossed over the canyons of the Chicago River, remembered the 1968 Democratic-convention riots and the then mayor, Richard J. Daley ("Don't take a nickel, boys. Just give 'em your business card."), and fulfilled a lifelong dream of doing business in the Tribune Tower.

Having recently published a book, I went there for a radio program, which reminded me of an uncomfortable job interview. An assistant escorted me to a studio, where I was left to idle with my nervousness, my tepid glass of water, and my freshly shined shoes. With the air of a personnel chief, the show host entered the studio, flipped through the book as though it were a padded résumé, asked questions that sounded like inquiries into my accounting grades, and then said it would be six weeks before the network would decide whether or not to air the interview. Right then, I knew I wouldn't be playing in Peoria.

Departing O'Hare the next morning, I crossed the Great Plains on American Airlines, although it felt like a prairie schooner as we sailed above a patchwork quilt of farmland squares. I landed in Rochester, Minnesota, which looms from the flatlands as though a cyclone had delivered a Big Ten university to Oz's Emerald City.

Rochester is home to the renowned Mayo Clinic, the Lourdes of medical pilgrimage. Alas, I wasn't there for a second opinion but to see an institution I had worked with professionally, but knew only by its fine reputation. I thought, too, that I might find the local book climate warmer than that in Chicago.

The campus of the Mayo Clinic engulfs the grid of a small American town. Many of the buildings are linked with basement tunnels, where I encountered an underworld race clad in bathrobes and slippers. The older buildings package immortality in the façade of Depression-era red brick, although one of the newer glass-and-chrome towers has an atrium sculpture that looks like a glass-and-bead dragon that escaped from a Chinese new year's parade.

Voltaire said that "the art of medicine consists in amusing the patients while nature cures the disease." Indeed Mayo has been host to many ailing potentates and others on the grand tour of medical tourism. But the genius of the clinic is the commonsense legacy of the two Mayo brothers, Charles and William, who learned the arts of medicine and surgery from their father—also from Rochester. "It never occurred to us that we could be anything but doctors," is one of their remembered aphorisms.

I toured the Mayo brothers' offices, preserved as a small museum. From the curios on their desks, and the pictures on their walls, I sensed them to have been men of infectious optimism, who even from the cauldron of World War I trenches gleaned surgical advances. Their portraits convey an absence of jealousy, trust in subordinates, and the operating touch of watchmakers. Their pluck and luck turned fields of corn into one of the few utopias that accepts Medicaid.

That evening I gave a reading from my book at a dinner

that was attended by a most-congenial group of heart surgeons. (I kept to myself that line of W.C. Fields: "After two days in hospital, I took a turn for the nurse.") I admit to taking secret pleasure in watching them enjoy salmon, Scotch, and a second desert. Reflecting in the glow of these new friends, I was sad to leave Rochester, and the next morning went reluctantly to the airport, as if setting sail for Cape Horn. In a way I was, as I took a quirky succession of flights to Argentina, the land of Ferdinand Magellan's southern passage.

En route, to prolong the warm confines of Lake Wobegon, I read stories by Garrison Keillor ("No innocent man buys a gun and no happy man writes his memoirs.") and stopped long enough in Miami to cruise the Art Deco beachfront—another of God's waiting rooms, although this one has more neon and beer on tap. Having tasted fall in Chicago, winter in Minnesota and summer in Florida, I then woke up in the Argentine springtime, where the clouds of economic discontent made it feel like yet another Kansas town beset by twisters.

If ever a country needs a magic cure, it is Argentina, which for the last decade has tried to ride the wave of global prosperity to the realms of economic respectability, as if the wealth of nations can be conjured from over-the-counter options. For a brief shining moment, it had a balanced budget, a currency pegged to the dollar, increasing oil production, and the divine intervention of foreign investment. But on closer inspection, the books might well have been cooked at the Enron Corporation, as the collateral for the country's $123 billion in debt proved to have the same illusory assets as one of Kenneth Lay's partnerships.

Only after I left Buenos Aires did the country default on its bonds, devalue its currency, cut its democracy adrift, and send the past-due invoices to the middle class, which this time, instead of embracing military dictatorship, rampaged through the capital district as though the bulls of Pamplona were collection agents.

Buenos Aires evokes the same remembrance of trips past as does Chicago, only here I recalled my honeymoon spent in a city bankrupted by the Falklands war. On this Sunday in the capital, I walked with friends in the sunshine past crowded cafes into the Recoleta Cemetery, a city of the dead that lays claim to immortality with opulent crypts and tombs like Roman villas. At Mayo life everlasting is divined in magnetic resonance imaging; here the citizenry puts its faith in Grecian urns. One of the headstones we passed was that of Eva Peron. Like so many in Argentina's political past and present, she had tried to amuse the patient electorate. But as with many cure-alls—political or otherwise—the show tunes amounted to little more than whistling past the graveyard.

La Vie Suisse
(2006)

I KNEW WE had stayed too long in Switzerland when my wife brought to the dinner-table conversation the idea of buying a chalet. By that point we had spent ten years in Geneva and had devoted many marital conversations to discussing the best way to survive the Swiss winter. Despite having the reputation as a mountain redoubt, Geneva is actually set in a moist valley that each November is sealed with a blanket of winter fog, lasting, with few exceptions, until late February. The average winter day in Geneva is about thirty-five degrees Fahrenheit, damp, sunless, and windy. Come Friday afternoon much of the city, to use the local expression, 'goes up'—either in search of skiing, sun or both.

Partly because our children were not skiers before the age of six, and because for a long time school convened on Saturday mornings, we had dodged the ski question with the odd day-trip to the mountains. Within an hour of our house are some the world's great ski resorts: Chamonix, Megève, Morzine, and Flaine are but a few of the French stations that are reachable on a morning drive. Trying new slopes on each excursion turned many ski trips into elusive searches for holy trails. To be sure, during these epics, the children learned to ski, and I managed to turn car packing into one of those obscure Olympic competitions—Romania's one shot at a medal. But skiing loses its magic when you start judging the slopes by their accessibility to parking.

What put a chalet on my wife's agenda was a short hiking vacation in Saanen, the Swiss town next to Gstaad, the unpronounceable resort of the rich and famous. (Locals say "sh-taad.") Not feeling the pressure to impress Roger Moore, a local favorite, I had booked the family into the Saanen Youth Hostel, which is a rambling chalet on the edge of town that has mattresses as hard as stale bread rolls. During our short week in residence, we played about four hundred games of ping-pong, tried to speak Czech to the family at the next table, and spent several days of a golden autumn trekking among that area's grassy peaks.

Having been raised on Sunday driving tours around New England, my wife judges most towns by the age of their wooden houses. Thus, to her, Williamsburg rates higher than, for example, Las Vegas. Walking through Saanenland, she noticed great pastures dotted with classic Swiss chalets—complete with geraniums and cowbells on the façades. On the train ride home she framed the health, education, and welfare of our children in the context of allowing them to escape the Geneva murk in the confines of an authentic chalet. Only someone grumpier than Heidi's grandfather could disagree, and the following weekend we were back in the mountains, this time in the company of a real estate agent.

Prior to this appointment, in what to me seemed like Samara, I had checked the price of a chalet in Sanaan and discovered that the 'starter' mountain houses were priced between $1 and $2 million. In Gstaad, it isn't uncommon for buyers to spent several million dollars for a chalet, only to tear it down after closing and rebuild something more suitable on the same land. In towns on the farther edges of Gstaad's gravity, however, chalets were listed for under $200,000—it being understood that Roger Moore or Barbara Walters would only pass through such villages at three thousand feet, while landing in their private jets. But my wife didn't think much of my suggestion when I remembered a chalet beside the train tracks with a large for sale sign nailed over the front door.

The real-estate agent, whose professional qualifications included a very short skirt, showed us three houses in the Alpine-perfect town of Rossinière. They ranged in prices from $200,000 to $300,000, which was still more than we wanted to spend. One was spacious, and the other had been "renovated," agent-speak to describe any home improvements done during the 1960s. When it was clear that we were not enthusiastic about the artificial bricks, the agent confessed that she had one more house for sale, but didn't think it was something that would interest us. She apologized in advance for its rundown condition and its location near the railroad station, but did utter the magic word that it was *old*. In fact, we were led to the house along the tracks with the for sale sign and entered to find a large puddle in the upstairs hall.

Keep in mind that Switzerland is not Soho. No one buys a wreck of a house to fix it up. In Geneva, anyway, many of the houses are identical, and all are finished with tiled roofs and kitchens. But this chalet, around which we were puddle jumping, was a mess. Many of the rooms were piled with several generations of junk. The front yard, sloping down to the tracks, had old barbed wire and a few car batteries. The roof was corrugated tin, like you see on shanties in Mexico City. Insulation consisted of green carpeting stapled to the walls. To enter some of the rooms, many of which had low ceilings, we had to use skeleton keys, which were about the size and shape of the mouse remains in many corners.

Needless to say, my wife was charmed. On the front of the chalet, in French that looks like Latin, were carved inscriptions that described the construction of the house for a village notable in either 1636 or 1686 (we still can't read the third digit). When we peeled back the wall-to-ceiling carpeting, we could see the original seventeenth-century wood in seemingly pristine condition. The kitchen and the bathroom were swathed in linoleum, but then so was our first house in Brooklyn, which, unlike this staid Swiss establishment, had also come with multi-colored lights—as you would find in a Caribbean disco. Even the train running through the front yard contributed to our delight. The tracks did not belong to the Swiss mainline between Lausanne and Zurich, but were the narrow gauge of the Montreux-Oberland-Bernois (known affectionately as the MOB). Once or twice an hour a train looking like a pastoral street car would rumble past the house, prompting the children to rush to the windows and wave at the passengers and engineer.

We offered the selling family the Swiss equivalent of $81,245. As I told my wife, if we just offered $80,000 they would assume we were lowballing them. With a more precise figure, they (being Swiss) would assume we had commissioned engineers to calculate what it would cost to install tile on the roof and in the bathrooms, and had deducted that from the asking price, which was about $175,000. A few weeks later, the miniskirted agent called to say they had accepted our offer and hoped to close within the next several weeks. We dickered briefly over the detritus around the house, and the stoves—great wood-burning kilns—and fixed the closing as the day before Christmas.

My wife and I had never bought property in Switzerland, and thus the closing process was a mystery. No contracts were exchanged between buyers and sellers. We did receive a document describing the dimensions of the house and yard (which turned out to include a stream and an orchard), and instructions on how to find the office of a notary. On the afternoon of December 24, we arrived and were shown into unheated chambers last used, at least to my mind, in the novels of Charles Dickens or Honoré de Balzac. Various concerned parties assembled, including many heirs of the sellers, who turned out to be dead. Neither side came with a lawyer.

The notary could have been the grown up Oliver Twist. He wore a rumbled tweed suit, various vests, and a tie that wandered around both sides of his faded collar. I don't remember anyone turning on a light. In the winter half-light, the notary read aloud the contract, which was bound like the Magna Carta. It included not just our names, but also those of our parents, and our mothers' maiden names. Everyone present signed the proclamation with a fountain pen, except for one of the heirs, who presumably opposed the sale or the price, and refused—although that concerned no one and the closing continued until the last of the seals was pressed into the parchment. We were given a great fistful of skeleton keys and shook hands with the sellers, including an older man, in tears, who said he had been born in the house and wished us well. We all went next door for a drink, and then we drove back to the chalet, which despite it being Christmas Eve, was dark, cold, and covered with a thin layer of snow.

In the five years that we have owned the chalet, we have spent many free weekends hauling trash to the dump and ripping carpeting off the walls. That first winter, no water flowed through the pipes, which, oddly for a mountain chalet, lay above ground out the back door. Mostly, however, the surprises ran in our favor. Under the linoleum and all the green carpeting was indeed well preserved wood. A neighbor explained that, as the house had never been centrally heated, the freezing weather each winter had killed the bugs. My wife and son, armed with a $20 caulking gun, fixed the dripping roof, which then lasted another four years. With a sledgehammer, we were able to knock through the stonewall that separated the previously distinct sides of the two-family chalet. Admittedly, the hole in the wall makes the kitchen look like a coal mine. But we installed track lighting over the shaft, to give it the feeling of an archeological site. Even the defrosted bathrooms returned to life, and we learned to tell time by the sounds of the passing trains.

YOU WOULD THINK any family retreating to such rusticity on the weekends spends the rest of their week in a large city. But the fact is that our house in Geneva is in another small, pristine village, although here vineyards surround us instead of mountain forests of evergreen. We moved in 1991 to Laconnex, which is twelve kilometers from the center of Geneva, itself hardly a city. Despite the presence of the United Nations and a busy airport, Geneva is not much bigger than most American suburbs. Its population is less than 250,000 and the entire Lemanique basin, which stretches into neighboring France, has less than half a million people. As a result, less than five miles from the center of Geneva are a series of ancient villages. Laconnex, west of the city in landscape like that of Beaujolais, can trace inhabitants to the fourteenth century. At the same time the population is 565, and the classes in the village school are so small that they need to double up with another grade.

Historically, Laconnex is a French village. Indeed the border with France lies beyond the town vineyards. The Republic of Geneva, a free city, only joined the Confederation Helvetia (the real name of Switzerland) in 1816, after the Congress of Vienna and another of Turin, which then buffered the new Swiss city with a few surrounding French villages, including ours. Even now almost half the families live off the land—if not from cultivating grapes then from selling plots to local builders. The rest, like me, commute to desks in Geneva, although the traffic is so light that, on most days, I go into the city by bicycle. The village has one store, a *boulangerie*, and one restaurant, which is owned by the commune. Most of the wine is also consumed locally. When we arrived in 1991, the harvest was sold to a cooperative near Geneva. Now village wine is sold under five private labels. At first, the white wines tasted like lighter fluid, and the reds were closer to paint remover. Since then, the local *viticulteurs* have ripped out a lot of their old vines to plant new varieties, and more of them are installing the equipment to produce and bottle their own wine. Now we can drink pinot gris, pinot noir, merlot, and assorted local blends that are as good as many of the higher priced wines found across the border in Burgundy.

How anyone makes a living selling Swiss wine is another question. The better producers in town sell about 10,000 bottles a year for an average price of $9 a bottle. But from that

$90,000 they have to rent machinery, tend the vines, buy the bottles, and print the labels. To make ends meet in Switzerland, most farmers collect federal subsidies. After fifteen years in the village, I still cannot find anyone to tell me how the subsidies are calculated or when they are paid. They do not come from the town budget, but from Bern, the Swiss capital, and I know that the vintners in our village manage to buy cars, houses, and shoes for their children. But that is all I know of this subterranean source of income. Why are subsidies paid? Without aid to the farmers, the fundamental aspects of Swiss rural life would be lost forever. No one can build a house or a business on agricultural land around most Swiss villages. In the United States, where every man is a king, you can build in any field, anywhere. But not in Switzerland, which preserves the quality of is landscape by restricting building to prescribed acreage. As such, Laconnex looks much as it did in the eighteenth century. Indeed many of prominent families in town were here a hundred years ago, and in the same houses. But without subsidies to the farmers, the farmland would have to be sold, Laconnex would look like Levittown, and Geneva would be another French suburb.

Although Switzerland is best known for the shadowy capitalism of its banks, on another level the country could well be described as communist—perhaps not in the sense of Marx and Engels, but in that the highest form of government is the commune (which roughly translate to township). In our case, that's the commune (read village) of Laconnex, to which we pay the bulk of our taxes, and which, in turn, makes the key decisions about our lives. If you become a Swiss citizen (the process takes twelve years), the commune has to agree to support you in your old age. But it is also the village that recycles the garbage, puts out the fires, and maintains the graveyard. Admittedly, the canton of Geneva organizes the schools and runs such necessities as police and hospitals. But to most citizens the face of government is the municipal town council, made up of nine villagers, which has authority over building permission, civil defense, school maintenance, local sports, social programs, traffic, environmental protection, and the local pursuits of happiness (a political idea of Jean-Jacques Burlamaqui, who was Swiss).

Every year the municipal council publishes an annual report for the village. Before me are the 2004 accounts, which summarize the state of this small Swiss union. Some of the points covered in this report are: the mayor's office hours, the cost of renewing a passport, dog licenses, voting procedures, communal buildings, police interventions, the volunteer fire department, school issues, a list of children who turned eighteen, sporting events, village parties, humanitarian aid (1 percent of the local budget), traffic problems, drainage issues, social services, matters at the town dump, public transport, and supervision of the town-owned restaurant. Village revenue amounted to CHF 1,856,458 of which CHF 1,818,758 was spent, leaving a surplus of CHF 38,700. On its balance sheet the town reports CHF 13.7 million in assets of which CHF 10.5 million are local buildings, including a brand new gymnasium, which the town financed with a CHF 3.5 million bank loan. Older residents, without children on the football team or taking gym classes, thought the new facility extravagant, as it includes a house for a caretaker, a field with artificial turf, a restaurant, and expensive picture windows. Previously the town football facility was a shack with a dingy locker room and an adjoining wet bar. But Swiss villages measure each other's wealth by the prominence of their local football teams. Thus each villager had to assume new borrowings of CHF 6,194 (about $5,000) for the glory of Football Club Laconnex.

WHEN IT COMES to paying taxes and voting abroad, Americans living in Switzerland have the worst of both worlds. Under the tax treaty between the two countries, Americans pay their income tax in Switzerland, and then get a credit against taxes due in the United States. The United States is one of the few countries in the world that imposes tax on citizens who live and work abroad (other countries see expatriates as a way to boost exports), and Switzerland, despite its tax-haven reputation, is one of the few countries with a tax on global assets. But despite such tax burdens, Americans in Geneva have a hard time voting in either country that collects their money. Essentially it is a system of double taxation without representation.

To vote in U.S. elections requires receiving an absentee ballot from the election district of your last permanent U.S. address. In our case, we lived in Brooklyn, where we voted at Public School 61 on old voting machines with heavy levers and faded curtains. After moving abroad, we received absentee ballots in regular fashion. But then they stopped arriving, and the local consulate said that voters had to reapply for ballots for each election. Needless to say, the Board of Elections for King's County in New York (Brooklyn's married name) is not in the habit of responding to letters addressed from Switzerland. Before the last presidential election, because I was in New York on business, I went to their offices in downtown Brooklyn and stood in line for an hour before I could tell my electoral history to a distracted clerk. Her answer was that I should go back to Switzerland

and write another letter. A second clerk, overhearing my frustrations, invited me to a remote, gray metal desk, where I sat patiently while she rounded up ballots for my wife and me. I even voted mine on the spot. Absentee ballots may have decided the 2000 presidential election, but I am sure that not many of the five million Americans living abroad have the time or energy to secure a ballot, even though they out-number the population of the original thirteen colonies that became the United States.

By contrast, Switzerland votes early and votes often. Referendums decide most important questions, so every two months or so citizens go to the polls to decide whether the army needs more jet fighters or whether unemployment benefits should be increased. The Swiss voted against joining the European Union but *for* joining the United Nations, which is a large local employer. Recently, certain cantons, including Geneva, decided to extend the right to vote at the local level to foreigners who have been resident in the canton for more than seven years. In our case it would mean we could vote in village elections. But that would not include the right to cast votes on various national referendum issues, such as the question to be decided this month on whether to dismantle the border checks between Switzerland and the European Union. (The decision was yes.)

Despite its reputation for isolation, Switzerland has the world's second oldest democracy, a confederation that dates to 1291. Only England can claim a longer democratic tradition, but then the Swiss have never had a king. When drafting the American Constitution in summer, 1787, a number of delegates, including Benjamin Franklin, wanted the U.S. government to mirror that of Switzerland. Franklin favored a unicameral legislature and a federal council instead of the presidency. But he lost this argument to James Madison and John Adams, and the United States got its bicameral legislature and presidency, which Thomas Jefferson, also an admirer of the Swiss political system, called "a bad edition of the Polish king." To this day the federal Swiss government in Bern is run by such a rotating federal council, from which, about every year or so, the president is chosen. In effect, the presidency is just one of the many portfolios managed by the national council. Some years I know the name of the Swiss president, and other years I do not. I am unaware that the position comes with a private plane or a house, and it certainly is not news if the Swiss president visits Geneva—even Laconnex, for that matter.

A few years ago Ruth Dreifuss had the top job. That was unusual because she was from Geneva, a woman, and of Jewish origin; in general, presidents are men from the German-speaking part of the country. In my mind Dreifuss distinguished herself in many ways, but never more than when she had to welcome the Chinese leader Jiang Zemin to Bern. He was there on a trade mission, but near where he planned to give his speech there gathered a group of Chinese dissidents, demonstrating for something like Tibetan independence or other freedoms. Jiang Zemin complained to Dreifuss about the demonstrators and asked that they be removed, forcibly if necessary. He also threatened to cancel his speech. Politely, Dreifuss explained that the demonstrators were breaking no Swiss laws and that they were entitled to their opinions, just as he was. The demonstrators remained, as did Dreifuss, while the Chinese leader stormed away, berating the Swiss that they "had lost a friend." No one seemed to care.

Politically, Switzerland stands apart—from the United

States, from Europe, from whomever—perhaps making it the only gated community in the world with its own flag. What pays for its independence of mind is an economy unburdened with either heavy debt or outrageous expenditure for weaponry. With few natural resources in the country, Switzerland trades in watches, banking services, pharmaceuticals and tourism. It maintains its own currency, the Swiss franc, and generally only admits foreigners into the country if they have either money or a specific job. Although now a member of the United Nations, Switzerland adheres to its historical neutrality, but not pacifism, as witnessed by its army, which drafts all nineteen-year-olds for six months of active duty, and by its reserves, which can mobilize an army in a week's time. But without foreign entanglements, an expensive standing army, interest payments on national debt, or vast social security costs, the country can afford to plant trees along most highways, pay its teachers well, and run trains on time to all corners of the country, including those that pass in front of our chalet.

For now it has chosen to stand parallel but outside the European Union, which, in turn, believes that Switzerland enjoys the political and economic benefits of the Union without paying any of the costs. The Swiss, however, are leery of full membership, which could mean giving up both banking secrecy and agricultural subsidies. Nor would Switzerland embrace warmly the ideas of open immigration, especially if countries like Turkey eventually win EU membership. Call it religious or racial intolerance, but Switzerland is not a nation of immigrants. Many Portuguese, for example, have lived and worked in Geneva for several generations but many of them are still not Swiss citizens, and, socially, they remain an isolated subculture. During the war in Kosovo, many Albanians came to Switzerland as refugees, but now, quietly, most have been sent home. Geneva is an international city, where a third of the population is of foreign origin, largely because of the UN presence. When we moved to Laconnex, a friend said that it was a village known to accommodate outsiders. But at our chalet, one of our neighbors scorns us, and I can only think it somehow relates to feelings of historic isolation. Why should foreigners live in one of the oldest Swiss houses? Maybe we simply have a cranky neighbor.

PERHAPS TO BLEND more easily into the surroundings, I spend a lot of time reading novels and histories that describe either what the French call the provincial life or what it is like to be an American abroad. In recent years I have gone through periods reading Henry James, Edith Wharton, and F. Scott Fitzgerald, all of whom had uncertainties about life in foreign lands. (In *Tender is the Night*, Fitzgerald writes about Switzerland: "This corner of Europe does not so much draw people as accept them without inconvenient questions.") More recently I have found myself in the company of Honoré de Balzac, the nineteenth-century French novelist of the *Comédie humaine*—in which I sometimes feel I have a cameo role as either a banker or an awkward foreigner.

Balzac was born and grew up outside Paris, in the kind of provincial village that so often appears in his novels. Oratorian Brothers taught him school in a harsh setting. Honoré (he adds the *de* later, to give his background what Basil Fawlty would call a "touch of class") escapes a lonely childhood, first into the arms of a neighbor (he's twenty, she's in her forties— "*Here's to you, Mrs. De Berny*") and then to spend ten years in Paris, failing at the venture of capitalism. Of the city he writes: "I knew well the importance to me of this Faubourg, this seminary of revolutions, with its heroes, its inventors, its men of practical wisdom, its rogues and criminals, it virtues and vices, all hemmed in by misery, subdued by poverty, steeped in wine and ruined by brandy."

Balzac tries ghost writing, printing, rare books, and financial speculation, but survives on advances from his mother and his lover. In his late twenties, to stay ahead of the debt collectors, he turns to serious literature, which he writes between midnight and late afternoon, feeding his imagination with dim candlelight and strong coffee.

The more I read Balzac, the more I divide the lives that he describes between the worlds of love and debt—two of his more compelling interests. Balzac himself was often in love and in debt, and he worked feverishly to escape the enchantments or entrapments that both offered. At his writing table, he was a genius; beyond it, a fool. During his days, he ran up debts—investing in things like Sardinian mines—and chased inaccessible women (countesses, married women, and the like), as if a character in one of his novels. Only, at night, in his novels does he correct his failings at business and love.

A biographer, Stefan Zweig, writes of Balzac's failures: "What he had lost as a man of business he had gained as a man of letters.... He had learned the tremendous, the demonic significance of money in a materialistic age, and he knew that the struggle waged around a bill of exchange or a promissory note, the tricks and stratagems employed in small shops no less than in the great counting-houses of Paris, involved as great a play of psychological forces as did the adventures of Byron's corsairs or Sir Walter Scott's blue-blooded knights."

Although I first took to Balzac to understand the village life that I often found lost in translation, the deeper I got into the *Comédie humaine,* the more I found it that it better described my days at work in a Swiss bank. Indeed I found it a better guide than those tracts pursuing excellence or coloring my parachute, as, for example, when Balzac writes:

> A banker is accustomed to weigh and balance different pieces of business and to set interests in motion, just as a writer of vaudevilles is trained in creating situation and moving his characters about the stage.... Monsieur de Nucingen, purely a banker, with no inventive capacity outside his calculations, like most bankers, believed only the safe investment.

Indeed, the mistake most people make about Swiss banks is to think of them as banks at all. They rarely lend money, and then usually to a client who has more than the loan on deposit. Swiss banks are a cross between savings banks and brokerage houses. Yes, like Swiss lawyers and doctors, bankers here take an oath of secrecy, but all that often hides is poor investment decisions rather than things like Nazi gold. In general, however, Switzerland lay over Balzac's horizon, although in *A Harlot High and Low*, he recommends it for marriage prospects: "It's the air of Switzerland, you grow thrifty there.... Why don't you try it, child! find yourself a Swiss, and perhaps you've got a husband! for they haven't learnt about women like us yet....In any case, you'll come back in love with what can be written in ledgers, a refined and lasting love!"

Throughout his novels Balzac explains the intricacies of bankruptcy or a love affair, or both, as when he entitles a chapter: "How bedrooms are often council chambers." Indeed, in most of the marriages that Balzac describes, including his own, there is a debtor and creditor. He describes a suitor,

Charles Grandet, in one courtship: "Eugénie had no place either in his heart or in his thoughts. She had a place on his ledger as a creditor for six thousand francs." But the prospective mother-in-law sees the gentleman's prospects in a different light: "The Hôtel d'Aubrion was mortgaged to the hilt, and Charles was marked down to clear it"—thoughts that may have been close to Balzac's own as he pursued his courtship of Madame de Hanska to the Ukraine and then brought her back to Paris as his wife, to his own house, then heavily mortgaged. (He wrote once: "But, as there are no accredited experts in intrigue or graduate masters of passion, a banker [or for that matter a novelist] has little guidance when he's in love and cannot be expected to manage women.")

At age fifty-one, blind and debilitated, Balzac died a short time after his arrival from the Ukraine. Creditors made the most of his estate, except what he left to his readers. Zweig sums him up: "When he transmuted his imaginative gift into literary production it brought him not only monetary rewards, but imperishable fame; when he tried to transform his illusions into money he succeeded only in adding to his debts and multiplying his labors."

ONE OF THE surprising qualities about Switzerland is its absence of history. You would think that being located at the crossroads of Europe it would have battlefields, museums, and other historical markers that would fill up many weekend afternoons. But Geneva has always struck me as far from the frontlines of history, important as the city has been in the trade and finance of European business. About an hour from our house in the French Alps is the mountain valley of Les Glières, where the French resistance in 1944 held out against the Nazis. But the last battle fought in Geneva was in 1602, and the initial weapon used in that engagement, between the Genevois and the nearby Savoyards, was boiling soup. Napoleon recognized the strategic values of the Valais—the valley that leads from Switzerland into Italy—but after 1816, Swiss neutrality became an article of faith in European confrontations. Switzerland fought in neither the first nor second world wars, a fact brought home to me most mornings when outside our front door I pass a water trough on which is engraved the date 1914. Clearly that summer the owner of our house (then a barn) was thinking more about his cows than the ultimatum delivered following the assassination of the Austrian archduke.

One of the few historical figures associated with Geneva (aside from Voltaire, who lived across the border in France) is Germaine Necker, known to the world as Madame de Staël. She was the daughter of Jacques Necker, Louis XVI's minister of finance at the time of the French Revolution, who fled the Directory to his summer chateau de Coppet, on the shores of Lake Geneva. Swiss by origin, Necker had made his fortune and reputation in France, where, during the early days of the Revolution, he was seen as a possible savior of the debased currency that had progressively ruined the monarchy and then the democracy. His wife, Germaine's mother, was also Swiss, and she achieved Parisian fame for her salon, which attracted on a weekly basis some of the great French minds to the Necker household. It was in such an intellectual atmosphere that Germaine grew up in Paris, rivaling her mother for the affections of her father, whom she adored. "Warm, generous, vivacious, spontaneous, effortlessly brilliant yet never pedantic," is how one biographer describes Germaine, "although she quite lacked her mother's beauty, she attracted all who saw her." The same account says of her mother: "When God created Madame Necker, he dipped her first, inside and out, in a bucket of starch." Her husband's wealth, however, attracted more dinner guests than his wife's piety kept away, although Madame Necker, a confidant of Marie Antoinette, did once confess: "I do have atheist friends. Why not? They are my unhappy friends."

Instead of inheriting her mother's frosty personality, Germaine took up the mantle of her salon, especially after she married a Swedish prince and diplomat, Eric Magnus de Staël Holstein, one of her few bad decisions. "It was said," Maria Fairweather writes in a recent biography, *Madame de Staël*, "that while Monsieur de Staël had married Necker's millions, Germaine had married Paris." About that time she wrote to her father: "True pleasure for me can be found only in love, Paris or power." She found all three among the likes of Talleyrand, Lafayette, Condorcet, and La Rochefoucauld-Liancourt, who gathered regularly in her salon. She was attracted to the men of the so-called Third Estate, the professional classes, accomplished thinkers, writers, lawyers, and financiers. (The First Estate was the church; the Second was the nobility.) It was assumed that she had been a lover of Talleyrand, although Fairweather notes their differences: "Where she was passionate, direct, tactless and utterly loyal, he was delicate, oblique, diplomatic and unscrupulous." She also noted: "Some thought her an intriguer, but no one had any doubt about her political experience, her acute intelligence, her liberal views, or her love of France —and few were immune to her extraordinary charm." But the one who was immune was Napoleon Bonaparte, and his rise to power led to her exile in Geneva and to her wanderings around Europe.

In the early days of Napoleon, she had tried to win him to her cause of liberalism, if not something more intimate.

But Fairweather writes: "She was everything he disliked most in a woman—outstandingly intelligent, outspoken, imprudent and lacking beauty." She was among the first to judge his tastes for imperialism over liberty, saying of his single-minded ambition and calculating coldness that it is "like an icy sword that freezes as it cuts." She did remain on good terms throughout her life with Napoleon's brother, Joseph, who sometimes tried to broker a rapproachment between the First Consul and his recalcitrant, independent subject. Napoleon once asked her brother: "What is it that she wants?" When those words got back to Germaine, she scoffed: "It is not a matter of what I want but what I think." She knew what she was confronting when she accepted the responsibility of opposition to Napoleon. She reflected: "One must choose in life, between boredom and torment." Napoleon was certainly capable of providing torment and vowed to crush Madame de Staël, to which she bravely responded: "There is a kind of pleasure in resisting an iniquitous power. Genius too is power." Fairweather writes of Napoleon: "His social manner was uneasy but not timid, there was a haughtiness about him when he was reserved, although he tended to vulgarity when at ease." Madame de Staël was more blunt about Bonaparte: "he was undoubtedly resolved on constant war, interspersed with those moments of peace which have always increased his power more than the battles themselves." In the end, it was written: "The crucial difference between them lay in her love of humanity—which he despised."

Napoleon was right in thinking that exile to Switzerland would condemn Madame de Staël to a life on the periphery of Parisian ideas and power. She had once said: "The spectre of boredom has pursued me all my life." Nor did she warm either to the Genevois or to the environs of Geneva, with its climate that while, sparkling in summer, can be dreary in winter. In many ways Germaine was a modern woman who loved ideas, liberty, her friends, good writing, men (at times) other than her husband, and the confluence of a literary and political life. By contrast, she found the Genevois to be *haute bourgeois*: "Their love of equality is no more than a wish to bring everyone down; their love of liberty is mere insolence; and their high minded morality—boredom." Once during her long years abroad, her son approached Napoleon with the idea of letting her return to Paris. But Bonaparte was unrelenting: "She has an unbridled mind, she has never understood the meaning of subordination." On another occasion he said she "is a machine of movement, stirring up the salons." In fact, although she would have been loath to admit it, exile suited another side of Madame de Staël: one that was reflective, which allowed her to become a noted historian and novelist. She published an important history of the French Revolution, based on her conversations with many of the protagonists. Byron admired the heroine of her novel *Corinne*: "She is sometimes right and often wrong about Italy and England; but always true in delineating the heart, which is but one nation; of no country, or rather of all." Talleyrand, who is given an unflattering feminine portrayal in her novel *Delphine*, was less charitable about the writings of his old lover, telling friends: "I hear that in her novel, Madame de Staël has disguised both of us as women."

In exile, Germaine also became a reluctant traveler, skirting the Napoleonic empire to visit the important thinkers of Germany, Italy, and England. She found the chateau in the Geneva suburbs confining: "Coppet is like living in a convent, while Geneva is, of all the places known to me, the most uncongenial to my tastes, my habits and my thoughts." Wherever she went, she caused a sensation as Napoleon's severest critic. Fairweather writes about her trip to Germany: "Reports and rumours flew around: she was a bluestocking, she was the most famous Parisian saloniere, she was brilliant, she was a Jacobin, she was a Republican, she was in trouble with Bonaparte; and though she was no beauty, she was a great seductress—was Constant really her lover?" She lingered for months at court, charming allies and enemies alike, working on her books, speaking her mind. "The republic of German letters," she reflected, "is truly astonishing, but I think that the aristocracy is not very cultivated; the thinkers are all underground while the grenadiers march over it." After her whirlwind left Weimar, Schiller wrote to Goethe: "I feel as if I had just recovered from a severe illness." But she was ahead of her times, as she herself admitted: "Exile severed the roots which bound me to Paris and I became European."

As a foreigner living in the Swiss countryside, the question I am asked most often is whether I plan to stay. Noted salesman, Willy Loman, once observed of his Brooklyn residency, that he "felt kind of temporary about myself." I feel the same way living abroad, no matter how familiar I find the bread in Switzerland or the countryside. Most of our friends are from the village, and I would be happy to spend the rest of my life in their company, given their warm and friendly compassion, qualities few outsiders associate with the Swiss. I like it that I can bike to work and that the malls are closed on Sundays. Switzerland is a civil society, with a functioning democracy, good schools, and no interest in invading countries like Iraq. On the downside, at least in my case, it's a corner of a foreign field that largely isn't mine.

Quirky as it may seem, one attraction to life in Switzerland, and Europe beyond its borders, is the rail network, which not only takes me on weekends to the chalet, but which connects Geneva to the four corners of the continent. Sadly, European trains are more expensive than the new discount airlines, so I don't ride them as often as I would like. But in the last few years, I have taken the family around the Balkans on a succession of decrepit sleepers, and last October my younger daughter and I took trains and ferries from Geneva to the Greek island of Rhodes, off southern Turkey. Geneva is not on the European main lines, so to go anywhere means changing trains in Basel, Paris, or Milan. But it is still a pleasure to arrive or depart in the great European stations, which figure so prominently in fiction or Impressionist paintings. If I have a complaint about European railroads, it is that the overnight trains leave late and arrive early. London to Edinburgh, for example, is barely six hours. When I went last year on a sleeper to Florence, I was ready to start my sightseeing at 6:45 A.M., which is one way to beat the crowds around Brunelleschi's Dome.

No doubt I am partial to European trains because I first saw Switzerland and the Continent in 1970 on trains that took our family from Luxembourg to Venice, and included side trips around Yugoslavia and Italy. During my junior year abroad, in London and Vienna during 1974 to 1975, I spent more time in train stations than museums, something I now regret. But the year on the rails filled in the blank spaces of my mind's European map, and included stops in Scotland and Smolensk. It also gave me a lot of time to read, to connect the landscape of northern France to Maupassant or that of southern Poland to Primo Levi.

For Christmas 2003, my father gave me *Trains of Thought*, the literary memoirs of Victor Brombert, now a retired professor from Yale and Princeton. He had heard Brombert speak in Princeton, where my parents live in retirement, and later tracked down his memoirs, which near the beginning describe earlier rail journeys: "My early political education in the 1930s had much to do with border controls, visas, and the sound of sternly polite questions asked across the threshold of a compartment that for an interval of time ceased feeling cozy." Brombert's parents were Russian Jews, who learned of the 1917 Revolution while on their honeymoon in Denmark, and who then raised their son in Berlin and Paris, before having yet again to flee war in 1940, first to southern France and Iberia, and then by ship to the United States.

In the book's twist of fate, Brombert enlists in the American army, lands at Normandy as an infantryman and translator, and fights his way across Europe, along many of the same tracks that earlier had carried him in flight from German aggression. The book eloquently describes his adolescence in Paris, his wartime experiences in the Bulge and across the Rhine ("There could not have been a worse assignment that the Hürtgen forest...nothing could compare in brutal discomfort and senseless sacrifice of lives with what several of our divisions, soon torn to shreds, experienced in the slime, cold, and fog southeast of Aachen..."). He concludes with his academic career in the United States, where he finished as chairman of the Council of Humanities at Princeton. In one passage he writes about the ending of Gustav Flaubert's *Sentimental Education*, in connection with his family's flight across prewar Europe: "Our story was different. Yet we also somehow did not lose our innocence on that winter afternoon near Gare Saint-Lazare. Whenever I teach Flaubert's novel, I feel that I have a special understanding of that last chapter. The lived experience and the literary one now color each other. Perhaps this is the best way to read books." But one of the bonds of this disparate, transcontinental life is the rail miles covered. He writes: "Lived life and literary realities seemed to exchange their resources. Between the two was a shuttle of words and restless trains of thought."

Much of what Brombert describes about prewar Europe echoes my father's own stories about riding bicycles and trains around prewar Nazi Germany, seeing Hitler on the main street of Bergesgarden and sensing intimations of war from the anti-Semitism that passed along the bunks of the youth hostels where he stayed. As it turned out, my father's war against fascism was fought on Pacific islands, not continental Europe. But the thread of European and American trains was a constant theme in my childhood, and when he would take the children on business to Chicago or St. Louis, we would hear what it was like to change trains in Paris or Geneva, where he and my grandmother spent several summers. He can certainly relate to the last lines in Brombert's memoirs, which connect the Princeton Dinky (a one-car commuter train) to the Orient Express: "It reminds me of the child I was and have remained, of that same child who stayed awake all night in the sleeper so as not to lose one exciting moment of the journey."

Brombert's odyssey began in central Europe and ends in Princeton, where I often visit my parents on trips back to the United States. For the time being my own journey has gone in the opposite direction, one that started on the Long Island Railroad and is continuing in the Swiss countryside, married to the MOB. But in between we have both glimpsed some of the same grade crossings and lonely stations, attended either by flashing lights or guards impassively holding those railroad signposts. I can relate to his sense of excitement, conveyed by a sleeper rushing through the night, be it across the Great Plains of North Dakota or among the Tuscan Hills south of Florence.

For now, anyway, the framed windows of my train rides are in Switzerland. But even when I am heading up to the chalet, riding along the shores of Lake Geneva, either my book or my imagination usually has me somewhere else. Yes, the French Alps are spectacular, the lake boats sublime, and Montreux has palm trees. But as Brombert writes of his own daydreams: "My trains of thought most often carry me home again. Writing and traveling have much in common for me....As I dream, I get lost; as I write, I discover. The old train stations inhabit me because they were all at once places of departure, of transit, and of arrival."

Acknowledgements

As MUCH AS I ENJOY things like night flights across Russia and Armenian taxi rides, I confess I am nervous when faced with the prospect of written acknowledgements. My fears are those of omission. I dread not mentioning somebody here who has had a hand in helping to shape this book. So let me begin with an anonymous thank you to those who gave me hands in places like Serbia, Armenia, Lebanon, and Okinawa. It's always a great pleasure for me to be in a far-flung land and to find a willing driver, an accommodating desk clerk, a friend of a friend, or a fearless guide. Many of these scouts are mentioned here in the book, but for those omitted, please know that I retain a keen sense of gratitude for the favors large and small.

In particular, I do wish to recall some particular help along the many miles of this book. When I got back from Armenia, Harut Sassounian, the President of the United Armenian Fund, took the time to read the manuscript, offer some suggestions, and recommend other histories of Armenia that I might read. Jeff Kisseloff, a scholar and indefatigable researcher on the Hiss case, kindly read the Alger Hiss chapter, and pointed to numerous ways that I could improve the text. I am sure that those who disagree with my conclusions on the case will find even more faults than did Jeff, but I appreciate his help, as well as that of Tony Hiss, Alger's son, whose books on the case and other subjects are well worth reading. Tony is always generous with his time, and I admire his persistence to clear his father's name. Alex Kishaba made all the difference for me on Okinawa. He is chairman of the Ryukyu America Historical Research Society, and I found him thanks to a letter of introduction from another friend, George Feifer. Alex drove me around that remote battlefield, showed me campaign maps that he had stuffed in his briefcase, and made clear a battle that was as deadly for members of his family as it was for American and Japanese soldiers. On that same trip, I met the Australian journalist and author, Murray Sayle. Together we toured southern Japan, including the contemplated invasion beaches and ground zero at Nagasaki. I drove and Murray held forth on the theories of Admiral Mahan. In Nagasaki we shared bowls of *champon*, a soupy dinner than lingers in my mind, as does Murray's warm friendship and his thoughts on the Second World War.

I always enjoy traveling in Serbia, in part because it feels like going home. Descendants of my grandfather's brothers still live around the country, and all of them reached out to make that trip an extended family union. In particular, I want to thank my cousin, Slobodan Stanojevic, his wife Milica, and their son, Milan, for their generosity and careful planning. Boba's brother Stasha Stanojevic, another cousin, also lead the way on the roads south of Belgrade. My happiest times of Balkan travel, from Macedonia to Montenegro, have come in his company. Mary Nicklanovich Hart, editor of *Serb World USA*, vastly improved the Serbia chapter, with her sense of history and clarity. In Lebanon, the historian Judith Harik and her husband Anton welcomed me to their lovely home in the Chouf Mountains, and nudged me into corners of that war-torn country that I might otherwise have missed.

The production and editing of this book has passed through many hands, all of which draw my admiration and gratitude for their stout professionalism. Michael Martin, an American writer and editor who lives in Amsterdam, did the heavy lifting with the early drafts of the manuscript. I love his way with words, his long query e-mails that force me back to original sources, and his gentle way of correcting my many errors of grammar, spelling, and sentence structure. He's a fan of the Cincinnati Reds, but otherwise faultless. Likewise, Sandra Costich, who must dream of perfect sentences, ran her blue pencils over nearly every line, and each is better for her sense of language, her humor, and her fly-paper memory.

Al Cetta had hoped to design the manuscript, as he has earlier books of mine, but bad luck with his health forced him to watch the production from the sidelines. I have missed his collaboration here, as Al goes the extra mile when he has a book in hand. But my sister Nanette who first designed books in the 1970s, picked up the layout and brought to the project what I can only describe as "the Stevenson drive"—which means late nights at the computer, dozens of questions about type and style, and her own sense that the craft of bookmaking is as important now as it was when manuscripts were illuminated. Our younger sister Julie is a constant source of books and encouragement, and many chapters here start and end with her reading lists, if not her amusing take on life. I appreciate the suggestions that John Silbersack brought to the manuscript, especially as they reconnected a friendship that began when we were in grade school. Likewise, my friend and now fellow expatriate, Tom Wallace, was unflagging in his enthusiasm for the essays, with many excellent suggestions for books I should read or paths I should follow. I admire Judith and Ernest Peter, at Pathway Book, for the cheerful way they take my phone calls and solve problems. My business partner, Stephen Beekman, pushes me with his exacting standards and inspires me, and many others, with his magnanimous humanity.

This book was written at a difficult professional time in my life, when I found myself needing to recycle a career in finance and banking into other pastures, few of which could be described as green. As such, I can't say I have always been a cheerful household companion in recent years, and more than once, while writing in my home office, I have shouted into the void for children to "keep it down," a reference to noise that comes from an active house of four teenagers, not to mention cats, a dog, and countless guinea pigs. But if I struggled with my syntax and frustrations, the children (Helen, Laura, Henry, and Charles) pressed on with their schoolwork and outside activities with a purpose that became for me an inspiration. It's a lot easier to work on a manuscript when you are trying to measure up to the excellence of your children, and in their disposition and drive they never let me, or my wife, down. We marvel at their creative resources, their friends, their sense of many languages, and their fortitude. Now if they could only make their beds or take showers that do not threaten the water tables of Switzerland.

When this book is published, my wife, Connie, and I

will have been married for twenty-five years. Her story and mine, of recent years, is best told in the chapter "La Vie Suisse," an account of the pleasures and perils of living in a foreign land. We still have anxiety about attending French-speaking dinner parties, and that may explain why more and more our idea of a great evening is to read books in front of the fireplace. Connie reads everything, including what I write, and in the last twenty-five years she has crossed out the word "but" about ten thousand times. You would think by now I would have dropped it from my vocabulary, but then too you think I would have mastered by now the atomic codes of the dishwasher or the launch sequence of the washing machine—both of which Connie reveals in long, countertop instructions whenever I am left alone at mission control. That she does so cheerfully, despite her lingering doubts that I will ever feed the cats correctly, is testament to a nature that is unflappable, devoted, hardworking, imaginative, and loving, for everyone in her family. In twenty-five years I haven't quite converted her into a fan of the New York Jets, but wait until she gets a Joe Namath jersey for our anniversary.

Lastly, although the word fellow traveler felt out of favor in the shadow worlds of the 1930s, it does apply here to the enthusiasms of my parents, Nick and Shirley Stevenson, now in their 90th year. They met in 1931, when they shared the same seventh grade homeroom in Montclair, New Jersey, and now they live down the road from that junior high school, in Princeton, New Jersey. My parents don't travel as much as they used to. But they are still travelers at heart, and during many weeks my father drags his cane and briefcase up the stairs at Princeton Junction Station and onto a day coach of New Jersey Transit, for the commute into New York. For his work as president of the Association of Macular Diseases, he gives inspirational talks around the United States, relying on the kindness of strangers to read airport departure boards and to drive him to seminars. When I visit my parents in Princeton, we spend a lot of our time talking around the kitchen table—with me telling many of the same stories that are here in this book. Ours is a family of travelers' tales, and all of us have complicated and strong opinions on the best way to read timetables or fly from the United States to Europe. I realize that most readers will see this book as what might be called a collection of historical travel essays, but any Stevenson will recognize it as just a long after-dinner conversation, those that we have shared in Sands Point, at the condo, and now at the Windrows. Keep in mind that the family, especially my mother, puts great stock in the phrase, "Wuz you there, Charlie?" In that sense, this book is an attempt to get there, if not home.

–Matthew Stevenson, Laconnex, Switzerland,

December 10, 2008